FANGA

FANGASM

SUPERNATURAL
FANGIRLS

. . . . .

Katherine Larsen

and Lynn S. Zubernis

UNIVERSITY OF IOWA PRESS, IOWA CITY

University of Iowa Press, Iowa City 52242

Printed in the United States of America

Printed on acid-free paper

Library of Congress Cataloging-in-Publication Data
Larsen, Katherine.
Fangasm: Supernatural fangirls / by Katherine
Larsen and Lynn S. Zubernis.
     p.   cm.
Includes index.
ISBN-13: 978-1-60938-198-1 (pbk.)
ISBN-10: 1-60938-198-X (pbk.)
ISBN-13: 978-1-60938-215-5 (ebook)
ISBN-10: 1-60938-215-3 (ebook)
 1. Fans (Persons).   2. Supernatural (Television
program: 2005–).   I. Zubernis, Lynn S.   II. Title.
HM646.L37 2013
302.23′45—dc23   2013010121

CONTENTS

. . . . .

Acknowledgments vii

Prologue ix

1. Falling Down the Rabbit Hole 1

2. Seeking Asylum 19

3. Get a (Sex) Life 38

4. Hollywood Babylon 59

5. Fear and Loathing in Vancouver 76

6. Don't Ask, Don't Tell 95

7. Coming Out in LA 116

8. Playing the Fame Game 141

9. Stuck in the Middle (with You) 167

10. Working for the Man 185

11. The Sweet Spot 203

12. The Monster at the End of This Book 228

Glossary 241

Index 247

ACKNOWLEDGMENTS

· · · · ·

Thanks to our families for their patience (and for not giving up on our sanity) throughout our five-year road trip through fandom. We couldn't have done it without their support and the support of the rest of our SPN Family—the cast, the crew, and our fellow fangirls who've come along on the journey. People on both sides shared their insights and feelings about the show that's changed all our lives in so many ways, with remarkable candor. Thanks to Eric Kripke, Sera Gamble, Jensen Ackles, Jared Padalecki, Misha Collins, Jim Beaver, Richard Speight Jr., Chad Lindberg, Matt Cohen, Danneel Ackles, Samantha Ferris, Gabe Tigerman, C. Malik Whitfield, Todd Stashwick, Samantha Smith, Fred Lehne, David Mackay, Betsy Morris, Jason Manns, Steve Carlson, Brian Buckley, Serge Ladouceur, Jerry Wanek, Chris Cooper, Maryanne Liu, Lee-Anne Elaschuk, and Clif Kosterman for sharing their insights. We're also grateful to our talented photographers, Lizz Sisson, Chris Schmelke, and Karen Cooke, for their contributions, and to Maryanne Benetatos for transcribing endless hours of interviews. Special thanks to Catherine Cocks at the University of Iowa Press for taking a chance on us—and to Tony Zierra and Elizabeth Yoffe and Bhavna and M. Night Shyamalan, for daring us to tell the real story.

PROLOGUE

· · · · ·

"Turn here, turn here!"

"Where?"

"Right there, right there, ohmygod you're gonna miss it!"

Kathy yanked the wheel of our rented PT Cruiser sharply to the right, tires screeching as we drove way too fast through the unfamiliar streets of San Diego. Lynn scowled from the passenger seat, clutching the door handle as the car barely held the turn. In the back seat, Sabrina wisely stayed silent, hoping we'd make it to our destination in one piece.

At 4 A.M., the massive glass and concrete convention center up ahead was still a dark outline against the sky. We lurched into a spot in the deserted underground parking garage. Easy! We were feeling confident that we'd be first in line as we hurried up three flights of stairs and onto the darkened sidewalk, repeating our mantra "please let us be the first ones here, please let us be the first ones here." The area outside the convention center was eerily quiet as we headed down the sidewalk. It was too early for the trolley, too early for the traffic and crowds that would soon clog the streets. Even the street sweepers hadn't shown up yet. We threaded our way through the previous day's debris—discarded flyers for new television shows, promo cards in the shape of coffins, souvenir buttons, colorful miniposters for upcoming films. Geek garbage.

Our instincts told us that three women in an unfamiliar city at 4 A.M. should be careful, but we silenced the pesky little voice of reason. If we'd had good judgment, we wouldn't have been in California at all. None of us had the excess money or the time to fly three thousand miles across the country to go to a fan convention, and we knew we were going to pay for it in all sorts of ways. But not right now.

"We did it," Sabrina whispered to Kathy. Even Lynn—never a morning person, let alone a 4 A.M. person—started to smile. Then we turned the corner. Our self-congratulatory grins faded. There was already a line.

Welcome to Comic Con, one of the biggest fan conventions in the world, attracting over 140,000 people each year. We'd never even heard of it until three weeks before, yet there we were, trying to catch our breath and rein in our disappointment.

As we took our place on the pavement in the dark, Lynn catastrophized. It's what she does. "No way we'll get the seats we want," she grumbled, glaring at all the people who had apparently dragged their groggy asses out of bed even earlier than we had. Or maybe they had never slept at all. "We'll probably be a hundred rows back." (In fact, there were only about seventy people there. Lynn also exaggerates.)

"They're not all going to the same panel we are," Kathy snapped, grudgingly forced into an optimistic role that was wholly unfamiliar to her. Sabrina just yawned, perhaps in lieu of taking sides. After all, she barely knew us. In fact, we had only met the day before. That, of course, didn't stop us from offering her the second bed in our hotel room and cramming ourselves into the other so that Sabrina could join us in our early morning quest. She's a fellow fangirl, and that's enough for us.

It would be another two hours until the main doors opened, so we had time to strategize. We may have been new to fan conventions, but we recognized a siege when we saw one. The Powers That Be (TPTB) want and need to control the fans. The fans want and need to get close to the objects of their affection and are willing to do battle for that privileged position. Recognizing this dynamic, we had gone on a reconnaissance mission the day before. We'd scouted out the most direct route from the front doors to Room 6CDEF, where the panel for our favorite television show and most recent obsession, *Supernatural*, was scheduled for the next day. We'd timed it and planned it and practiced it until we wouldn't have to think, until the procedural memory would carry us to our destination quickly and seamlessly when the time was right. We'd laughed at ourselves more than once and promised never EVER to mention this to our kids and significant others. We may even have entertained the nagging suspicion that all the practicing we were doing exemplified the very definition of "over the top." Then we practiced again.

When the doors finally opened at 7 A.M., we took off, running the preplanned route through the sprawling convention center along with the rest of the crowd. "Walk, people, walk," the groggy security staff called out behind us, their admonitions falling on hundreds of determinedly deaf ears. We careened up stairs and around corners, not daring to slow down, not pausing to catch our breath. Suddenly an imposing group of Comic Con staffers appeared and began to herd us into yet another line, this one for Hall 6CDEF. This time, we were the tenth, eleventh, and twelfth in line. Lynn was relieved. Despite the early hour, she brightened at the prospect of being right up front. And Kathy was relieved that Lynn was relieved.

Many other fans would not be so lucky. The line for Hall 6CDEF would eventually number in the thousands, snaking back on itself several times, as more fans than the room could hold tapped their feet and bit their lips nervously, hoping to get inside. Many of them would make it in only to stand far at the back, having to settle for seeing their favorite actors on a screen once again. Many wouldn't get in at all because of people like us, who lined up at 4 A.M. to see a panel that would not begin until 3 P.M.

But we were looking forward to a good day. Yes, we'd have to sit through panel after panel on things that held little interest for us in order to keep the good seats we'd worked hard for. But we were five feet away from the stage where our favorite actors would eventually be sitting. This is the very definition of fangirl heaven.

With one hitch.

How were we supposed to introduce ourselves to the other fans surrounding us, who were happily exchanging information and sharing the fangirl moment? As Dr. Larsen and Dr. Zubernis, academics writing a book on fandom? As Kathy and Lynn, obsessed fangirls and prolific fanfic writers? Who were we that day? We sat there worrying, struggling with an identity crisis that had just begun but would not soon end. That was our first Comic Con, in July 2007.

This is the story of two reasonably intelligent women who fell hard for a television show called *Supernatural*, a sci-fi genre series that follows demon-hunting brothers Sam and Dean Winchester on a road trip across America "saving people and hunting things." Kathy is a university professor with a PhD in eighteenth-century English literature, who eventually found herself teaching courses in writing, celebrity, and fan culture. Lynn is a psychologist, a professor, and a researcher with a PhD in clinical psychology. We're serious-minded, middle-aged women with kids, partners, careers, and responsibilities.

We're also fans. Not casual armchair "oh-that's-a-fun-show" fans. *Serious* fans. Fans who make evening plans around air dates of their favorite show. Fans who preorder the DVD sets months in advance (and snag the downloads as the episodes air anyway). Fans who would travel across the United States and Canada in the years to come—to conventions, movie premieres, fan gatherings, television studios, small-town theater productions, and sometimes just to meet a fellow fan at Starbucks. Everywhere we've looked, others are proclaiming themselves fans as well—*Harry Potter* and *Twilight* fans lining up for the newest book or film, fans turning out by the thousands to mourn Michael Jackson and Whitney Houston, fans gracing the covers of magazines from *Entertainment Weekly* to the *New York Times*. *Fifty Shades of Grey* started out as *Twilight* fanfiction; fans turned it into a bestseller. Fandom, it seems, is a phenomenon. But what is it that draws so many of us to become fans?

In those moments when we had to extract ourselves from fangirl mode and return to the world of academics, we questioned our own evolution as fans. Why had this show become so important to us? Why were we, and many others, so passionate about what we were fans of? Why were we willing to camp out on a sidewalk before sunrise, foregoing money, sleep, and dignity just to have front-row seats at the feet of actors Jensen Ackles and Jared Padalecki?

Surely someone had figured this out by now. We were certain that we had perfectly good reasons for leaving some of our good sense behind us outside the San Diego convention center—we just needed to find them. We obviously knew how to do research, so that's what we did. Sure enough, we found articles on being a fan, though not nearly as many as we expected. Some of what we found seemed plausible, but none of it reflected our own experience. We couldn't find ourselves—our fangirl selves—in the research. Some theories downright annoyed us. And most academics, we felt, had missed the point of fandom entirely, at least our version of fandom. So we decided to write a book of our own on fans—one that we thought, rather naïvely, would set the record straight. We would figure out what being a fan was all about, and we would get it right! So we hit the library and the Internet, accumulating stacks of articles and hundreds of pages of research. We typed and revised and theorized, quoted and footnoted, and ended up with an academic text crammed full of the current research on fandom.

This is not that book. This book is a lot messier. It's a book about celebrity and fame and power and our attempt to negotiate the unfamiliar terrain of the entertainment industry. It's about sex and desire and being a woman and the shame that we feel about sex and desire and being a woman. It's about friendship and validation and finding people who "get you." It's also about losing friends, fighting on street corners in unfamiliar cities, and bumping up against those who steadfastly do not "get you." It's about discovering who you are or who you want to be instead. It's about the excitement of being passionate enough about something to throw caution to the wind and indulge—and about the price we pay when we do.

BONUS for *Fangasm* readers: free download of
Jason Manns's popular song, "Soul," at
http://jasonmanns.com/fandom.
Enjoy the beautiful music.
"Fangirls got soul!"

FANGASM

ONE

. . . . .

Falling Down the Rabbit Hole

Long before we started writing about being fans, we simply lived it. And there was nothing intellectual or rational about it, as our 4 A.M. dash to Comic Con makes clear. What is it about being a fan that makes us, and so many others, push the boundaries of common sense to pursue the emotional rush of fandom? What was compelling enough to make us trade our briefcases and textbooks for autographs and plane tickets? And why are we all so ashamed of it?

Case in point: Kathy was standing in a friend's kitchen after Thanksgiving dinner. The evening had been filled with good food and good conversation. Everyone had that warm, collegial feeling that comes of having passed plates, exchanged jokes, and shared bits of their lives. After the meal Kathy stood at the kitchen sink, sleeves rolled up and ready to help with the inevitable aftermath: dishes. As she traded off washing and drying duties with her friend's sister-in-law, the talk turned to the safe ground of the latest *Harry Potter* film. They both admitted their fondness for the books and the films. They discussed the characters, plot twists, the increasing darkness of the novels. Finally her friend's sister-in-law hesitated then leaned toward Kathy somewhat conspiratorially and asked in a lowered voice: "Do you ever go to the fan sites?"

The sister-in-law was clearly worried that she had gone too far. From the look on her face, you would have thought that she had just asked if Kathy had ever mainlined heroin or had a penchant for rubber. Kathy smiled reassuringly. No, not *Harry Potter* sites, but she did know of them. And yes, she had been to others. The sister-in-law's sigh of relief was audible. And then they talked. Really talked. About finding community and kindred spirits, about fanfiction and flame wars and metacommentary (see the glossary for definitions of these and other colorful words in the fandom vocabulary). In short, they discovered that they spoke the same language, even if in slightly different dialects: the language of fandom.

It seems too obvious to point out that most of us are fans of something—the local football team, model railroading, Elvis Presley, Anthony Bourdain. We're Gleeks and XPhiles and Parrotheads. We Rock the Red (yes, Washington Capitals fans, we're looking at you) and root, root, root for the home team. And when we find something we like, we want to share our enthusiasm with someone else who "gets it." Cheering together—or criticizing together—is a bonding experience. But fandoms are not all alike. Sports fans generally get a pass. (In fact, to be male and not a fan of some team somewhere is the more questionable position.) Craft fans at least have something to show at the end of their quilting, beading, or scrapbooking day. Dog enthusiasts have the backing of no less than the Westminster Kennel Club to validate their devotion. Opera, ballet, and theater fans (they might call themselves aficionados) have the weight of cultural approval on their side. But fans of a television show, especially one that falls within the sci-fi genre, are often viewed as a disquieting breed apart.

Attempts to validate fans inevitably come up short, falling victim to the same attitudes that they seem to be questioning. Even the documentary *Trekkies*, which at first seemed like an attempt to explain and vindicate fans of *Star Trek* and all its spinoffs, wound up mocking them instead. The stars of the original show actually provided thoughtful and moving commentary on the fans that they came to know over the years. But the filmmakers chose to feature instead the fringe elements of the fandom: the Florida dentist and his family who dress in *Star Trek* uniforms 24/7 and run a *Star Trek*–themed dental practice, the couple who dress the family dog in a Starfleet uniform, the young man exhibiting what seems to be an obsession with the stitching on his new *Star Trek: First Contact* uniform. The final effect was that these people made viewers uncomfortable and then made them laugh. The current crop of television shows that appear to celebrate nerds and geeks sometimes perpetuate the stereotypes instead of challenging them. *Big Bang Theory*'s Sheldon does for geeks what Jack did for gay men on *Will and Grace*. We love the character in no small part because he fits our cultural construction—and allows us to laugh.

In fact, laughter seems to be the order of the day as soon as you admit to being a fan, with everyone from newspaper editors to the local grocery store clerk reminding us that "it's not a coincidence that 'fan' derives from 'fanatic.'" But perhaps it doesn't. *Merriam-Webster* stands on the side of etymological uncertainty by saying it is "probably" short for "fanatic," and the *Oxford English Dictionary* identifies "fan" as an American term first used by baseball reporters. That sounds benign enough until we look at the selection of citations that follow the definition: "trainspotters and manky fanboy geekoids" and "spikey haired, bespectacled fanboys." And it turns out that laughter is still better than some of the other reactions to fans.

The Minneapolis-based blog Citypages ran an article identifying the "Top 7 Scariest Fandoms," presumably as a public service to the "rest of the world." If you're a female fan, the ridicule can be particularly scathing. The celebrity website ROFLRAZZI posted a photograph of a group of "Twilight Moms" tearfully awaiting the arrival of twenty-something actor Robert Pattinson and Taylor Lautner, on the cusp of turning eighteen. The article, provocatively titled "Boo! For pedophilia double standards," insisted that "if this was men cheering for 17 year old girls, someone would call the cops." Fans of Brooke Shields, Britney Spears, and Miley Cyrus would presumably also have been subject to incarceration at various times. Nevertheless, hundreds of commenters referred to the women who were fans as creepy, ridiculous, and unattractive, accusing them of being horrible parents who should be tending hearth and home instead of lining up to see actors. Perhaps most striking was the reaction to the death of a woman at last year's Comic Con. Crossing the street to get back to her place in line for a *Twilight* panel, she was struck by a car in front of horrified fellow fans. Online comments to news of her death ran from "Well it's not a bad start," to "She was in her 40's and obsessed with twilight [sic] did anyone honestly think she'd be smart enough to get out of the way of a fast moving vehicle?"

Given the culture's clear discomfort with fans, it's a wonder that any of us admit to being one. And yet fans keep film studios profitable, television shows on the air, *Fifty Shades of Grey* on the shelves, and gossip magazines and blogs in business. We might make fun of the guy dressed up as a Wookie at Comic Con or the co-worker who watches *Here Comes Honey Boo Boo*, but odds are more people can name all the Kardashians than can name all nine Supreme Court justices. Whether we want to admit it or not, most people are aware of popular culture, if not infatuated with it. We tend to laugh (or worse) at people who *can't* join the water cooler conversation about what Britney Spears did over the weekend or what happened on the latest installment of *Snookie and J Woww*. Thus we mock the overinvested and shun the underinvested.

Has it always been this way? In the early nineteenth century, the Romantics gave us our first taste of modern celebrity culture and, with it, the first negative views of fans. In Germany, Johann Wolfgang von Goethe's *Sorrows of Young Werther* inspired a contingent of fans, mostly young men, who imitated both the protagonist's morose mood and his sartorial sensibilities. The fans were said to be suffering from "Werther-Fieber" (Werther Fever)—perhaps the precursor to the modern affliction of "Bieber Fever." Lord Byron may have spawned the first fangirls—squealing, swooning, and desperate to get into his apartment and into his pants. As soon as fangirls were born, of course, so were the derisive comments about their "consuming passions." Byron was repeatedly accused of leading his readers into a state of "hysterical excitement" and producing a taste "for extreme sensation." (Sound familiar? Who knew that Stephanie Meyer was following in Byron's footsteps?) Attitudes toward fans have changed little in the intervening years—especially when it comes to those "swooning fangirls."

And if fans are not busy being oversexed, the media tell us, they are rapacious, needy, and worse. The day after the death of Michael Jackson, a writer for the *London Times* proclaimed that "Fans Killed Michael Jackson." Other journalists who stop short of categorizing fans as murderers nevertheless accuse them of being geeks, losers, and social rejects or hysterical, crazy stalkers. Some of this is the fault of a little mind game that we all play in the interest of not bogging ourselves down with too much heavy-duty thinking. Psychologists know this as the "availability bias." What we generally have available to us are the most salient images: hysterically sobbing teenagers, fangirls fainting at Beatles concerts, the stalker who tried to break into an actor's home. These images, unfortunately, become representative of "fans" instead of just isolated examples.

If we're being honest, we all tend to shy away from those who allow their enthusiasm slips to show (Tom Cruise on Oprah's couch, anyone?), who are too fervent, too dedicated, too much of anything. We're uncomfortable when someone seems overly passionate, even about things that we clearly need to survive (you know, like chocolate). Even though we need food, we still have cultural rules of etiquette demanding that we eat relatively slowly, no matter how famished we are, and that we resist the temptation to steal a particularly delectable morsel from our neighbor's plate. We're expected to eat as if eating wasn't the most important thing in the world, even if at that moment it is. We're expected to act detached even when we feel anything but. Anyone who violates these expectations can expect ridicule, whether they're *Hobbit* fans waiting impatiently for the release of the film or *Star Wars* fans who know all the specifications of the Millenium Falcon or *Supernatural* fans who watch twenty-two episodes back to back in DVD viewing marathons. We might know a little bit about that last one.

We have yet to come across more than a handful of fans who contend that *Supernatural* actor Jensen Ackles is their soulmate or have offered up thousands of dollars for the coffee cup that Jared Padalecki discarded at a *Supernatural* convention. But nobody can accuse fans of a lack of investment or of not being willing to put their money where their passion is. At a convention in Vancouver, a fan bid $8,000 for Padalecki's thirtieth birthday goodie bag. The money went to charity, but the fan was paying for a hug from the birthday boy as well as making a contribution to a good cause.

While the vast majority of fans remain sane in the midst of passion, the tendency to characterize fans—especially female fans—as "rabid," "demented," "obsessed" stalkers or just plain "batshit crazy" persists. Even the fans themselves can't quite decide whether to scream their glee about fandom from the rooftops, apologize for it, or just pretend that they're not fans at all.

Given those disparaging descriptions, it's hard to imagine why anyone would choose to be a fan. The thing is, it's never a conscious decision: we don't get to choose a fandom. It chooses us.

2005: We could say that it was our friend Lana's fault. At first, we watched *Supernatural* (known within the fandom as "SPN") mostly because she begged us to. Not that we didn't appreciate the way Sam Winchester's emo bangs fell in his oh-so-handsome face or Dean Winchester's amazing green eyes with eyelashes that any woman would die for. We're not blind, after all.

Throughout the first season, we'd catch an episode here and there, enough to know what Lana was talking about when she described the

Left, Jared Padalecki (Sam Winchester) and right, Jensen Ackles (Dean Winchester).
Courtesy of Elizabeth Sisson.

show's well-developed mythology or actor Jared Padalecki's well-developed biceps, but we were still far from being fans. Lana didn't give up though. She burned soundtrack CDs and mailed them off to us. And she never stopped talking about the intricate plot and the fascinating characters and the brilliant directing, even when most of the conversation was embarrassingly one-sided.

Looking back, we probably should have realized that we were teetering on the edge of a cliff ourselves, primed for something that would distract us from the complexities of our lives. Some people buy sports cars when they're having a midlife crisis. Some people have affairs. Some start drinking. We fell for a television show. Fandom, for both of us, had been a refuge in the past in times of crisis—from the raging hormones and constant doubts of adolescence to the terrors of grad school statistics. It had provided a welcome respite during some rocky patches in both our lives. Now, as midlife loomed, we were both in need of a refuge once again, as well as a place to figure ourselves out for the second time. Who were we now, after defining ourselves as partners and mothers for decades? What did we like, want, need, desire? What made us laugh, tugged at our heartstrings, turned us on?

At just the right time, along came Lana—and *Supernatural*. The same thing happens to countless fans in every corner of the world on a daily basis. It might be an obsession with *The Hunger Games* or *Harry Potter*, the latest boy band, or the local college basketball team. It might be *Star Wars* or *Star Trek* or *Twilight*. For us, it was a relatively unknown sci-fi genre show.

Why *Supernatural*? Volumes of fan-written essays explain the appeal of the show: solid writing, an intricate mythology, meticulously researched urban legends, and monsters both literal and metaphorical. Classic rock. A badass 1967 Chevy Impala. Sibling rivalry, unresolved oedipal drama, reluctant heroes. A story of family ties, love, and loyalty. An emotionally intense relationship between the two main characters that generates enough chemistry to power a small city. Cinematography and directing that make each episode look more like a 42-minute feature film. Two very hot actors.

And then there's the allure of the romantic hero, which has as much appeal today as it had two hundred years ago when Byron and Werther created such mayhem. We are still drawn to the loner with a mysterious past that renders him both fascinating and unattainable. It's a past that haunts him, preventing him from fully joining in "normal" life. He feels deeply and shows little. *Supernatural* presented its viewers with not one but two variations on the romantic hero in brothers Sam and Dean Winchester (and then, in a stroke of genius, cast Ackles and Padalecki to play them).

The Winchester brothers appealed to us—and lots of other women—for multiple reasons. Yeah, they were hot. But we could also relate to them.

Supernatural writer and showrunner Sera Gamble described the inherent heroism in the two main characters, both of whom are damaged.

Dean is the more damaged of the two. He's had to put his own needs aside for his entire life, which tends to cook up an interestingly fucked up kind of person—and in this case, has ended up making him instinctually heroic. Selflessness is a huge part of heroism. We often say in the writer's room, when the two of them are in disagreement, that as long as they're falling all over themselves to save each other they can go pretty out there with the misguided ideas; their actions will still maintain a core of heroism.

Putting your own needs aside for your entire life is something that many of us have done too.

The Winchester brothers were also appealing to all those who have ever felt like they don't quite fit in with the rest of the world. Maybe your imagination takes you places where nobody else goes. Maybe you don't fall in line with society's expectations of what it means to be a man or a woman or you've experienced difficulties that set you apart. Maybe you just happen to have the specifications of the USS *Enterprise* memorized or can rattle off every detail of the last episode of *Doctor Who*. Sam and Dean Winchester don't fit in either. They're outsiders—but they're also heroes. And they're what we all recognize as family. Sera certainly understood the show's appeal. "The theme of being alone in the world, having lived a different life than anyone else—that was there from day one. It's the core of the series."

Many shows meet these general qualifications. Only once in a while does something grab you so completely that the word "obsession" starts to seem appropriate. Rationally, we knew that there were explanations for why we suddenly fell down the rabbit hole of *Supernatural* fandom. None of those theories mattered to us at the time. Falling into fandom is like falling in love. We don't always make the smartest choices or make those choices for the best of reasons (Kathy's Keanu Reeves phase and Lynn's fling with *Interview with the Vampire* are cases in point). Decisions are made with the gut (or lower), not with the head. We were simply hooked.

In fact, we soon discovered that we were hooked in a way that our friend Lana was not. She's always on the lookout for something new—a more fascinating premise, a more talented band, a prettier boy—and she's willing to expend time and effort dragging the rest of us along with her when she finds it. She's more of a buffet fan, happily sampling from a tantalizing variety of television, books, and movies and then moving along to the next offering to nibble some more. We, however, are perfectly content to eat the same delicious meal again and again, digging in with both hands, getting sticky and gooey and messy and . . . oops—were we letting our enthusiasm show too much there?

We're not the only ones. *Supernatural* is in its ninth season and has become increasingly popular worldwide, winning not one but two People's Choice awards in 2012 (including Best Network Drama) and 2013 and snagging the cover of *TV Guide*'s very first "Fan Favorite" contest. The show has a reputation for having some of the most devoted and passionate fans. And while we were merrily indulging in being two of them, other researchers had not checked their academic credentials at the door. The relatively new field of "fan studies" has been developing over the last twenty years, with University of Southern California media studies professor Henry Jenkins leading the way. Academics were just as taken by *Supernatural* as we were, adopting the show as a critical favorite. Jenkins, like us, fell hard for the show, describing why it inspired him to "more or less inhale Season One" in his online blog:

> On one level, it is made up of classic masculine elements—horror, the hero's quest, sibling rivalry, unresolved oedipal dramas—but on another level, it seems ideally suited to the themes and concerns which have long interested the female fan community. Heck, this series is one long hurt/comfort story. Every episode seems structured as much around the character moments as around the monster of the week plotlines. Everything here seems designed to draw out the emotions of the characters and force them to communicate with each other across all of the various walls which traditional masculinity erects to prevent men from sharing their feelings with each other. Dean in particular seems to hate "chick flick moments" and has a running commentary on how much he would like to avoid getting in touch with his feelings but this doesn't prevent us from having some real emotional revelations in almost every episode.

The show seduced not only academic superstars but seasoned entertainment writers. Karla Peterson, then entertainment critic for the *San Diego Union-Tribune*, confessed that this was the first time she had "come out" as a fan in over twenty years of writing criticism for the paper. The emotional impact of the show convinced her to confess.

> It's not just that I like the show, or that I think it has artistic merit, this show *moves* me, I look forward to this show in ways I don't to other shows I like. When I'm doing anything for the first time, what I really want is for

the "fasten your seatbelt" light to go off. I want to sit back and know I'm in the hands of people who really know what they're doing. And within the first ten minutes, I thought, "It's off." I'm on board and I'm comfortable. These people knew what they were doing. You have character development, drama, comedy, the scary. I'm in love with how the brothers feel about each other. The costumes were perfect, the music was perfect, it was all a self-contained fully imagined world from the first fifteen minutes, and when it was over, I thought—I love this show. It's like this perfect snow globe that you can be a part of and it's a total escape because it's so well done, and I really feel like I'm in good hands when I turn myself over to that show. I trust that show.

Every fan has a list of personal reasons why their fandom resonates. Whatever the reasons you become a fan, one aspect is clear. In fandom, one thing usually leads to another. Once you're hooked, you want more. More information, more pictures, more viewings, more of everything associated with the show. Our forays into research uncovered some theories about why, though we didn't necessarily like what we found. One of the earliest psychological explanations of being a fan is Lynn McCutcheon's "Absorption-Addiction" model. The name itself was enough to make us nervous. This absorption, McCutcheon says, is like an addiction, leading to increasingly extreme (sometimes increasingly delusional) behavior in order to get a "fix." Fans become psychologically absorbed with a celebrity as a way of establishing their own identity and finding emotional fulfillment. Okay, we can go along with some of that. After all, who wouldn't be absorbed by actors who look so fabulous?

Researchers have recently backed away from calling fannishness an "erotomanic delusional disorder" as they once did. They no longer contend that *all* fan behavior is pathological (perhaps realizing that they'd have to throw about 90 percent of the population under that particular bus). Researchers now estimate that fully one-third of us are affected by what they've tagged "Celebrity Worship Syndrome," and many more would categorize themselves as fans. We'd already established that we were at the head of the line.

There are well-researched reasons why most of us develop (healthy) attachments for things outside ourselves. From an evolutionary standpoint, we're built to become deeply connected to outside entities. The scientific

Addictive: Padalecki and Ackles. Courtesy of Christopher Schmelke.

explanation goes like this: the part of the brain called the mesolimbic system acts as a reinforcement circuit between the opiodergic system (which influences what we like) and the dopaminergic system (which influences what we want). So when we like watching *Supernatural*, we want it again and again, just as soon as it's available—if not sooner. This system developed to help us find our next meal, not our next fix of Sam and Dean, but anything that we want badly enough can trip the same circuits. Jeff Rudski, a psychologist who studies *Harry Potter* addiction, summed it up: "For fanatics, liking may trigger an unusually high degree of wanting" (quoted in *Psychology Today* [January 2011]). We weren't fond of being called fanatics, but we couldn't argue with Dr. Rudski's conclusion. We were definitely experiencing a high degree of wanting every time Jared and Jensen graced our TV screens.

Being a fan—of anything—entails a great deal of emotional investment. Some recent research on music fans found that the intensity of emotion created by live music lit up the brain's pleasure center, putting the fan on a roller coaster for the duration of each concert—an experience that feels great and makes you want to do it again and again. One music fan who had seen her favorite pop group forty-four times described it as an almost religious experience—pounding heart, tears, no words that could convey the emotion. We've seen the same thing happen to a *Supernatural* convention first-time attendee, after finally getting up close and personal with Jared Padalecki. Sometimes fans burst into spontaneous tears after such an encounter, rendered speechless by a celebrity's simple hello. (And yes, we may have experienced this phenomenon once or twice ourselves.) Sports fans experience a vicarious sense of success as intense as that of the actual players when their team wins, with the identical hormonal surges and the same sense of optimism about life in general. According to social identity theory, "involvement" is the degree to which we're intellectually and emotionally engrossed in something. When our team or television show or favorite movie or band is successful, involvement means that our own self-esteem gets bolstered right along with theirs. We feel better about ourselves, which explains why rooting for your chosen team in the Super Bowl is a national obsession. Whether you're a fan of the Phillies, the Grateful Dead, or *Supernatural*, fandom is deeply emotionally important.

Yet much of the research on fandom—as well as most of the articles in the popular press—continues to pathologize fans. Sports fan researchers have tied the level of emotional investment to what they call "fan dysfunction," which contributes to bad behavior such as heated arguments with other fans, radio commentators, or anyone who criticizes their team. They characterize the most deeply invested fans as "isolative, incapable of relationships and trying desperately to soothe an empty self" (*Journal of Psychology*

137/4 [2003]). Some of the earliest (and still the most talked about) research on why people become fans was done in the 1950s by Donald Horton and Richard Wohl, who called the one-way relationship between fans and the famous "parasocial interactions." They saw the false intimacy created by the fan's feeling of knowing the celebrity, and the celebrity's experience of the fan as a stranger, as inherently pathological in its one-sidedness.

Fans were characterized as lonely, desperate, delusional people who couldn't form relationships in "real life" and had to count on imaginary ones instead.

None of this lined up with what we were experiencing ourselves. Fans do tend to feel like they "know" the people they are fans of, but most are aware that it's the celebrity's constructed media image, not the real person. We were pretty sure that we hadn't become delusional enough to forget that we weren't bffs with Jensen Ackles or Jared Padalecki. But we couldn't deny that some of the Wikipedia descriptions of "fan" fit us perfectly, including a "focus of time and resources, a desire for social interaction with other fans, and the wish to acquire material objects related to the area of interest." We experienced all three.

Acquisition first. Lynn began in Barnes and Noble, casually wandering over to the DVD section while her kids were busy looking for books. There it was, calling out to her—the first season of *Supernatural* on DVD. She was on a tight budget with two kids starting college. She did not have money for indulgences, and this was most definitely an indulgence. She carefully weighed this decision for all of fifteen seconds then grabbed the DVD set off the shelf, heart pounding at the sheer feeling of wrongness, selfishness, rashness—closely followed by an unfamiliar rush of exhilaration and antici-pation. And for good measure, as she was throwing all financial caution to the wind, she bought both seasons of *Dark Angel* and Season 4 of *Smallville* (a quick look at Jensen Ackles's IMDB [International Movie Database] page should explain the additional purchases). Lynn clutched the bag to her chest as she walked to the car, hoping that neither of her children would ask what she'd purchased. It felt terrifying. She had just spent well over one hundred dollars that she could ill afford. It was also fabulously liberating.

Kathy wasn't far behind. Her investment involved more time than money. She stayed up late into the night trolling the web for any and all informa-tion, watching YouTube videos and creating folder after folder of images.

When she visited Lynn, the DVD stash came out. We settled in to watch the entire first season of the show from start to finish, stopping to ogle screencaps and closeups and slap each other on the shoulder when the sexual punch of Dean Winchester's pouty lips and pretty green eyes got the better of us. We sat there watching all day and into the night, until 4 A.M., slept for a few hours, and then got back up at 7 A.M. to start in again. At 6 P.M. the next day, we stared at each other. Lynn asked blearily, "Um, did we ever even eat anything today?" The answer—alarmingly—was no. We were beginning to realize that our investment was anything but casual.

As for the "desire for social interaction" with other fans, we had lots of friends in "real life," but most of them didn't share our fannish interests or even understand them. Initially we had each other and of course Lana, who'd landed us in this predicament in the first place. But the allure of fandom is finding others to raise your voice with, to celebrate with, to scream with. (Stand in the middle of the room at a *Supernatural* convention and you'll quickly realize that's no exaggeration.) Fandom offers the possibility of laying aside the whispering—or worse, the complete silence—that is usually the burden of the closet fan. It offers up community, support, friendship, reassurance, and *fun*. That all-important "you're not alone" feeling is hard-wired into all of us from way back, when being isolated meant literally not surviving. It can still feel that way. Ask anyone who was the odd girl out in middle school.

Community has always been integral to fandom. In the early days of organized fandom, fans kept in touch through snail mail. They joined fan clubs and eagerly devoured newsletters and whatever media coverage their favorite books, films, and television shows managed to garner. Enterprising fans typed up fanzines and circulated them to other fans. In the fanzines they discussed the books and shows and films they loved and wrote fanfiction to expand on the plotlines and explore the characters further, some of it not exactly G-rated (and thus both kept hidden and quite popular). Fans passed zines around at fan conventions too, clandestinely. Fans saw each other in person only at infrequent fan-run conventions or, in the case of music fans, at concerts.

By the time we rediscovered fandom, the landscape had changed radically—as had most of life—with the advent of the Internet. In 2007, *Supernatural* online fandom consisted mainly of the network's own site, the blogging and social networking site LiveJournal.com, and the message boards of TelevisionWithoutPity.com, TVGuide.com, and Supernatural.tv. This was a world where everyone watched *Supernatural* with a magnifying glass, wanted to have long intellectual discussions about the symbolism of the tattoos on Sam and Dean's (happily bared, muscular) chests, and read ten-chapter stories of the oh-so-very-fictional adventures of Jensen and Jared.

We couldn't wait to join in.

There's no one way to experience fandom. Each fan looks for something different when searching for a place to belong. Some fans go online to talk about plot twists, some to dissect cinematography, some to lose themselves in role-playing games (RPGs). Some want to criticize and some to cheerlead. Some want to create art, make videos, or write fanfiction about their favorite characters. We weren't completely new to fandom; in fact, we had met years before as members of a small fan mailing list, when we were both writing fanfiction for a little-known film. Since we were writers, we wanted a place to connect with other writers, which quickly led us to the online archive fanfiction.net and then to LiveJournal.com (LJ). LJ, with its mix of autobiographical journal posts and a vast array of fanfiction, fanvids, fanart, and commentary, instantly felt like the right place for us. Here, we decided, we'd make our fandom home. We signed up and dove in.

Several scholars have argued that fanfiction constitutes a site of resistance, a chance for fans to take control of characters and in some cases to fix what's "wrong" (at least as they see it) with their favorite shows, filling in gaps in the source text, providing backstory where none existed, fleshing out or inserting characters as needed in order to create a text that fits the needs of the reader. We're familiar with this from English classes whether we know it or not. Jean Rhys wanted to explore the character of mad Bertha Rochester in *Jane Eyre*, so we have *Wide Sargasso Sea*. John Gardiner thought it was valuable to have the "monster's" point of view in *Beowulf*, so we now read *Grendel* alongside the Old English classic. Fanfiction is also a mode of criticism and interpretation. One could argue that Michelangelo Buonarotti's statue of David and John Milton's *Paradise Lost* share many of the characteristics of fanart, putting a new spin on a familiar story. They rely on the collective knowledge of the original story to give their reinterpretations some of their power. The fear on David's face is not in the Old Testament, but it is powerfully present in Michelangelo's "reading" of the story. Fanfiction acts in a similar fashion, creating a powerful sense of intimacy as fans bond over a shared text. We can swap ideas about characters, who they are, what they feel. We are free to interpret and reinterpret collectively and individually.

Every fandom develops its own unique language and customs. While we were familiar with some pan-fandom terms and practices, we had also been away from fan pursuits for a while—and things change fast online. We had a steep learning curve. Was a picspam part of a new advertising campaign for canned meat products (Pick Spam!—shades of Monty Python)? Why did a bunch of photos labeled "biceps porn" seem so G-rated? And why were Jensen and Jared dressed as Carmen Miranda in that photo, and OMG are they making out in that picture? (What the hell is a "manip" anyway?) We were confused. For a long time, Lynn was convinced that the popularity of so-called "crack fic" attested to an inexplicable fandom fascination with drug use.

Considering the vast array of creative expression going on in the fandom, it took a month of exploration (known as lurking) before we felt comfortable enough to say anything, let alone post any fanfiction. While we contemplated, we read. And read. And read some more. The amount of *Supernatural* fanfiction out there was overwhelming. Luckily, fandom is accustomed to newbies like us and has developed all sorts of communities to help you find your way in the strange new land.

In fact, there is so much *Supernatural* fanfiction out there, and with such high demand for more, that an online community developed just to help you find exactly what you're looking for. Confused? There are communities to keep you organized and make sure that you don't (heaven forbid) miss a single thing that happens within the SPN universe. Visit all_spn on LJ for a rundown of all things *Supernatural*. Consult Spnroundtable for the latest meta discussion. Read the daily (and no, they never miss a day, amazingly) Spnnewsletter. Check out the Supernatural Wiki for a crash course on SPN-speak, the latest videos of Jared's appearance at a fan convention, Jensen's interview for Australian television, or writer Jeremy Carver's teaser hints about the new season premiere. Or if gossip and bitchslapping are more your thing, check out Fandomwank for the latest explosion of fan infighting or Fandomsecrets for true confessions of the kind of thing that you probably wouldn't tell your mother (maybe your therapist, but definitely not your mother).

Fans share their love of *Supernatural* with each other in a wide variety of ways. They write complex analytical essays known as meta, deconstructing the show's mythology, examining its metaphors, and taking episodes apart moment by moment to dig for deeper meaning. They make videos that are both technically breathtaking and emotionally gut-wrenching. They share original artwork that could be making the artists money instead of earning them kudos in LJ or Tumblr comments. Days, weeks, even months are spent in creating vids, picspams, icons, original art, and sometimes novel-length works of fiction. Not for profit (*Fifty Shades of Grey* notwithstanding), though the quality is often superior to what you'd find on the shelves of your local bookstore or any art dealer. Fan works are created solely for the pleasure of other fans—fandom, as they say, is a gift economy, not a market one. The only payback that fans want or get is the joy of sharing "the pretty." That's what we wanted too, much to the consternation of our families, who would have preferred that we actually make some money from the long days we were starting to spend researching and writing. To do other things like, oh, you know, buy groceries. Who needs groceries when you have Sam and Dean Winchester? We'd already established that eating is optional when you're in fangirl mode.

We didn't want to cook. We didn't want to eat. What we wanted was to share our love for our beloved show. We wanted to formulate creative hypotheses about why John Winchester turned his sons into hunters when they were still kids and why some demons had yellow eyes. We craved long conversations with like-minded people who could appreciate Sam's emo tendencies and Dean's propensity for being thrown into walls or Jensen Ackles's eyelashes.

We wanted, like anyone who's poised on the outskirts staring at the kids laughing on the playground, to be inside. Fandom is a community. We could see that clearly as we peered eagerly through the hole in the fence— you can walk down the virtual streets of fandom and wave at friends you see every day. Stop to chat with some about the latest news, whether that's the psychological implications of last night's episode or a breathtaking new piece of fanfiction or Jared Padalecki's latest haircut. Sometimes it's not about *Supernatural* at all—it's to ask how a presentation turned out, to give a hug and an "I'm sorry" in the face of a recent loss or a word of encouragement for a job interview. The sights and sounds of the neighborhood might be different from those in the neighborhoods we grew up in, but we could already see the way fans supported each other, encouraged each other, and looked after each other.

Of course, neighborhoods are also known for their shady back alleys and deadman's curve intersections and backstabbing disagreements between the neighbor on your right and the one on your left. Fandom, we soon discovered, is no different. For every love meme that gets passed through the fan community, there's an anonymous hate meme that rips people to shreds behind their backs, fueled by jealousy, insecurity, and the very passion that makes fandom such a powerful place to be. Of course, that didn't discourage us—we wanted in.

So in we went, rose-colored glasses firmly in place. We didn't realize what we were getting ourselves into—the joy the journey would bring and the real hurt it would cause us, the friends we'd make, the friends we'd lose, the relationships with family that would strain and sometimes crack in pursuit of the ultimate Fangasm.

TWO

. . . . .

Seeking Asylum

In May 2007, actor and object-of-our-affection Jensen Ackles traveled to England to appear at his first fan convention, Asylum. We, unfortunately, did not follow. Instead Lynn sat glumly in Starbucks frowning into her chai, while Kathy tried to turn the disappointment into constructive discussion. She didn't get very far.

"Why did they call it Asylum?" Kathy asked.

Lynn pondered. "Place of refuge? Fans coming together, feeling safe?"

"Place to house the crazies?" Kathy countered. Seeing the dismayed expression on Lynn's face, she added, "Too cynical?"

Kathy's cynicism is understandable given the stigma affixed to fans. We had succumbed to that nagging feeling of shame repeatedly when we were asked to explain yet again why we like a genre television show as passionately as we do. On the surface, we fell into *Supernatural* fandom because Sam and Dean Winchester are fascinating and compelling (and breathtakingly gorgeous) characters. We initially thought that we'd simply gain from the experience more photos to sigh over and more opportunities to dissect the show's mythology and more fanfiction to enjoy. What we actually got was something that we didn't even know we were looking for.

In fandom, we found a community of others—a group of people who, like us, had always felt a bit different. Many people who end up fans— particularly media or sci-fi fans—have experienced this sense of difference. And most of us have never talked about it. So fandom, with its radically different norms for self-expression and its overt acceptance of "difference," turned out to be as much about validation and acceptance as it was about the Winchesters. The research we'd found touched on only part of the story.

Celebrity worship, pathological or otherwise, is not the only reason why people become fans. Sure, we are fans of the actors. But there's a different pull toward fandom that has as much to do with finding like-minded fellow fans as with whatever it is we're fans of. Especially for women.

In an essay about being a media fan, Kristina Busse says that many women describe fandom as the first place where they truly created friendship ties with other women that were intimate and genuine. These friendships can actually be more intense than "real life" ones, with daily—sometimes constant—online contact. The relationships can also be more intimate, because women feel free to disclose things that they might not if they were face to face. Fandom is all about belonging—a feeling that's crucial for humans. We're not isolative creatures; we need connection in order to thrive. Being kicked out of the tribe used to mean being eaten by a bear. We haven't forgotten that evolutionary lesson.

And it's not only about physical survival: it's about psychological survival too. Isolated, we all secretly believe that we're freaks—that we're the only ones who have *those* feelings, *that* fantasy, *those* impulses—until we open up and somebody else says "Oh my God, that's exactly how I feel!" Until then, we don't believe it—we feel different, weird, abnormal. It's only within the group that we find validation. In his book *The Yalom Reader* psychologist Irving Yalom describes the feeling of "universality" that comes from sharing yourself and your life story with the group:

> "We're all in the same boat," or perhaps more cynically, "Misery loves company." There is no human deed or thought that is fully outside the experience of other people. I have heard group members reveal such acts as incest, burglary, embezzlement, murder, attempted suicide, and fantasies of an even more desperate nature. Invariably, I have observed other group members reach out and embrace these very acts as within the realm of their own possibilities. Long ago Freud noted that the staunchest taboos (against incest and patricide) were constructed precisely because these very impulses are part of the human being's deepest nature.

One of the most common secrets we have, Yalom says, is a deeply held conviction of inadequacy. Who hasn't wondered if they're really up to par, good enough, capable of tackling an unfamiliar challenge? We could definitely relate, having both struggled with feelings of inadequacy our entire lives. The other secret, according to Yalom, is almost everything to do with sex. Who hasn't wondered if what turns them on is what turns other people on? Sharing all those deep dark things that we're convinced make us weird, and finding ourselves not all that different, challenges the fear that we're basically unlovable. Expressing repressed emotions (known as "catharsis"), exploring the split-off parts of ourselves that we've always tried to deny, and realizing that others will accept us anyway—that's what everyone's paying for when they go to therapy. Fandom, we thought, offers a lot of the same things. We all long for a group of people who accept us, a place where we work through our "stuff" in safety. People who are drawn to any sort of group are looking for the same sense of belongingness that fans are. Fans didn't necessarily have more stuff to work out; they'd just found a different place to do it. A place that can help you feel better when you're not feeling all that good about yourself—without the down sides of drugs or alcohol or cheating on your spouse or running off to Bali. So researchers' contention that fans were isolative didn't pan out. Clearly, if we're including online interaction as well as in-person encounters, fandom is anything but isolating. Twitter, Facebook, Live Journal, Dreamwidth, Tumblr: each day there are more social networking sites, and every one of them becomes a home for fans. Fandom is the antithesis of isolation—it's all about community.

At first, sociologists had scoffed at the idea that a virtual community could provide any of the same benefits that face-to-face ones did. Could online communities really be considered communities? After all, you couldn't really "interact," could you? Research now shows that yes, you can—and we do. Communities are defined as networks of interpersonal ties that provide sociability, support, information, a sense of belonging and social identity. That describes exactly what we found in fandom. Within online fan communities, members police group norms and defend their electronic boundaries against outsiders, just as they do in their local neighborhoods. The sense of belonging is powerful—especially for women. Many of us no longer have the immediacy of neighborhoods and kids playing in the street that used to draw women together and create a bond of friendship among them. But we still have the need for those bonds, especially when modern life is more stressful than ever.

There's even research to back that up. A 2010 University of California–Los Angeles study found that women respond differently to stress than men do. Instead of the stereotypical "fight or flight," women often react to stress with the drive to "tend and friend"—that is, to take care of offspring and gather with other women, both of which produce a calming effect thanks to oxytocin. The researchers had noticed that when men were stressed, they holed up somewhere on their own. Women came in, cleaned the lab, had coffee, and bonded. Ninety percent of the stress research had been on men, so this came as a surprise. Friendships are critical to women's mental and physical health. The more friends we have, the less stressed we are and the more joyful. So why is it so hard to find time to be with our girlfriends? We regularly relegate friendships to the bottom of the priority list when we get busy. But we need to have unpressured space in which we can talk freely and bond with other women. It's literally a healing experience. That's what we found in fandom.

Television fandom may be one of the most powerful experiences of all. Not only is online fandom the sort of women's friendship community that helps us heal, but being a television fan itself has benefits. Researchers at the University of Buffalo's Center for Addictions discovered that watching your favorite TV programs provided an experience of belonging that the researchers called "social surrogacy." Remember those so-called parasocial relationships that early researchers were so down on? It turns out that they can actually fulfill belongingness needs—watching or just thinking or talking about our favorite show can create an experience of belonging that makes us feel less lonely and buffers us against feelings of rejection. People do form parasocial relationships with their favorite television characters or media personalities, but they're not as pathological as was once thought. These one-sided relationships show many of the psychological hallmarks of real ones—being in the "presence" of the parasocial partners or thinking about them brings the same benefits as being with "real" friends—people are more empathic, more open, less aggressive, and feel better about themselves. This also explains why people react to the cancellation of a beloved show as if it were the end of a relationship. It IS!

Television, the researchers say, produces particularly potent parasocial relationships. Viewers can immerse themselves in a recognizable world, where characters become intimate and comfortable. People wanted to think about—and write about—their favorite show more when they felt a need to belong, and doing so satisfied that need. And it's not just pure escapism or distraction—only indulging in your *favorite* show worked. Fans turn to their beloved shows when they're lonely, because they feel better when they do. Retreating to a familiar fictional world relieves stress and shores up self-control. In fact, watching feels as reinvigorating as actually hanging out with a loved one. This applies not only to fans with "low self-esteem," as some earlier studies had decided—it applies to everyone.

And this is important. Entertainment reporter Karla Peterson put it this way: "TV is this emotional currency you can share with so many different people, this wonderful web that connects us. For me, it's an ideal escape at the end of the day. I'm a working mom, and my day is very disciplined. I exercise, I recycle, I'm very conscious about every little aspect of my life, and my little escape is watching *Supernatural*, my Weight Watcher's Fudgsicle, and a glass of wine. You can take away my Fudgsicle, you can take away the wine, but you cannot take away my *Supernatural*."

Fans themselves are quite aware of the therapeutic value of fandom, and that their "use" goes up or down depending on how well their lives are going. Some fans "use" by posting on message boards and discussing plot twists; some express themselves through writing or commenting on fanfiction, creating fan videos, or making fanart, or interacting on Twitter or Tumblr; others watch the show or read the book or buy the movie and lose themselves in the fantasy. By the time the Asylum convention brought *Supernatural* fans together physically for the first time, we had started to make friends in the online community. We felt real there, comfortable with being ourselves and talking about what we really thought and felt and desired. It was, for both of us, one of the most liberating experiences of our lives. And we weren't the only ones.

Supernatural fan Wendy posted this message to her online fangirl "friends list" to celebrate her tenth anniversary in fandom:

LJ has changed my life in ways I never would have expected. I've met this amazing network of strong, smart, creative women. I've been able to ask for help when I needed it, but also to be the shoulder when someone else needed it. I've learned about myself, this country, this earth, from reading about other people's experiences. I've traveled all over the US, been to concerts and cons and people's homes. I've shaken hands with famous people and eaten in diners and frozen to death in lines. I've laughed and smiled more than I knew was possible. You guys have changed my life. You taught me that it's okay to be ME. You taught me about creativity and self-confidence. You taught me how to think and argue and decide for myself. You helped me to see that there is beauty in every day, whether it's something big or something small. You showed me that sometimes life is serious, but sometimes it isn't serious at all. You showed me that I never, ever have to be alone.

If you've never been part of a fan community, it's difficult to explain how unusual and powerful this sense of belongingness is. Kay also "found her-self" through fandom, which helped her negotiate real-life changes in her career and family, as her children grew up and her relationship with her husband evolved. Like us—and many other women—she was rediscovering and redefining herself after a lifelong struggle to be authentic.

It's really about creativity, personal relationships, and freedom of expression. I made a pledge to myself last fall. Be myself. Give myself permission to ex-press what I'm thinking and feeling—even if I think or know not everyone will agree with it. I'm almost being militaristic about this pledge to myself because I've spent so much of my life adapting to satisfy others. Another pri-mary motivation for me is the drive for differentness. I used to describe this by saying I loved to "collect" people who were oddballs. People who "didn't fit in." Recently I found the word "quirky" really fits what I meant. I love quirky. It fascinates me. I've always felt quirky and out of place—inside. I just hid it under a shell of mundane normal. And in the last 2–3 years that shell of mundane normal started to chafe me—significantly. And the final motivation I wanted to include was creativity and creation. Creativity (and imagination) are my ultimate drug of choice. And it seems to me that when people are free to fully express themselves, regardless of society's approval, some amazing creativity results. Here you can be yourself.

Mickeym described a similar sense of acceptance:

Fandom for me is a place to vent, to share, to find comfort and friendship and offer the same. It's a sounding board, social outlet, information source, entertainment source, message board and forum for many different topics. You all have helped me broaden my musical horizons, recced books and movies I never would've touched otherwise, and provided countless hours of entertainment through fanfiction, songvids, con reports, music and video uploads. Even when I can't go to an event, I always feel as though I'm there vicariously, because everyone is so generous about sharing photos and video. Through fandom, I've become more aware of things that affect me—politics, feminism, parenting, education, charitable organizations. I've had the opportunity to get involved by doing things I'm comfortable with and don't feel overwhelmed by. You've supported me through some of the worst moments of my life, and provided me with some of the best. More than anything, when I think of fandom I think of all the friends I have—casual and otherwise—and the feelings of acceptance and welcome and love that I get from them.

When times are tough, the pull of fandom is particularly strong. Fans post heartfelt stories of what fandom has meant to them in anonymous online communities like Fandomsecrets:

When I have something else to think about—a fantasy life I can retreat into if I'm writing—then I am genuinely happier. I threw away the depression pills and embraced fandom. I haven't needed the pills since; fandom really does keep me sane. It took me a long time to realize it but fandom makes me happier, so I shouldn't be embarrassed about it. Football hooligans are proud of what they're into, why shouldn't I be?

I was taught that to share left you vulnerable and that all vulnerabilities would be exploited. I could probably teach Dean Winchester a thing or two about erecting walls. But then I came here. I've seen people share their darkest moments, their innermost fears, all the things I was taught to hide . . .

I've seen people rally around to help others in genuine need. You taught me that my feelings and emotions are more than a weapon to be wielded against me. That there are people out there who genuinely care for others. Thank you to everyone whose writing, vidding and general creativity, whose wit and humour kept me going. Most of all THANK YOU for giving me a place where I felt I could be myself for a while.

The importance of fandom is clear in the icons that fans use as avatars when posting online, a visual means of communication that's a unique language as well.

Clearly, we were not the only ones to experience the unique value of

Our investment was far from casual. And we weren't the only ones.

fandom as a place to feel what you really feel, even if it's angry or terrified or selfish or sexual. We both had strong emotional reactions to fandom from the start—but from the start, they were different.

While hundreds attended Asylum in England, Lynn sat at home and moped and pined, envying those who were there. The only thing that seemed to ease her regret about not being there was tracking down every tidbit of information and every picture and video, so that she could tell herself that she didn't really *miss* any of it, just saw it through a camera lens instead of her own eyes. Luckily, almost every moment of the convention was indeed recorded for posterity and posted somewhere on YouTube thanks to both the obsessiveness and the generosity of fandom. There were vids of panel discussions, painstakingly recorded word-by-word transcripts, candid photos, and hundreds of posed "photo ops" of blissful-looking fans who got to have their pictures taken with Jensen Ackles. (This was before the Time of Twitter, which has now brought moment-by-moment con reporting to a grateful fandom.)

Kathy was more stoic (she would say rational). Lynn wanted to know everything that was happening. Kathy went with the "stick your fingers in your ears and pretend it isn't happening without me" approach, though she could not insulate herself entirely with Lynn feeding her information. At first what we saw seemed to confirm our blissful view of fandom as a place of total acceptance and mutual support. Then—unexpectedly—we were confronted with evidence that fans can be as ruthless and judgmental as any other humans. Our first taste of fan-on-fan attacks (known as "wank") happened when a young fangirl, overwhelmed with her adoration of Jensen Ackles, jumped on him, clinging like a monkey in a desperate attempt at a hug. In the hours and days following the convention, the legend of the fan "attack" grew exponentially online, morphing from the cautionary tale of an overly eager fan to that of a veritable superwoman, leaping from a staircase and tackling the hapless actor to the floor as he tried to escape into an elevator.

Sharon Vernon, a fan who later moved on to running fan conventions herself, described a harrowing scene: the girl leapt from the stairs on top of Ackles, who was knocked to the floor by the force of her ten-foot fall. The girl then wrapped arms and legs around the actor and refused to let go, hanging on even as he tried frantically to push the buttons on an elevator to get away and eluding the security people who tried to help. In true whisper-down-the-lane fashion, everyone's take on the incident (which went down in fandom history as the case of the Flying Fangirl), from fans who weren't there to celebrities who were, was different. The incident seemed to shake up the other *Supernatural* actors as much as the fans, contributing to a psychological "need to protect" on both sides. Even the actors who hadn't been there knew the story, just as all the fans did. Actress Samantha Ferris (who played sexy older woman and kickass hunter Ellen Harvelle) told us this version:

> Sci-Fi fans can be loyal and very intense, but they can be radical. Jensen got jumped on last year and it's sad because that was his first convention. He got hurt. Someone jumped on him from the staircase! And I know the other fans were mortified because they didn't want this one person to ruin it for them, but it does. Jenson was like "Woah, I'm not doing this," and so there was a lot of security after that. Jensen is not a small dude, and he and Jared are strong guys, but they can't take on a crowd. And with women freaking out, I mean guys can't even take on women at the best of times. And they're not assholes, they're the two nicest guys in the world, but they need to watch out for their own safety.

Actor Jim Beaver, who played Bobby Singer, hunter and substitute father for the Winchester boys across seven seasons, told it this way:

> I heard it from an Asylum staff person who was with Jensen when it happened. She said it was really embarrassing. He was going back to his room, waiting for the elevator, just casual. The door to the elevator opens and someone comes running up and jumps on Jensen with both arms and legs, and they both fall into the elevator and the doors close and Jensen and this girl are in the elevator and he's hitting the button and she's just on him like a spider monkey, and it was like a movie and no one could save him! Finally the door opened and they pulled her off him. They kicked her out of the convention and she spent the rest of the convention outside with a sign saying "I'm sorry, I'll be good."

Jim shook his head in sympathy for the hapless fangirl as well as the actor when he told us the story. Interestingly, it was Ferris—a woman—who responded more as the protective fangirls had. Beaver, a man, was far less eager to pathologize. Are women, we wondered, just more protective in general? Or are they quicker to turn on other women?

The Flying Fangirl, in fact, was barely old enough to be called a woman. From the stories we'd heard passed around by fans online, we had pictured a grown-up big enough to take down the six-foot-one-inch Ackles, not the young teenager who was there with her parents and apparently sat outside the convention doors all day, sobbing and begging to be allowed back in. It's easy to get overwhelmed with excitement when you're fourteen, after all. Lynn managed to stab David Cassidy in the stomach with the pen that she was trying to hand him for an autograph when she unexpectedly met him in person at that age.

Maybe Jim Beaver understood because he had his own story of being overwhelmed by fannish appreciation:

> Years ago, I was at the theater, running a spotlight for a blues singer named Linda Hopkins, and she did this show, and she was incredible. I had known her name, but wasn't really a fan. The show was over, and I closed up, and she was walking across the lobby, the audience had already left, and I did one of the least characteristic things I've ever done in my life. I saw her, and suddenly saw myself running to her. I grabbed her and told her, "I love you! That was such a great show!" That's all it was about, but I was taken aback by what I had done—then she just went on her way. I don't think she was particularly perturbed, but . . . I was like, what!? I look at that and I think, okay, I can see somebody suddenly running and jumping on the hottie.

The other Asylum guests were impacted almost as much by the unexpected display of fannish enthusiasm as Ackles himself. We asked musician Jason Manns, a friend who was walking with him at the time, what happened. "She just popped out and came at him," he told us. "I think she was trying to kiss him." It was an understandable impulse, to be sure. Giving in to it? Not so much.

"When she jumped up on him she kicked her legs around, and cracked me in the shin," Jason went on. "And Jensen stumbled backward. Security pulled her off—and I don't know how, but she got out of their grips and she came running toward the elevator. We were in there and it was like slow motion, the doors were closing, and it looked scripted, she got caught like halfway in so the doors stayed open, and they're holding her parallel to the ground screaming and they just carried her out!"

This was not exactly what Ackles and Manns were expecting from their first fan convention. At first they dismissed it as more amusing than scary—after all, isn't having an attractive young woman throw herself at you closer to fantasy material than to nightmare? Of course, we all know that fantasies work better when they stay just that. Manns said:

> Then the doors closed, and we're in the elevator thinking, what did we just get into? That was our first experience of a convention. That's why any videos from the concert, there was like a 60-foot gap between the audience and the stage . . . She was a tiny little girl, so it was only after, when we thought about it, that it really got scary. People who step outside the realm of normal society and behave in ways that people refer to as crazy—they *are* crazy, and that's how John Lennon got shot. After that point we were like, it was funny at the time, but now it's kind of scary and kind of dangerous. Everywhere Jensen goes since then, there is a big security presence.

We wondered what security at all the conventions that came later would have been like if Ackles's first con hadn't started off with such a bang—and how much that experience influenced the actor's conception of his fans. Did he worry that all of us were at risk of losing our composure and tackling him at any moment? When we asked Jensen himself (wondering if he was in fact expecting us to drop our audio recorders and jump him), he seemed to have come to terms with the whole thing.

"I laughed at that immediately as soon as I got in the elevator," he told us. "And then it was after that, I was like 'hmm, what's to stop her really jealous boyfriend from coming at me with a little knife?' Then I got a little freaked out, but I was like well, I guess if I got stabbed, I'd turn around and deck him."

Ackles clearly has learned a thing or two from playing Dean. He wasn't traumatized; the *Supernatural* fans, however, most definitely were. The young fan was unceremoniously kicked out of both the convention and the fandom community. Fans even made T-shirts ridiculing the "Flying Fangirl" and sold them online, encouraging fans to wear them to the next *Supernatural* convention just in case she got any ideas about attending. Apparently, in fandom it's one strike and you're out. We were shocked. Where was the acceptance and support that we'd come to value so much? Granted, tackling actors is never okay, but most fans could certainly relate to the impulse to give Ackles a hug, even if we'd never act on it.

The extreme hate leveled at the Flying Fangirl seemed out of proportion to the actual incident. We were struck by the sense of shame that the incident produced among fans. Fans—especially female fans—are so accustomed to accusations of insanity and prohibitions against being out of control that we have become hypervigilant for any evidence of those sorts of behaviors. The Flying Fangirl threatened to undo the assertion that fangirls are not crazy stalker chicks but rather women indulging in normal and healthy passions. That's entirely true 99.9 percent of the time. But all it takes is one extreme incident—like this one—for the outsiders to roll their eyes and say, "See? Fangirls really *are* crazy!"

Fans not only externalized their outrage onto the young woman but turned the actor's imagined fear and loathing on themselves as well, worrying that Ackles now subscribed to the idea that fangirls were not only insane but dangerous. This was our first exposure to internalized fan shame, which runs deeply through fandom and contributes to some of the most vicious fan-on-fan attacks. The defensiveness and shame were surprising to Lynn at the time, because she'd been lounging happily in her fandom "honeymoon phase" and still wearing her rose-colored glasses. In contrast, they were uncomfortably familiar, if only in a dimly realized way, to Kathy. (She would have ample opportunity in the coming months to examine her own shame more closely.)

In fact, women seem to be vulnerable to feeling ashamed of whatever it is that they use their leisure time for. Traditionally, the more leisure time women had, the more threatening whatever they did to fill it seemed. Women who spent time reading novels (or later seeing movies) were being unproductive—or worse. Things haven't changed all that much. We may in fact have more leisure time than in previous generations, but we are not necessarily allowed to enjoy it. Our culture sanctions "football Sundays" for men (and Saturdays and Mondays for that matter). But women may sneak off to their computers only after the kids are in bed, claiming a need to write emails or research cold remedies in order to have a clandestine rendezvous with their LJ friends or read some racy romantic fanfiction.

One fan told us:

> My family knows I like *Supernatural* . . . but they just don't get it and they find
> it silly and therefore they find ME silly and it shouldn't matter but somehow
> it still does. It's being looked at like you're a thirteen year old again with post-
> ers on your wall that you kiss every night. (Which I SO didn't do *coughs*)
> Because they just don't understand what it means being a part of fandom
> and what an incredible experience that is, being with people who share your
> obsession and who just *get it*.

Deirdre C, another fangirl, also married with children, described her psychological struggle this way:

> In my family, people are expected to be engaged productively, not wasting
> time with amateur fanfiction and flailing over pictures of cute actors. And I
> can see the point, in some ways. But on the other hand, I have the right to
> do things that make me happy, even if they aren't the things my loved ones
> would understand. Yes, it's no fun having to hide such an important part of
> my life. However, it's wonderful to have a place like this where I DON'T have
> to be the serious adult, the good parent, the perfect daughter, the charming
> neighbor. It's a safe zone, you know?

We knew. But as much as they enjoy fandom and recognize what they're
getting from it, fans are ashamed of their own enthusiasm, guilty about
spending time indulging in something as "unproductive" as fandom. We
were no exception. So the reality of a fangirl at Asylum—one of US—suc-
cumbing to what everyone kept insinuating were "dangerous passions" was
more threatening than might be expected. Of course, tackling people, no
matter how much you claim to adore them, is never going to be welcomed
by the person on the receiving end. No surprise there. But fandom is a
fiercely protective place. There are lines that fans are not allowed to step
over, even if you don't know where they are until you've crossed one. One
thing's for sure—if you do step over those lines, the fans themselves will
let you know.

In fact, we soon discovered that fans are as protective of their own fan
practices as they are of their chosen fandom and its celebrities, simultaneously defensive and ashamed. While fans constantly post online about how
fandom helped them feel less ashamed and more okay about themselves,

that doesn't mean that they want anyone else to know about how they got that way. The First Rule of Fandom is tell no one about fandom.

Another incident at Asylum drove this point home. Fans still tend to think of fanfiction as something done in secret, best kept to the warm cloistered depths of the fandom community so that it can flourish unobstructed. But fanfiction is an increasingly popular creative enterprise, added to the *Merriam-Webster* online dictionary in 2009 and discussed everywhere from the *New York Times* to *Entertainment Weekly* to *Time Magazine* (and in virtually every discussion about *Fifty Shades of Grey*). Everywhere, that is, except within earshot of the people who are being written about—like Jensen Ackles sitting onstage at the Asylum convention.

As we watched the videos of the convention online, hunched over Kathy's laptop, a fan stepped up to the microphone to ask Ackles a question. "What do you think of the fanfiction?" she asked pleasantly.

A loud gasp could be heard from the audience. That was the sound of the First Rule of Fandom being broken. Even as the question hung in the air, fans were mobilizing. Ackles, however, was nonchalant. "My favorite is Wincest," he said dryly. At the dropped jaws of the audience, he then added, "I just hope my grandmother doesn't stumble over it."

To understand the gasping and jaw-dropping going on in the convention ballroom (and in the online fandom that was following along), you need to understand that fanfiction comes in many different flavors. There's gen, fanfiction with plot and drama that doesn't revolve around romantic pairings. Sam and Dean, looking dashing as ever in their tight jeans and muddied T-shirts, hunt a wendigo and barely escape with their lives. Het fic pairs a male and female character romantically. Sam and Dean hunt a wendigo (still dashing) and then Dean hooks up with Layla for a night of steamy lovemaking. Slash takes two (usually straight) male characters and throws them into bed together. Sam and Dean (still dashing, jeans still tight) fight a wendigo and then Dean hooks up with (the equally dashing and male) Castiel, while Sam laments that far too many of his romantic encounters end up with someone dead. Gen is the least controversial type of fanfic, for obvious reasons. Slash is the most controversial, even today, and also the most popular in *Supernatural* fandom.

Some fic (canon) follows the script of the show. Other fic that diverges into an "alternate universe" is known as AU, a sort of write-your-own ending book that lets the writers make the show over into exactly what they want. Dean's a bounty hunter. Sam's a law student. Dean's a bounty hunter who needs a lawyer but can only afford a law student. (Readers of *Fifty Shades of Grey* know that the books started as AU *Twilight* fanfiction.) In genderswap fic, one of the boys wakes up as a girl and the other proceeds to tease him—sorry, her—unmercifully and buy lots of Victoria's Secret panties. In crack fic, anything can—and does—happen. Dean gets turned into a dog, and Sam loves him anyway. Sam gets cursed by a witch and has to get laid *right now* or die, so Dean . . . well, you get the picture.

And then there's that "other stuff," which raises eyebrows among nonfans and fans alike. In hurt/comfort (H/C) fic, someone is afflicted with illness, injury, disability, or a supernatural curse (in fannish parlance, "whumped") and then is comforted. The hurt is often graphic and extreme, which makes this a controversial fan favorite. Some online communities for fics explore Dean Winchester's unfortunate propensity for being thrown up against walls and ending up bruised and bloody and the equally common incidents of Sam Winchester getting himself strangled. PWP fic (Plot? What plot?) doesn't require a plot because it's usually so scorchingly hot that it would melt your ability to understand the plot before you could make sense of it anyway.

RPF (real person fic) features the show's actors in various fictional adventures. Admittedly, the real people are often unrecognizable in the fictional stories, as happily acknowledged up front by the writers and understood by any fanfic reader. None of the fanfic authors claimed to know "the boys," as every writer, director, actor, publicist, journalist, production assistant (PA), and dog walker call Ackles and Padalecki. Neither did the fanfic writers claim to have any clue about what the actors actually get up to in their off-screen time. As far as we know, nobody believes that Jensen is actually a secret agent working covertly for the Central Intelligence Agency or that Jared is romantically entwined with Paris Hilton—or, more commonly in fanfic, his co-star Jensen (a pairing known affectionately as "J2" or "JSquared"). But RPF makes some fans uncomfortable simply because it's written about real people, who might conceivably stumble upon a pornographic tale of their exploits with someone they may or may not even like, let alone want to tumble into bed with. Or their grandmothers might stumble over it—awkward.

And then there's Wincest. While the fans gathered at the Asylum con gasped in shock, Ackles had referenced the most controversial *Supernatural* fanfiction of all—stories that imagine a romantic relationship between brothers Sam and Dean (combine Winchester and incest: voilà, Wincest!). Wincest is controversial because it's . . . well, incest. True, it is fictional character incest, and without reproductive risk (though fictional character reproduction isn't exactly a big concern, come to think of it), incest between equals if you will. But incest nevertheless. Never mind that even popular hip hop songs celebrate getting it on with a young woman and her sister and that male fantasies of what happens when a man meets a willing set of twins are the subject of stacks of straight-male porn (and eventually even winked at in the Season 3 opener of *Supernatural* itself). We've already established that what's good for the gander isn't necessarily okay for the goose.

Some online communities are devoted to Wincest fic, and other communities are devoted to protesting it, resulting in periodic rants within the fandom that bounce back and forth between "Ewwww, don't you have any brothers?" and "It's fiction, stupid! I don't actually consort with vampires either." (This is not, in case you're wondering, an aberration unique to the *Supernatural* fandom. Similar communities exist in many other sibling-populated fandoms including *Harry Potter* [Twincest], *The Vampire Diaries*, and bands such as My Chemical Romance and Good Charlotte, among others.)

Most of the fans, following along through written online accounts of Asylum instead of witnessing the exchange, never actually heard the fan's question or Jensen's response, let alone saw his telltale smirk. Once again, the actual events got lost and replaced with the fandom's more paranoid shame-tinged version. ("She asked Jensen about Wincest, OMG!") This fan was ostracized as swiftly as the Flying Fangirl, even though she hadn't attempted any actor-tackling. Fans struggled with the internalized shame of being a fangirl, projecting their fears onto the actors and expressing their discomfort in a plethora of humorous icons.

Meanwhile, Ackles and friends at Asylum continued to have fun with their burgeoning knowledge of oh-so-secret fan activities. Joining musician Jason Manns onstage for a song later that evening, Jensen quipped, "I'll sing it from *this* side," making a show of not getting too close. Jason took

Fangirl? Who, me?

up the joke with an admonition to the fans as he strummed his guitar: "No pictures with little innuendos, we're sharing a microphone, completely platonic—just be sensitive." Jensen alternated between singing harmony and keeping his distance from Jason with a knowing grin.

Around this time another harsh reality intruded on our safe and accepting community. It's one thing when fans police each other. It's another when the censorship comes from outside the seemingly safe space of Live Journal. In 2007, corporate pressure on the part of LJ owners Six Apart to silence the non-mainstream voices that have made Live Journal their home resulted in a random crackdown on both individual users and entire communities. It's no coincidence that Live Journal is a largely female fannish space, and Six Apart seemed quite happy to be the unofficial police of female sexuality. The internalized fan shame only made it easier for them. Kathy replaced her brand-new fanfic tags with the infinitely more PC "bunnies, rated g for goodie two shoes, unicorns, and unoffensive material" and changed her location to "undisclosed" lest the LJ police come to find her with guns blazing. All over this insulated little world we'd discovered, people were locking their doors and changing their names. The psychological benefits of finding a place where "you can be you" and share your love of all things *Supernatural* seemed about to be blown up in an online witch hunt that left fandom vacillating between terrified and furious. But rather than abandoning their "safe spaces," fans found ways around the invasion. In the end, uniting against a common enemy served to bring the virtual fandom community closer together. At the same time, our own sense of community intensified, and our determination to keep researching the "real story" of fandom intensified with it.

Meanwhile, in the real world, we had each other. We continued to make frequent trips to each other's houses for "girls' weekends," which meant nonstop watching of *Supernatural*, loud and frequently R-rated squeeing, and very little of anything else. As we sat huddled around Lynn's computer late one night reading fanfic, we got a call from Lana, our SPN enabler, giving us the heads-up that Jensen was set to star in a local Fort Worth production of *A Few Good Men*. She wondered if we'd like to go with her. We wondered if this was a rhetorical question.

The road trip was beginning.

THREE

. . . . .

Get a (Sex) Life

On our first fannish excursion to Fort Worth, we were already struggling to balance our fan lives with our real-life responsibilities (mother, partner, friend, professor), torn between the first love thrill of fandom and our sometimes debilitating guilt about indulging our passion—a guilt that we suspected might not be so strongly felt if we had been avid knitters or gardeners. As a matter of fact, Kathy was an avid knitter and gardener and never did feel guilty about that—perhaps because those pursuits spoke to home and family. Her kids could help in the garden; they wore the sweaters she knit and accompanied her on forays to sheep farms. These were wholesome pastimes. Fandom, in contrast, was a kid-free zone.

Our significant others were variously tolerant, confused, or amused. Our children were less amused, grumbling about being deserted in the middle of family obligations and more than a little worried about their mothers' priorities. Even our fellow fangirl friends, Lana in particular, weren't exactly on the same page. If we were doing fandom right, then we were doing everything else wrong, or so it seemed.

We made our first mistake with Lana even before we boarded the plane for Texas. Lynn had bought us matching shirts that read simply "/Writer." Undecipherable to nonfans, it said it all to the initiated: Slash Writer. We thought that they were clever. Lana did not share our opinion. In fact the shirt managed to offend her in two ways. There was no third shirt, and she felt understandably left out of our little joke. Worse yet was our disregard of her feelings when it came to slash. Lana was a slash writer herself—indeed we had both written fanfiction with her in the past, in other fandoms. But in *Supernatural* fandom, the default romantic pairing at the time was either fictional brothers Sam and Dean or real people Jared and Jensen. Lana did not approve of either. She said nothing, and we were too clueless at the time to realize our blunders. They would not be the last ones we made over the next twenty-four hours.

Lana wasn't the only one to see certain aspects of fandom differently; as soon as we hit the road, our own divergent personalities started to become clear. Arriving at the Casa Mañana theater on our first night in Fort Worth, we walked through the same lobby, saw the same people, and had vastly different reactions to what we encountered there. Lynn saw a throng of kindred spirits who shared her passion and couldn't wait to get to know as many of them as possible. Kathy saw "fangirls" subscribing to all the negative stereotypes (nerdy, socially awkward, and no doubt living with at least half a dozen cats) and sought to distance herself from them. "That's not me!" she told herself, conveniently ignoring the fact that we had flown one thousand miles to ogle One Good Man. It turned out that Kathy's reaction wasn't uncommon. Perhaps still smarting from the Flying Fangirl fiasco, more than one discussion thread on the new Live Journal community dedicated to Ackles's run in *A Few Good Men* included admonitions to other fans to "behave." But these admonitions were even stricter. Be quiet. Be calm. In other words, don't act like the fangirls and fanboys that we were. One person even reminded us to dress appropriately, perhaps assuming that we were too uncultured (because of our affection for a television show?) to know how to behave in the more rarefied space of a theater. Of course this advice was being given by another fangirl, but one thing we learned quickly is that fans know how to compartmentalize and can "other" with the best of them.

Fans' need to police fandom and Kathy's discomfort were both manifestations of that internalized fan shame that we saw demonstrated at the Asylum con. Part of the discomfort is the niggling worry that we're being selfish, frivolous, unproductive—that, God forbid, we're doing something *fun*. Part of it is the knowledge that we're hooked on a sci-fi show, of all things. Part of it is the fear that creative practices like fanfiction or fanart or fanvids will be ridiculed. But part of it runs deeper, especially when women are fans of a television show which stars actors who look like Ackles and Padalecki or any other attractive celebrity. That part has everything to do with sex—which for women has everything to do with shame.

Fanboys are no strangers to fan shame. But while male media fans fear being perceived as not sexual enough (the stereotypical fanboy virgin living in his mother's basement), female fans seem fearful that being a fan makes them too sexual. The entire culture seems to share that fear. Fangirls aren't sedate, controlled, calm, or quiet—therefore, they must be crazybadwrong stalkers who can't tell the difference between fantasy and reality (and thus are at serious risk of doing something shamefully, frightfully, and overtly sexual, though nobody seems clear about what that dreaded thing might be). Fan shame for female fans often seems inextricably linked with shame about sexuality.

We figured this out in a Starbucks (where else?) at the Dallas airport, while we were waiting for Lana.

"That's it!" Lynn exclaimed to Kathy over steaming cups of coffee and chai. "It's all about SEX!"

"Shhhh," the woman sitting next to us admonished.

Sex is still a bad word almost everywhere, especially when spoken by women. We need only look at recent politics to be assured that, despite the "progress" of the last several decades, women are in many ways just as constrained as ever. In June 2012, the Michigan State Legislature barred representative Lisa Brown from speaking on a new abortion bill after she used the word "vagina" on the house floor. Such language, she was told, "violated the decorum" of the House. Discussing affordable access to contraception in front of House Democrats earned Sandra Fluke the label of "slut" from an offended Rush Limbaugh. This gets even more confusing when you factor in television networks that market actors who look like Padalecki and Ackles or studios who cast the likes of *Twilight*'s Robert Pattinson to appeal not only to young girls but to their mothers. We are told to look and like, but when grown women succumb (and admit) to desire, TPTB get nervous. Something about turning men into lust objects apparently is unsettling and needs to be controlled. Thus, "Twi-Moms" are depicted as creepy, ridiculous, unattractive, and bad mothers to boot. In a particularly scathing comment on the phenomenon of Twi-Moms, one man asked, "Do these women have no shame?" And even though a recent *Entertainment Weekly* commentary, "Hollywood Gets Wise to Women," seemed to celebrate women's right to gaze, it concentrated more on women finally being treated to the strong female characters that we presumably all want rather than on women's "right to a cheap thrill." Validation, when it does come, arrives more often than not with a dollop of derision.

Research tells us that women are more prone to shame than men, though we didn't really need research to tell us that. Even Freud weighed in on the subject, calling shame a "feminine characteristic." Few would disagree that we live in a patriarchal society. That means that female identity is under constant surveillance, leaving women to struggle with who we are and whether who we are is "okay." Many of us are good at constructing false selves to hide behind, facades that align with the way the culture tells us we "should be," which gains us approval but cuts us off from the real self underneath. Shame is the thing that keeps us in denial about who we really are and also makes us want to hide that real self from other people. Unfortunately, when you can never be real with anyone, nobody can ever make you feel validated or accepted for who you really are. Shame is an isolating experience, the opposite of belonging. That's why finding fandom, with its "safe space" and accepting community, can feel so compelling for women. We'd spent our lives being good girls, doing well in school, defining ourselves as loving wives and self-sacrificing mothers and hard workers. But who were we underneath all those carefully constructed oh-so-pleasant facades? Why did we feel not-quite-okay when we'd played by the rules all those years?

Let's get back to sex for a minute. As Irving Yalom identified in his research on why people are drawn to join groups, one of the things that we all need validation about is sex. We all fear that we're just a bit too "out there," that what turns us on isn't what turns other people on. The only thing that makes those self-destructive feelings go away is finding a group within which to share who you really are—warts and all. People inevitably discover that they're not so "out there" after all. That discovery normalizes and validates, allowing people to feel a whole hell of a lot better about themselves.

Both women and men struggle with cultural norms that are imposed on all of us when it comes to sexuality. But in spite of the strides made in acknowledging (but still not celebrating) women's unique sexualities in the wake of the so-called sexual revolution, a double standard still exists. Men have few social prohibitions against having a strong sex drive, masturbating, or using porn or erotica to get off. Women remain more socially restricted when it comes to sexual behaviors and even sexual desire. For women, the accepted norms hold that women want to be the objects of desire—that we want others to desire us. We're almost never encouraged to be the *subjects* of our own desire, which makes it hard to connect with our own bodies and our own sexuality. Young women aren't socialized to get in touch with what *we* want but instead to concentrate on what *others* want—to be objects instead of subjects. Women end up focused on how we look and who we can attract and how to make other people feel good, instead of what attracts *us*—hell, sometimes we don't even know! Fandom, in contrast, is all about what attracts *us* and makes *us* feel good. In the broader culture, women are used to having our desires constantly policed with the scary threat of "slut shaming," from middle school clear through adulthood. We're certainly not encouraged to be "kinky," although research shows that women's fantasies are every bit as kinky as men's. We're discouraged from even talking about sex, and certainly not openly or honestly. Fandom provides some of that missing conversation, changing the norms to allow women to get in touch with their own desires and openly express their genuine selves, including their sexual selves. Online communities tend to encourage more free and disinhibited, more direct expression. Women can begin to embrace their own sexuality and include room for activities or fantasies that they might otherwise have disowned, denied, or suppressed.

The accepted wisdom of the culture holds that women don't like to look— fandom turns that so-called wisdom on its ear. Hell yes, we like to look!

Fans create and post both G-rated and more explicit photos and fanart of their favorite characters and actors for the enjoyment of other female fans, something that rarely happens in real-life social interaction. We're used to what feminist research calls the "male gaze" turned on women; fandom turns the "female gaze" right back on men. Within the secret space of on-line fandom, objectifying instead of being objectified is normalized. Some fans see this as a way of challenging the status quo. One comment on a fanvid of attractive male television characters in various compromising (and half-dressed) positions said: "I feel perfectly justified in an eye-for-an-eye way. Because for me, what this vid says is that we can objectify you just as well as you can objectify us. This is brutal and honest female desire. It may not give fangirls any moral high ground (the opposite) but then, being morally superior has never been a tool of emancipation."

Fans—and many researchers—see fanfiction as a similar tool for chal-

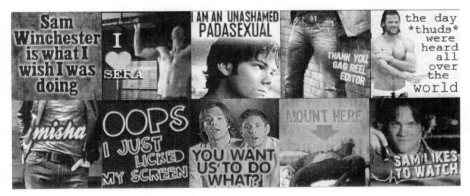

Of course we watch for the plot . . .

lenging the status quo. The fanfiction community is largely a community of women. Plenty of fanfiction is G-rated: rich character studies and suspenseful case fics and heartwarming childhood tales. Plenty of it is anything but, exploring sexual themes that run the gamut from vanilla to oh-so-kinky. The entire world now knows that some of that fanfic explores bdsm (bondage, discipline, sadomasochism) themes, thanks to the popularity of fanfic-turned-bestseller *Fifty Shades of Grey*, but that only scratches the surface. Slash, hurt/comfort, threesomes; wings, tails, tentacles; werewolves, vampires, demons; you name it, and there's fanfiction about it. Unlike the woman in Starbucks, the response of fellow fans is often closer to "gimme more" than to "shhhh."

A 2011 research study out of Hunter College found that the majority of female fans believed that being in online fandom had changed their attitudes about their own and others' sexuality. Fandom helped them discover and accept their own fantasies and turn-ons and gave them the permission to acknowledge themselves as sexual beings. They described these changes as liberating and rewarding, saying that they felt more "in touch" with their desires and needs. They also felt relieved of shame and embarrassment and freed from social proscriptions that limit women's expression of sexuality. They were less frightened of their own desires and more confident in general. While women may be socialized to view sex only in terms of relationships and romance, women have as wide a range of sexual fantasies as men do—including many that are "taboo." Women just feel more guilty about them. Even masturbation is perceived as non-normative for women. But in fandom "I'll be in my bunk" is said with pride, often as thanks to an author for a particularly "inspiring" fic. We found the freedom of expression, sexual and otherwise, that exists in fandom to be nothing less than life-changing. We could be real and honest. We could be lustful, resentful, sexual. We could be angry at a culture that had constrained us and giddy at finding a subculture that didn't. That we were writing and reading slash only intensified the sense of liberation.

Slash is one of the most popular types of *Supernatural* fanfiction (with sometimes vocal opposition from people like our friend Lana) and a common practice across a wide variety of fandoms. There are all sorts of explanations for why women would want to write fictional stories about two men getting it on (including the tried and true "Hey, nobody questions it when guys go gaga over two girls getting it on"). Somehow it seemed a lot weirder when women tried for quid pro quo, even though we realized that was unfair. Why do so many of us find slash so hot? We weren't just intrigued by that question from a detached, academic researcher perspective. This was personal. *We* found slash hot and had already had a tough time explaining why to the few people outside fandom that we trusted enough to try. There was already a fair amount of academic theory out there about why women read and write slash, but much of it didn't ring true for us or for the other women we knew in fandom. We agreed with the research that basically says that slash and fanfiction and the arts in general can be understood as activities that "pick the lock" of our brain's pleasure centers. This line of research says that women enjoy slash fiction for the same reasons they enjoy the romance novels that used to be found in every drugstore and bookstore. In fact, it turns out that slash fiction and romance novels often follow the same formula—both are wish-fulfilling fantasies designed to lockpick the pleasure centers of female brains (male wish-fulfilling fantasies are somewhat different, as anyone who's ever known a male probably knows). In both romance novels and slash fiction, the hero possesses the same attributes. He's a warrior—tall, strong, handsome, muscular, sexually bold, confident, and smart. In other words, like the Winchesters. The basic story is also similar—a love story, a relationship that's unique, a couple who slowly realize that they're soulmates and overcome obstacles to find their happy ending. Slash may or may not include explicit sex, but if it does, the emphasis is often on the emotional more than the physical.

Some of that research fit for us, but we wanted more than an explanation. We wanted validation. So after we'd hit the books and done the traditional sort of research, we tried a more direct approach—we asked some of our fellow fangirls: "Why do you write slash?"

Sarah talked about writing fanfiction, including slash, as a way of becoming part of the participative community of fans. "I write fan fiction because it allows me to belong to a collective creative consciousness in a way that nothing else I can imagine does. And when I succeed in writing something that means something to someone else's canon, that resonates, or illuminates, I am becoming part of this elusive but completely vital *thing* that is fandom."

"I think the only answer I've ever been able to come up with to that question is 'I cannot NOT write it,'" said one friend. "It's like an itch under my skin and voices in my head and feelings of the characters pressuring me to be put on paper. Also, hot men together make my pants happy."

Another gave us a David Letterman–esque countdown, with typical fannish humor, about all the cultural inadequacies that slash "fixes" (thanks to former LJ user sl-cross, wherever you are!).

5—Traditional pornography is crude and unimaginative. Tab A into slot B. *yawn* Slash is to me an exercise in erotica, and the difference is that erotica is rich with emotion, not just the physical.

4—Traditional TV and movies so often use what I call "cookie-cutter" females. They do not reflect anything close to me, or how I think, and are often quite shallow characters. I cannot relate to them. The male lead(s) usually have far more interesting dynamics going on between them. Like most women, I love the intricacies involved in relationships.

3—Two hot men together is naughty and fun and I want to watch. It's the same for guys and seeing two hot girls together. It feeds the voyeur in me.

2—Male slash is the height of sensual romance. What you need is two males who have very different viewpoints, who struggle against all odds together, often struggle against each other, but are extremely loyal, and most important of all—will gladly die for each other. Throw in a healthy dose of angst, tragedy, conflict, heroic deeds. All slashed males have been shown on the screen in that iconic picture of two men standing back to back with weapons drawn. All that is missing is sex . . . which slashers provide because we know that just causes more tension in an already complex relationship, and forces male characters to deal with *gasp* their feelings on an intimate level. Slash gives them a vulnerability never to be seen on the screen, and the risks they face are greater because of it.

1—Slash writers break social taboos about what women are supposed to be like. I think we are a necessary and inevitable reaction to pop culture. I enjoy the fights, action, violence and gore as much as any boy. Depicting two men together allows me to write about sex in a way that I could not do with a man and a woman. The boys can be meaner and rougher with each other and act out aggressive behaviour that blurs the lines of consensual sex. With Dean and Sam, the ultimate societal taboo of incest is explored, and not presented as a bad thing most of the time. *horrors* It is a guilty pleasure to read and to write. *egads but SPN fans are rebels*

We agreed—at least, our secret online identities did. Within the "safe space" of online fandom, female fans refuse to be told what they can and can't like, whether it's slash or something else. To put it in more impressive-sounding terms, we proclaim our rebellion against constricting social norms by celebrating a subversive sexuality—with slash, Not-Safe-for-Work (NSFW) fanart, hurt/comfort, bdsm (long before *Fifty Shades of Grey*), explicit het fanfiction, any kink you could possibly imagine (and you some you probably couldn't)—or whatever else floats our boat. And then something magical happens—others in fandom let us know that whatever that is, it's okay. In fact, more than a few fellow fans have harbored a secret liking of whatever-it-is themselves. They jump online to say "OMG yes, me too!" or "OMG, so hot!" or "OMG so dirtybadwrong, gimme more!" Everyone engaged in the conversation feels validated and normalized and just a little bit less weird.

As one fan said, "Shaming women for their sexuality seems to be universal. It was fanfiction that opened my eyes and heart to the wide range of 'normal,' and fandom that freed me to know myself as a sexual adult."

When we asked why they write fanfiction, many fans talked about the joy of self-expression—of writing the stories they wanted, or sometimes *needed*, to tell. Creating and sharing fanworks is a social activity. Fans have described it as part of a long history of women's "secret" art—from quilts to pies to hats to writing. The communal aspect of fandom gives writers and artists a built-in audience, as fans comment on and expand on each other's work, validating each other in the process. One fan said, "Fandom sets your fantasies free and gives you a peer group that you can talk freely about without feeling shame."

Sometimes the stories that fans write are just for fun, or to fill in plot holes that a television show or film or book left gaping, or just to toss two good-looking men into bed together. Sometimes they also contain a component of self-healing, similar to what happens when psychologists use narrative therapy or expressive writing to help people figure out who they are and to feel better about it. A stack of research out there on the therapeutic effects of writing about the bad stuff that happens to all of us along the way shows that people tend to feel better and do better when they can express their genuine emotions. We're all the narrators of our own life stories, figuring out who we are in the telling. It turns out that it's even more effective to re-write our stories as fiction. Dealing with past hurts or broken relationships or just trying to figure out who you are for real? Writing a fictional story of Sam and Dean Winchester enduring something similar—and coming out on the other side—can help the writer come out on the other side herself.

For women, mapping our experience onto male characters can be especially empowering, freeing ourselves from cultural expectations about gender.

We had plunged into *Supernatural* fanfiction headfirst. After a few months of lurking and reading, we took a deep breath and started to write it. For us, there was no question as to what we wanted to write. We were slash writers—always had been. We wrote Real Person Slash (RPS). We wrote Wincest. We were both damned.

Kathy's first piece of fanfiction was so angsty that it had Lynn sobbing all day at work. The comments on the fic took up four LJ pages, and Kathy's friends list grew by leaps and bounds. Soon we were both writing and posting fic and starting to feel like we really knew the people reading and leaving feedback. We felt accepted, comfortable, validated. The fandom felt like home. We also quickly gained reputations both as decent writers and as women with no boundaries who can't hold their liquor, after Kathy drank far too many blue martinis with her hubby and was foolish enough to post the following helpful advice about knowing when you've read too much *Supernatural* NC-17 fanfiction:

1. Every word is a dirty word. Most verbs, adjectives, adverbs and nouns, because basically *everything* sounds dirty to you by now.
2. You name your hands. You name them Jared and Jensen.
3. You make emergency runs to the supermarket for batteries. Lots of batteries.
4. Samndean is all one word because, well, yeah!
5. Your water bill has gone up astronomically. You chalk it up to a spike in the number of cold showers you've been taking lately.

So yes, in case it's not clear yet—fandom is sometimes all about sex. Those critics gnashing their teeth about Byron inciting the feminine masses and those censors cutting Elvis off at the waist might have been onto something. Sex might not be the motivating factor when you're a forty-something straight dude painting yourself green to go root for the Philadelphia Eagles (though Freud might have something to say about that), but for many women in media fandom it is all about sex, in one way or another. Willfully ignoring that is to miss one of the important aspects of fandom as well as several truths about women and desire and sexuality that, like fandom itself, are more often than not buried under layers of propriety.

All well and good, in the safe space of online fandom. But try to bring those fannish practices into the harsh light of "real life" and fans balk, overcome by that internalized shame they can't quite shake (as the hapless questioner at the Asylum con found out firsthand). In fact, fangirls feel so ashamed that they're convinced that the celebrities feel the same. Again and again at *Supernatural* conventions, a fan steps up to the microphone to ask the actors, "What's the weirdest thing a fan has ever done?" Clearly this carries the assumption that fangirls are constantly doing something odd and shameful, if not outright illegal or immoral. We wondered why nobody asked, "What's the best, most unselfish, most flattering thing a fan has ever done?" Let's talk about the charity endeavors, the fan support of the show and actors' other projects, the compliments. Or is it all about proving that "those other fans are weird, unlike Little Miss Normal—i.e., me!"

As we arrived in Fort Worth and took our front row seats for *A Few Good Men*, we were relishing the joys of being with fellow fans but struggling with our guilt about ogling a hot actor. We were simultaneously giddy with anticipation and still feeling a little silly about it when the play began. Almost immediately, we found ourselves less than three feet from our TV boyfriend himself—Jensen Ackles, in the flesh!

We were not only a few feet from Ackles but literally three feet from his backside. As in there he was, standing in front of us in his costume dress whites, gesturing and stalking back and forth across a stage that was low enough that we had a bird's-eye view of his dress-white-encased ass the moment he bounded onto the stage. And then he bent over. Lynn gasped out loud, breathless. Kathy looked over once to make sure that Lynn had not actually passed out then sank down a little deeper in her seat, trying to pretend that the up close and personal moment meant nothing to her and that she was just there for the brilliant Aaron Sorkin dialogue. Objectifying? Who, us? Later that night, in the safety of online fandom, Kathy had no problem at all with giving voice to her inner fangirl and happily posted all of the most important details of the evening: Jensen was even better looking in person. Jensen's girlfriend was there: Jared wasn't. Jensen's ass looked fabulous in dress whites. The unfortunate haircut couldn't detract from his good looks. (And did she mention that he was better looking in person?) Oh, and a play apparently occurred while she was staring at Jensen.

It felt good to be able to share the squee with the rest of fandom, and we sat up half the night hunched over Kathy's laptop disseminating the details of the evening to the fans who were waiting at their computers with bated breath. We knew firsthand how that felt. We were so busy sharing our experience with fans online that we were oblivious to the fact that we were further alienating Lana, the real-life friend who was glaring at us from across the room. She wasn't an active part of the online community and didn't appreciate us spending most of the night typing up reports and happily answering the comments as they poured in. We were paying more attention to our own sudden influential status in the fandom (first to post!) than to our friend. This was our second blunder. By the time we finally closed the laptop and called it a night, our friendship with Lana was already threatened.

We woke up the next morning still giddy from seeing Ackles in person and still oblivious to how angry our friend was. We had some time to kill after breakfast before heading to the airport, so we went in search of the *Dallas Morning News*, which was rumored to have a review of the play's opening night. The search led to a Barnes and Noble, where Kathy also checked out the magazine section.

"They have a *Smallville* magazine and not one for *Supernatural*?" she said incredulously to Lynn.

"Were you at the play last night?" a disembodied voice asked. A petite young woman popped her head around the end of the row of magazines, smiling at us.

And that's how we met Allie, who had driven all the way to Texas from Mississippi to see Jensen in person. She had set aside a whole week to spend in Fort Worth, planning to see three or four of Ackles's performances, and wondered why we flew all the way to Texas for just one. We started to wonder the same thing. After all, we were already here. Why not stay an extra day and see another? Pretty soon we were making phone calls to see if there were any tickets available for that night's performance and rearranging our travel plans.

Lynn pulled out her cell phone and tried to talk US Air into changing our flight.

"Seriously?" Lana asked in disbelief. "You're staying another day?"

"Why not?" we countered, while Lynn was on hold. And yes, we were a bit defensive.

"Well, I can't change my plans," Lana stated emphatically. She had planned this one day as a layover between home and the rest of her vacation plans with other people. There was no wiggle room in her travel plans.

"Okay," we said in unison, but it wasn't. Once again, Lana watched as we indulged ourselves without her.

Lynn went back to her conversation with the ticket agent. She looked exasperated then frustrated. Finally she put down the phone. "Yes!" she said, grinning. "Flight changed!"

Lana scowled and said nothing.

This was our third mistake and, as it turned out, a crucial one. When we parted, Lana was on her way to the airport and we were happily on our way to the theater to pick up two of the last six tickets for that night's performance. In our excitement, we completely failed to notice that Lana was upset, feeling left out once again. And Lana was not the only one who was angry. The cellphone conversations in which we broke the news to our families that we'd extended our stay in Texas were uncomfortable to say the least.

"But my AP French exam is tomorrow," Kathy's daughter pointed out, her voice icy.

"But I thought you were driving me to the football game tomorrow," Lynn's son complained.

"That's great you're having a good time, but what do you *mean* you need to stay an extra day?" her partner Doug asked when Lynn gave him her modified ETA.

"Fine with me," Kathy's husband offered, the only real voice of affirmation we heard.

Our families' reactions tempered our fangirl euphoria. Were we doing something wrong? Was it a stupid decision to stay an extra day? There was no doubt in our minds that it was a selfish choice, and that didn't sit well with either of us. But was it really a big deal? Twenty-four more hours to see an entire additional performance of the play we'd flown across the country to see seemed like a good trade-off. At least that's what we told ourselves.

Allie didn't let us stew about it for too long.

"C'mon, girls," she encouraged, "let's have some fun."

We shook off our lingering guilt, climbed into Allie's jeep, and drove off to explore Fort Worth. We spent the rest of the day with Allie, fangirling it up—sometimes loudly and somewhat lewdly. We compared notes on Jensen's assets (acting and otherwise) from the night before. We debated the plot twists of the last season of *Supernatural* and our hopes for the new one. We shared recommendations for the best works of fanfiction we'd read, gleefully noting our agreement on some of them. Then Allie popped a CD in and played us the very unofficial anthem of the fandom, a gloriously irreverent song penned and recorded by fan Virginia Tingley called "The Ballad of Jared and Jensen." We quickly learned the words, opened all the windows, and began to sing along.

> This is the story of two straight men,
> They're straight, they swear, except for when
> They meet each other and Jared's so pretty and so is Jen
> So they can't really help it, but here goes, you guys,
> Here's my love story . . .
>
> Jared's got this girlfriend
> And he likes her, sure he does, cuz she's a girl
> And he loves girls—and his dogs—and candy—and Jensen
> Because . . .
>
> Jensen and Jared are in love
> Don't try to deny their epic romance
> Jensen and Jared are in love
> Even Kripke can see it
> Which is why he puts all kindsa hella awesome
> Sexual tension into his show
> Even though the characters are brothers . . .

This is what being a fan is all about. It's meeting someone else who "gets it" and then indulging in ways that women—especially grown women who should "know better"—never do. Driving around Fort Worth with someone we met in a bookstore that morning singing the silliest of songs at the top of our lungs, feeling reckless and free, and, for a little while at least, successfully squelching the guilt that kept threatening to bubble up and take over.

And guilt eventually did take over. While we were sipping Texas-sized margaritas at dinner that night, Kathy's daughter called, the first in a series of calls that one or the other of us got over the next year from distraught children, partners, and co-workers at conventions from the East Coast to the West. Kathy sipped harder on her drink, tried to help from a thousand miles away, and—as soon as she could find some privacy—cried. By the time we headed to Casa Mañana for that evening's performance, Lynn (who does not hold her liquor well) was overly emotional about everything and Kathy was trying desperately to find her lost happy place, caught between feeling bad after talking to her daughter, anticipating feeling even worse when she got home, and wanting to enjoy the moment. After all, we were seeing Jensen again. Life was good.

And it was getting better. Thanks to a heads-up posted by a well-connected fan, we (unlike the rest of the audience) knew that Jared Padalecki and his then girlfriend, actress Sandy McCoy, were headed to Fort Worth, presumably to surprise Jensen at the play. Armed with this last-minute intelligence, we kept an eye out for Jared as we once again enjoyed watching Jensen. When intermission began, Lynn was off like a shot, scanning the lobby for Jared. At six foot four, the guy's not hard to spot.

Meeting the objects of fandom face to face can be a powerful experience. Lynn was still smarting from her failure to meet Ackles after the opening night performance. We had waited by the stage door, only to be told by a Casa Mañana employee that there would be no autographs because of an opening night party. Lynn wanted to wait anyway, since logic dictated that sooner or later Ackles would have to leave the building, opening night party or not. Nevertheless, she went along with the plan to meet with other fans at a nearby pancake house, all the time biting her lip and trying not to listen to the little fannish voice inside of her screaming "Noooooooooooo!" The actors did come out and sign autographs only minutes after we left, and Lynn's regret at missing the opportunity plagued her in the days that followed, especially as she heard the stories of other fans who had more determination and didn't succumb to the desire to go eat pancakes.

Clara, a fan who at the time was sorely in need of something good happening in her life, was one of the lucky ones. She traveled all the way from Canada to Fort Worth to see Ackles, and she didn't come empty handed. Having the opportunity to give something to someone you fan in exchange for the many hours of pleasure they've given you is a satisfying experience. Clara brought a special gift for Jensen.

I explained to the florist that I would like to purchase some flowers and the reason why. She created two lovely bouquets. After the opening night performance of Jensen's play, I was waiting at the stage door when he came out. He came right over and I said to him, "Hi, Jensen, these are for you with love from Canada." He smiled, thanked me, wanted to know what part of Canada I was from and then—and this will always endear me to that wonderful human being—he held my hand for the longest time, while he talked with other fans. It was just so lovely and light hearted and sweet. A very fond memory for me of a magical night.

In contrast, Kathy had no interest in meeting any of the actors (bordering on a pathological fear), due in part to overwhelming shyness and in part to a desire to "stay cool" and not act "like a fan." When Lynn realized that no one had yet recognized Padalecki, who was standing in the candy line greeting Jensen's father with a fond "Papa Ackles!" she decided that it would be a good time to say hello. Kathy decided that it was a really good time to hide in a corner of the lobby. She was having none of it. And Lynn was having none of Kathy. She rolled her eyes, grabbed Kathy's camera, and trotted off to say hi. Jared and Sandy were genuinely surprised to have anyone want to talk to *them* and were happy to talk to Lynn. They all agreed that Jensen was doing a fabulous job.

"It was really nice of you to come out and support Jensen," Lynn said, genuinely impressed by Jared's surprise visit.

Jared broke into a grin. "Of course I'd come! He's my bud."

Lynn could only grin back, imagining the rest of the fandom going "awwww" over that response. Then she remembered that she had gone to the trouble of confiscating Kathy's camera, so she probably should use it.

"Would you mind if I took a picture?"

"Of course, sure," Jared agreed.

This was obviously the answer that Lynn was hoping for. But then an odd thing happened. Lynn had second thoughts—not because she didn't want a picture but because she didn't want to ruin Jared's so-far successful attempt at staying incognito. Now that they'd had even the briefest of conversations, Jared was a "real person" standing right in front of her, a guy nice enough to fly across the country to support his best friend instead of a celebrity on a television show.

"Wait," Lynn said. Jared raised his eyebrows. "Are you sure? I mean, nobody has really recognized you, but if we take a picture, they might."

Jared just grinned wider, and Sandy jumped in to take the camera, thinking that Lynn would want to be in the picture. But while Lynn is less photophobic than Kathy, for the most part she too avoids stepping in front of the camera. She quickly backed away, shaking her head. Sandy and Jared were understandably confused. What kind of fangirl was this anyway?

Luckily, our new friend Allie stepped up to the plate and offered to pose with Jared (not exactly a hardship, since she's an enthusiastic Sam girl). Sandy snapped the picture, and Lynn and Allie hugged them both good-bye. Sure enough, within a few minutes, the rest of the fans in the lobby figured out who that tall guy getting his photo taken was, and Casa Mañana security came to usher Padalecki back into the theater.

"What are you doing out here?" the security woman admonished.

"I had a baseball cap on. I was flyin' under the radar," Jared protested, Texas drawl in evidence.

The security person scoffed. A baseball cap is not going to hide a man six foot four, especially when half the women in the lobby are his biggest fans.

Meanwhile, Kathy continued to cower in the corner. Her anxiety about getting up close and personal with celebrities is shared by many fans. Sometimes it's safer to leave them contained by our television or movie screens, where nothing can tarnish their reputation or knock them off their pedestal or interfere with our fantasy of what meeting them would be like. In Kathy's case, it was more the fear of sounding like an idiot. Meeting the objects of our affection can be exhilarating, but it can also stir up the fan shame that we keep bumping up against.

Another fangirl who traveled to Fort Worth for the play was already something of a Big Name Fan (BNF) in *Supernatural* fandom. Andie had created a popular online serial adaptation of *Supernatural* starring modified Ken dolls as Sam and Dean in all sorts of comic adventures that the actual show didn't dare tackle. She called it Plastic Winchester Theater.

"I came up with the idea for the plastic!boys," she told us, "because there wasn't any merchandise available for SPN. While shopping at Goodwill one day, I noticed a bin full of Ken dolls and the idea sprang into my head that I could make my own Sam and Dean dolls."

Plastic Winchesters: Sam, Dean, Castiel, and Bobby are ready to play. Courtesy of Elizabeth Sisson.

Like that of any other sort of fanwork creator, Andie's goal was to entertain other fans. "The ability to make someone who is having a rough time or a bad day laugh is indescribable," she said. "It just fills me with joy."

Andie had her Plastic Winchester dolls in her purse that night at the theater, sharing with other fans the excitement of seeing the inspiration for the Dean doll in person. That all changed when Andie unexpectedly ran into actress Danneel Harris, Jensen's girlfriend, in the Casa Mañana ladies' room.

We were in each other's space for less than three seconds, but that's all it took to begin the deflation of my previously shiny attitude. She gave me a look—a dismissive, fangirls-are-so-STUPID kind of look. In three seconds I went from Cinderella at the ball to Cinderella cleaning the chimneys. I felt ashamed of being a fangirl. Danneel Harris wouldn't fly to Texas to watch an actor in a play. Danneel Harris wouldn't write about it later in her LJ. Danneel Harris wouldn't carry around Ken dolls in her purse. I felt stupid. I felt embarrassed. In that moment I swore I was done being a fangirl. I was done with Plastic Winchester Theater, done with LJ, done with anything that could give me the stigma of a fan.

The sense of shame was so powerful that it almost immediately catapulted Andie from fannish euphoria to fan hatred (and therefore self-hatred). Harris hadn't said a thing, and we're quite certain that she didn't send a glare in Andie's direction, but fans are so primed for criticism and judgment that we tend to see it even in ambiguous situations when it's not really there. We imagine that people are looking down on us, especially those on the celebrity side of the fence. (Never mind that most celebrities, including Harris, have had their own fangirl and fanboy moments.) Once Andie returned to her seat, she was able to shrug off the shame and get back to the squee, largely by reminding herself of all the good things about fans.

"I realized I could never look down on any of them," Andie said. "By the end of the night, I had no shame putting Plastic!Sam on Real!Jared's seat in full view of Danneel, Jensen's parents, and anyone else . . . This was me, take it or leave it. I was never going to have this opportunity again, and hell if I was going to blow it because I was too embarrassed/self-conscious/hesitant."

Lynn was feeling the same sense of determination—this might be her only chance, after all, to meet Ackles. After the performance we once again headed to the stage door, resolved not to be left out of the meet and greet this time. Unfortunately, it turned out to be the one night when Jensen didn't come out to sign autographs, much to Lynn's dismay. Instead, there was an after-party in the lobby, which happened to have floor-to-ceiling windows the length of the theater. We watched from a discreet distance while Jensen and Jared laughed and talked animatedly inside, looking thoroughly happy to see each other again. There was no way we weren't going to watch, but we did have a few uncomfortable moments, wondering what we looked like peering voyeuristically through the windows—and what it must have felt like to the celebrities inside the virtual fishbowl.

We stuck to our plans and flew out the next morning, although the play was set to run for another five days and we *still* hadn't met Ackles. Our new friend Allie stayed in Fort Worth for the rest of the week and managed to catch Jensen at the stage door after several performances. We were happy for her, though the itch of regret was rubbed raw by the knowledge that we could have stayed longer and done the same. Seriously? One night we missed him coming out to say hi to go have pancakes and the next turned out to be the only night he didn't come out to greet fans? Lynn grumbled about it all the way home.

Our trip to Fort Worth changed the trajectory of our fandom journey. We now knew firsthand how gratifying it was to meet other fans in person and to share our experience with our online community. We'd had a small taste of being BNFs—and we liked it. We also knew, as hard as it was to believe, that Jensen Ackles was even more drop-dead gorgeous in person.

We also had another, more intellectual revelation. We had already decided to weigh in on the academic discussion of fandom and had stacks and stacks of research to back up our decision. Maybe, we thought, instead of just an article, we'd write a book—one that would set the record straight about who fans are once and for all. Our book would be different—we would write it from the inside, as fans ourselves. We also began to think that our book could be different in another way. We realized that talking to the other side of the fandom equation—the actors and directors and writers—might be possible. Jared and Sandy's openness and approachability were an unexpected encouragement to do just that. The seeds of our book started to take root as we left hot, dusty Texas and reluctantly returned to the East Coast and real life.

At this point in our fannish odyssey, we began to tell everyone that we were writing a book on fandom. But while the explicit goal was the lofty-sounding "to rehabilitate the image of fans and set the record straight," the implicit goal that we never acknowledged, even to ourselves, was already taking shape—and it was way more fannish than academic. How the hell were we going to meet Jensen Ackles?

FOUR

Hollywood Babylon

We returned from Texas filled with regret.

Lynn had sampled a little bit of it while missing out on Asylum but gulped down a bitter helping when we failed to meet Ackles in Texas. All the way back to the East Coast, and for weeks after, she berated herself for choosing pancakes over Jensen on opening night and for returning home rather than staying for additional nights (and thus additional opportunities for in-person meetings). The regret was painful. At the time, plenty of things in our lives were stressful, and the heady feeling of forgetting about all that stress and enjoying fannish euphoria instead was hard to give up. Both of Lynn's children were at a difficult transition time, she was contemplating a job change to another university, and her partner had just started a new professional practice. Stress, it seemed, was everywhere she turned—except in the safe, exciting, liberating, satisfying space of fandom. Lynn's decision to do the responsible thing (by not staying in Fort Worth even longer) instead of the fannish thing felt logical and "right" and at the same time emotionally "wrong."

In retrospect, the addiction model isn't entirely inapplicable here. Giving up a coping strategy, when it's the only one working for you, is both difficult and painful. It took Lynn months to get past the resentment of missed opportunities. Every time she read a fan's report of meeting Ackles at *A Few Good Men* or saw a video of the actor smiling and signing autographs, relaxed and happy (and wearing only a tight white T-shirt, just to twist the knife), Lynn felt literally sick with envy.

"What's the matter with you?" her daughter asked, frowning. "You got to go to this really cool thing, you should be happy."

"Why are you still even thinking about that quote-unquote missed opportunity?" Doug asked, frowning even more. "It's over. Let it go."

This seemed like good advice. Unfortunately, it was easier said than done. Lynn felt guilty, yet she kept wishing that she'd done things differently and wondered if she'd get another chance. The intensity of that discomfort left a lasting impression. Lynn tacked a saying up on her office wall as a reminder. "Deathbed words: I went to too many concerts. Said no one ever." Substitute "fan conventions" for concerts, and the message rang true. Lynn vowed to reach out and grab whatever opportunities presented themselves in the future, even if the impulse to do something for herself made her feel more than a little guilty. When your identity is wrapped tightly around doing for others, suddenly prioritizing running off to fan conventions feels like a cosmic shift of gigantic proportions. Lynn felt selfish, but the pull of fandom and the pain of regret were almost as strong. She tried talking about it with her kids and partner, hoping they'd understand. They didn't.

Kathy's regrets had less to do with missed opportunities to see her favorite actors. By indulging in her fannish passions, she had let her daughter down and feared she had created a rift that would always be achingly open. Her family's attitude toward what she was doing was always uppermost on her mind and drove her to keep fandom as invisible as possible, adding yet another facet to the fan/academic split that she was already beginning to experience.

We coped by focusing on the future. Anticipation in fandom is the antithesis of fannish regret—an emotion to be savored. The next episode, the next convention, the next epic piece of fanfic by your favorite author—there's always something to look forward to. It's one of the addictive properties of fandom, the constant desire for more more more. Fandom delivers on some days and not on others, with an intermittent reinforcement schedule that any psychologist can tell you is the most powerful way to keep you coming back for more.

While we waited for our next *Supernatural* fix, we got serious about writing a book about fandom from the inside, in terms that didn't have to do with erotomanic delusions or stalking behavior. We also got more serious about filling what we saw as a gap in the academic literature on fans. Academics kept writing about the reciprocal relationship between the creative side and the fans. From pop culture references to the creators' willingness to "give the fans what they want," the creative side increasingly seemed to be seeking out and putting to good use their understanding of fans. Joss Whedon, Russell T. Davies, J. J. Abrams, Eric Kripke (*Supernatural*'s creator), and a growing group of television show creators and film makers are self-professed fanboys who grew up to make programs that others could relate to as fans. Media theorist Henry Jenkins coined the term "convergence culture" to suggest that this new group of creative talent actively seeks and nurtures a reciprocal relationship with fans, because they "get it," but there was little actual discussion with those on the famous side of the fence. Clearly, we could make a valuable contribution to the field by doing just that—talking to them. Jensen Ackles just happened to be on the creative side of the fence. Purely coincidence.

As we pondered and plotted and looked for opportunities to get up close and personal with actors, our road trip through fandom continued. A month after we flew back from Texas, we got another phone call from Lana (who was miraculously still speaking to us). The Internet was filled with shockwaves of squee as the fans learned that the world's biggest fan convention organizer, Creation Entertainment, was planning a con that would feature *Supernatural*. Creation is the gold standard for conventions in the United States, responsible for the largest *Star Trek* convention, among others. We were beside ourselves that they'd recognized *Supernatural* for the cult hit it was rapidly becoming. At this point, we knew nothing about Creation cons, so once again we looked to Lana for advice. She was an experienced con-goer and understood the strategizing that was required to get the best tickets. Most of the fans stayed on the edge of their proverbial seats (and hovered over their computers) for weeks waiting for the website to change from "On sale soon" to "Purchase tickets." We were no exception. Four of us—Kathy, Lynn, Lana, and Kate (another good fandom friend)—took turns refreshing the website constantly for nearly a month, waiting for that magical moment when we could finally hit "Buy." Lynn got an entire week on monitoring duty once she was done teaching and was checking obsessively enough that she snagged tickets in the second row, much to everyone's squee. We had five months of anticipation to enjoy.

We couldn't wait to see both the *Supernatural* stars in person and to be surrounded by fellow fans again. November seemed far off, however, so when Lana called yet again to pass on the rumors that a *Supernatural* panel

would be held at San Diego's annual Comic Con in July, Lynn was determined not to miss out. She snuck onto her computer in the midst of the
family vacation at the beach to snag two passes. She got up early, before the
kids were awake, feeling as if she was making a clandestine, possibly illegal,
purchase instead of buying tickets for a fan convention. Kathy was still suffering the fallout from the trip to Texas and resolved not to go, in an attempt
to be responsible and grown-up (and not to get into any more trouble). Of
course she *wanted* to go. She was also uncomfortably aware of how her decision in this instance did not align with the rest of her life. She was not and
never had been the traditional "wife," taking care of her man. Household
chores and childcare had always been divided equally. She was a product of
the Women's Movement and many a women's literature class. She refused
to read her children *The Giving Tree*, balking at the lesson of female mar-
tyrdom that it espoused. And yet here she was, denying herself, her own
fan shame overriding her values and principles. But when Kathy's husband
found out about the opportunity that she was resolutely turning down, he
was having none of it. He called Lynn to assure her that he was on board
with it. Despite his supportiveness, Kathy's guilt was relentless. Mothers,
she told herself, must always put each and every member of their families
before themselves. Her husband telling her that of course she should go
was not enough. It was one voice against an entire culture. And plenty of
voices were certainly out there ready to judge, as the scathing article about
the Twilight Moms had showed us. But even Kathy was not made of stone.
She finally relented after much coaxing, and the second stop on our *Supernatural* road trip was set. She even allowed herself to get excited. Comic Con
here we come!

To add to the delicious anticipation, Sabrina, a *Supernatural* fangirl we'd
met online, let us know about another potential opportunity to meet the
elusive Jensen Ackles. She had tickets to a private screening of an indie film
starring Ackles, *Ten Inch Hero*, in Los Angeles two days before Comic Con.
Would we like to come out to LA early and attend that too? How quickly do
you think Lynn was on the phone snagging us tickets?

Two days later, we were on a flight to California. Kathy began quietly assuming the role of organizer. She made arrangements to rent a car, printed
out detailed maps (necessary in the days before the ubiquitous GPS), and reluctantly got behind the wheel once in LA. When her husband was around,

she always had him take care of these things. Lynn had always done the same and was even more clueless than Kathy about anything automotive or navigational. So Kathy was on her own and forced to take on those responsibilities herself. For someone who was almost debilitatingly shy, this was no mean feat. Fandom was giving Kathy a measure of self-confidence that she rarely felt in her real life. In fact, fandom was giving that to both of us, though we didn't realize it at the time. While we tended to think of ourselves as challenging stereotypes about women being dependent, helpless, silly, and not so smart, in reality neither of us had much experience doing things on our own or giving ourselves credit for what we did do. We were always feeling like imposters, merely passing as intelligent or capable, always more than willing to downplay our own achievements. We fought against the stereotypes, but in more subtle and insidious ways we embraced them wholeheartedly. Fandom gave us a reason to get out of our comfort zones. Want to see Jared and Jensen in person? Then get on an airplane and rent a car and book a hotel and GO! Want to write a book? Figure out who you need to talk to and pick up the phone and just DO it.

Falling for *Supernatural* and into fandom changed us in ways that we never could have anticipated, and the change was already beginning. Being our real selves—and figuring out for the first time what we really wanted—gave us the validation that we needed to start feeling *good* about ourselves, a sense of competence that marriage and kids and grad school and careers hadn't given us. The good feelings had a ripple effect, starting online but then spreading outward to every area of our lives. More and more, we knew who we were—and what we wanted. And we were determined to get there. That California highway turned out to be more than just a road between LA and San Diego.

Once we were on our way, the fun started for real. We were happily on the same wavelength again, sharing the squee and the feeling of freedom that being on our own gave us. Everything was amusing, and everything was an adventure. We giggled. We were lewd and rude. We made suggestive remarks about the hot dog that we ordered at Pink's (two dogs, one bun—the slashy jokes knew no end). We stayed in a Sam and Dean motel (meaning one that had seen better days long ago) and thought it was the best thing in the world, posing for pictures in which we gleefully poked fingers through the holes in the bath towels they provided.

The indie movie *Ten Inch Hero* was funny and unexpectedly moving. Jensen Ackles was expectedly gorgeous; so was his co-star and real-life girlfriend, Danneel Harris, who was there at the screening along with most of the cast (other than Ackles, alas—foiled again!). After the screening, the producer and director surprised us by inviting everyone in the small theater to the after-party at the Bungalow Club a few blocks away. We found ourselves once again in close proximity to people who knew people.

"We're invited to a party with Jensen's girlfriend?" Lynn asked incredulously, as we walked to the club.

"There she is, one of you go talk to her," Sabrina urged. "Tell her how much we liked the film."

Kathy looked paler than usual. "I need a drink," she muttered, heading for the bar.

Sabrina gave Lynn a gentle (okay, not so gentle) push toward Danneel and her co-stars. Clutching a drink of her own, Lynn squared her shoulders and repeated her mantra "No Regrets."

Being nervous about approaching the celebrities at the after-party was probably another manifestation of fan shame. As soon as people are "famous," we tend to deposit them on a pedestal and then crane our necks to look up at them, leaving us in the uncomfortable position of one-down. It's exhilarating to get close enough to stare, but at the same time our awareness of the inferior position is uncomfortable. Never mind that we're the ones who created the dynamic in the first place—its existence helps to explain both the concept of celebrity "worship" and the evil glee that everyone appears to take in watching the celebrity on the pedestal tumble off.

Nobody seems immune to being flustered by celebrity encounters. Certainly not us. Lynn has been around actors and on film sets; director and filmmaker M. Night Shyamalan has been a friend for decades. Lynn's son had a principal role in *The Sixth Sense* and worked on other films and television shows. You might think that she'd be used to being around celebrities. She had no problem storming the men's room at the party (when nature calls and the women's room is occupied, you do what you have to do) and even enlisted the help of one of the film's actors, a complete stranger, to guard the door for her. But getting up the guts to approach Jensen Ackles's girlfriend was another matter entirely. Remember the old advice about imagining your audience in their underwear when you feel nervous giving a speech? The idea is to remind yourself that we're all human, with similar underclothes and anxieties. But all that logical knowledge goes out the window when you're a passionate fan. Our only conscious thoughts at that point revolved around "This is Jensen Ackles's girlfriend, OMG I'm talking to Jensen Ackles's girlfriend."

We were also pretty sure that Danneel had better underclothes than we did.

It might have helped us at the *Ten Inch Hero* premiere to know that many of the people who make *Supernatural* have fan histories of their own and have been similarly tongue-tied.

Actor Jim Beaver told us he had a long history of being a fan.

I was a huge John Wayne fan. As a young man, I felt like the two worst things that could ever happen would be if my dad died or if John Wayne died. I remember when Wayne was in his final illness, I was doing a play in Dallas, and I played a jailor, and they had it set up so that before the audience came into the theater, I was just on stage pacing outside this guy's cell for forty-five minutes every night. One night just before I went out, there was some news on the radio about how Wayne was really sick, and I remember pacing for those forty-five minutes and pleading with the cosmos that he'd be okay—and it's weird because there I was, acting, and in the middle of a performance, so you would think I would have been able to separate.

He couldn't, of course, and neither could we. We knew actors were just people, we knew *Supernatural* was just a television show. It didn't matter. The emotions were there just the same. In fact, part of the fun of being a fan is knowing in the rational part of your brain that celebrities are just people but hoisting them up onto a pedestal anyway, against your better judgment. Then crossing your fingers that they can keep their precarious balance up there. Our friend Night now has fans of his own, but he remembers vividly what it's like to be a fan himself. He describes being a fan of Michael Jordan when he was young as almost like a religious experience, a need to believe in something, to project all your aspirations and beliefs onto someone bigger than life. Night was so invested that he would rise and fall with how well Jordan did and felt lucky that he always did well. Whether you're a sports fan or a media fan, if you're invested, your emotional well-being is tied to the fortunes of whatever you're a fan of. No wonder, then, that we're a bit in awe of those we keep on that pedestal.

David Mackay, *Ten Inch Hero's* director, told us that he keeps a concrete reminder of his own long history of being a fan. "I got the autograph of the first kid who asked *me* for an autograph. This person came up to me and said I love your movie so much, would you please sign my program? I said absolutely, but will you please sign my ticket as the first person that ever asked me for an autograph?"

Talking to Danneel might have been easier if we had understood that being an actor yourself doesn't change the experience of being a fan. Even after four decades of acting, Jim Beaver keeps a few fellow actors on a pedestal. He's still upset about missing an opportunity to work with one of his idols.

> There are a lot of actors still on pedestals in the sense of Oh my God, I would love to meet him. Toward the end of last season, I got asked to meet with some producers about a movie part. The problem was, I was doing the *Supernatural* season finale episodes, and this movie started in Vancouver just a couple days after I'd finish, and it's just really hard for me to be away from my daughter [then seven years old] as much as I have to be for *Supernatural*. So I didn't do it. Then I got up here and Jared said he'd just gotten this movie—and it was the same movie [*The Christmas Cottage*]! And I was like oh, I could have hung out and worked with Jared. I asked him who'd they get for such and such a part, and he said, Peter O'Toole. And I was like NOOOO! Because Peter O'Toole is one of those guys I would have—daughter schmaughter, I would've killed for that. And I'd just said, "Nawww, I don't think so."

Sounds like Jim got hit with a whopping dose of regret there. Lynn cringed in empathy.

The *Supernatural* actors aren't immune to their own embarrassing fan moments either. Samantha Ferris confided that she has a crush on actor Seth Green.

> He's really cute. I ran into him at an audition once, and me being this very vocal, outgoing person that I am, I just started talking and I talked myself so

far into the ground that I think in the end it just started sounding like vocal sex. I mean I was like "umm yeah I mean I took my top off for that show, and it's like not that I would take my top off usually, and . . . oh uhhmmm." It was pretty mortifying. And that's how I started the conversation, and then I just said, "I've got to go," and so he's like, "okay"? And so I was just like "bye!" It was horrible, and the audition room was quiet, and I'm not quiet, and I'm sure they all heard the whole thing, and I just thought to myself, you're an idiot!

That sort of scenario is exactly what we were worried would happen if we dared to attempt conversation with Danneel. The point is that for most of us it's not just meeting any old celebrity. That intense emotional thrill, and consequent inability to speak articulately, only comes from being up close and personal with someone *you* fan. As musician Steve Carlson told us, "I could meet the president tomorrow and it wouldn't faze me as much as meeting Stevie Wonder."

Exactly! Lynn was certain that she could chat comfortably with either Stevie Wonder or the president. But Jensen Ackles's girlfriend? Not so much.

Eventually Lynn managed to inch over to Danneel and say hello, with Kathy and Sabrina hovering nervously behind her.

"We just wanted to congratulate you on your performance," Lynn said, hoping that her voice wasn't trembling too much.

"Thank you so much," Danneel answered with a big smile.

Relieved, Lynn grinned back. Kathy and Sabrina grinned behind her. We even wound up chatting for a bit about the film and told Danneel to relay our congratulations to her co-star boyfriend. So now we'd had actual conversations with both Jared Padalecki and Danneel Harris. Maybe, we thought, we could find a way to have an actual conversation with Jensen Ackles too. Why not? We were determined at least to try. After all, the research was sorely needed, right? Right.

After the party, we emailed screenwriter Betsy Morris to tell her what we thought of the film. It was less terrifying to reach out to another writer than to an actor, so we figured why not? Maybe Betsy could give us some juicy behind the scenes tidbits about Jensen's role. You know, for research purposes. To our surprise, Betsy emailed us right back. We may have started out wanting some behind the scenes tidbits about Ackles, but we hit it off with Betsy in a way that transcended our original point of connection. Soon we were emailing back and forth, having long discussions about some of the things that we wanted to tackle in our book, including the way the production side understands the fan side. In our emails with Betsy, our research ideas began to expand. We knew how fans felt about their fannish objects, but what did the actors, writers, and producers understand about fans? Betsy was the first person we asked.

At the time, we knew very little about TPTB, other than that they existed and somewhere, somehow, were the mysterious beings who were pulling the strings. Betsy was the screenwriter of *Ten Inch Hero*, but she was also the marketing person for the little film—setting up the online blog, corresponding with fans, helping arrange screenings. We asked if she and the producers were aware of Jensen's fan following and if they were attempting to harness that popularity. This process, by which one fan community overlaps with another, is something we called "fandom bleed." Fans of a particular media text tend to have similar fannish histories. Many SPN fans cut their teeth on *Buffy, Stargate, Farscape, X-Files*, and *Star Trek*. In an interesting parallel, many of the SPN crew came from a similar background. Director and executive producer Kim Manners also worked on *X-Files* and *Buffy*. In the *Supernatural* universe, fandom bleed also includes being a fan of the actors' musician friends and any other film or television projects that the actors work on in between filming seasons. So SPN fans were on board with *Ten Inch Hero* before they even saw a frame, bought opening night tickets for horror films *Friday the 13th* (starring Padalecki) and *My Bloody Valentine* (starring Ackles) when they hit theaters, followed Jensen and Jared's musician friends as they toured, and lined up for autographs for anyone who ever guest starred on the show.

We asked Betsy whether the creative side was learning how to exploit these "bleeding fandoms." Will a filmmaker consciously go to one fan base in order to create another? Will those fans then be enlisted (not unlike street teams for bands) to spread the word, and will this sort of grass-roots movement be the way indie films and other creative projects become known in the future? At the time *Ten Inch Hero* was filmed and searching for a distributor, none of its stars was a big name, including Ackles. The director and producers weren't Internet savvy enough to tap into the SPN fandom that had already begun to develop and widespread recognition of the power of online fandom did not yet exist, so there was ultimately not enough fandom bleed to bring TIH a distribution deal. This was before the success of funding engines like Kickstarter, which do exactly that. In the next five years, the industry's perception of fans and fan influence would change dramatically—as would ours.

Our conversation with Betsy opened our eyes to the way the production side struggles with watching from the virtual sidelines as fans react to media content, sometimes violently. No longer do screenwriters, directors, and filmmakers have to wait for reviews or ratings to know what fans are saying about their works of art. It's right there on the Internet, tempting them to take a look at every turn. This theme was to be reiterated time and again once we got to Comic Con.

The next morning, we loaded our bags into our PT Cruiser and headed for San Diego. Even the infamous LA traffic jams didn't bother us—we popped in a Season 1 *Supernatural* soundtrack CD compiled by our friend Lana and belted out "Carry On My Wayward Son" as we inched along the highway. We were unabashed fangirls—giddy, pervy, and (at least within the confines of our rental car) absolutely shameless. We stopped for lunch in San Juan Capistrano and wandered around the mission, where everything reminded us of fandom. We checked out a few hot young priests, thinking of outtakes of Jared and Jensen in Chippendale "priest" gear, and stumbled on a strangely large vat of holy water that seemed tailor-made for the Winchester brothers. We got some offended looks when we giggled and took photos of it, but frankly we didn't care. In short, we were blissfully in the fan zone.

We arrived in San Diego still singing, ready for our first experience at Comic Con. Or at least we thought we were ready. Words of advice to the Comic Con uninitiated who are contemplating attending: if you hate crowds and traffic—don't come. If you like to sleep late and require regular feedings at normal intervals—don't come. If the thought of standing on a line that stretches for what is easily a mile is unimaginable to you—don't come. If, however, you like the idea of fans of all sorts coming together to celebrate their geeky, freaky fanboy/fangirl ways—come. If the sight of men in tights, multiple Jokers walking down the street, and furries and stormtroopers in pedicabs warms your heart—come. If the prospect of getting up close and personal with creative people of all stripes appeals to you—definitely come. The best thing about Comic Con is that we're all geeks there, on both sides of the panels. And it's okay.

Comic Con began as a showcase for comics and their producers but has become so much more. The event has been compared to the Super Bowl for geeks. Over the past forty years Comic Con has become not only a giant fan gathering but a giant corporate gathering, as TPTB began to get a clue about just how much money and influence geeks were wielding. The disconnect between fan and corporation, however, is often in stark contrast to the stated goals of bringing fans and creators together. TPTB have an uneasy relationship with the fans who make or break their media properties. From Facebook to Twitter to iTunes to Hulu, new media have changed the way fans and the corporate side interact, sometimes with such speed that neither side is able to keep up. At Comic Con that year, the public view of fans as geeks without lives, perpetually single and living in their parents' basements, was plastered all over the evening news programs, where Storm Trooper Elvises, caped superheroes, and furries figured prominently. Yet the power of the fans to disseminate information immediately, creating the buzz that will either make or break every new media offering, was an undercurrent of everything that went on at Comic Con, simultaneously embraced, banked on, and feared.

The rise and transformation of Comic Con closely mirrors the strange position of gossip columnists like Perez Hilton or Harry Knowles and his blog "Ain't It Cool News." Knowles went from an annoying fanboy with a computer to a powerful Hollywood insider. This happened not because studio executives realized that fans just wanted to share the love (and often the details of new projects before they hit the multiplex or the fall lineup) but because they realized that Knowles, with a following of his own, had positioned himself as an influential superfan who could make or break a project simply by word of mouth. There seemed no easy way to stop him, so they began to court him. They became unwilling bedfellows, uncomfortable with a model that challenged the time-honored unidirectional "Here, watch this, buy this!" interaction that had characterized their relationship with fans before the Internet. It was our first hint that ultimately the corporate side really didn't know what to do with the fans. Including us.

We've already fessed up to the calculated reconnaissance, meticulous planning, and Olympic-worthy running that we carried out during our first day there. In the midst of our route-planning to the ballroom where the SPN panel would be held the next day, Lynn just happened to pick up a flyer announcing a *Supernatural* autograph signing that wasn't listed in the program. What?? Cue squeals of joy. We immediately added to our reconnaissance a plan for the best route down to the Warner Brothers (WB) booth. And then we made sure we had the route memorized by running it a few times. Let us reiterate. We prefer to think of this as organization, not obsession. Whatever it was, the following day we were in front row seats in the cavernous hall, almost dead center. Strangely enough, all the other people around us were also *Supernatural* fans, who seemed to make up an unusually large proportion of attendees. We chatted, we discussed the Winchesters, fanfiction, Jensen's eyes. The usual. We played with dolls. Plastic Winchester Theater creator Andie was there with her pretty plastic boys, which included not only Dean and Sam but also Priestly, Ackles's character in *Ten Inch Hero*.

Andie is a BNF, famous for her meticulously staged comic-type animations, in which plastic Dean and Sam carry out their own monster hunts and negotiate the Barbie version of a complicated co-dependent relationship. At Comic Con, we were as much in awe of Andie as the rest of the fans were, posing for photos with her and oohing and aahing over her plastic boys. While she had struggled with feeling ashamed of her Sam and Dean dolls when she ran into Danneel Harris at *A Few Good Men*, at Comic Con Andie could bask in the admiration of her peers.

"My biggest moment came at Comic Con when the woman behind me in line to ask the SPN panel a question outed me as the Plastic Winchester Theater girl as I was walking to my seat," Andie said. "I will never forget the cheer that went up from the crowd and how at that moment I felt like a rock star."

At Comic Con, we also got to know Julia. A smart, articulate attorney as well as a passionate fangirl, Julia just happened to be behind us in line and helped out with our resolute determination not to allow thirty people to crowd in front of us just before the doors opened. We had ample time to get to know her as we sat through a day of panels waiting for *Supernatural* to take the stage. The system at Comic Con is basically a variation on squatter's rights. Your seat is yours as long as you stay in it: if you want to be front row for a panel that begins at 2:00 in the afternoon, you damn well better have ass in seat by 8:00 A.M.

The production team for the television show *Pushing Daisies* delighted the SPN crowd by handing out coupons for free pie, a *Supernatural* tie-in, which prompted Lynn to do some very bad Dean impressions and Kathy to do some eyerolling at Lynn. Author Laurell K. Hamilton endeared herself to the SPN slash fans by responding to a question about why there's a lot of gay male/male sex in her book: "Men like women. Men like to see two women together. I like men." By the time the *Family Guy* panel cleared out, the line of *Supernatural* fans hoping to get in wrapped around the hall (which sat approximately five thousand people)—twice. Lynn got a pass to go to the bathroom (shades of middle school). On her way back, she passed hundreds of fans still waiting in line, many wearing Sam and Dean T-shirts, distraught over the news that they probably would not get inside to see the panel they came for. Lynn clutched her bathroom pass guiltily and hurried back to her seat.

The panel that year included creator Eric Kripke, actor Jensen Ackles, and writers Sera Gamble and Ben Edlund.

Our divergent ways of enjoying fandom were in evidence once again at Comic Con. Kathy was content to sit back and absorb it all. Lynn was determined to film the entire panel so that she could watch it repeatedly in the afterglow. Lynn was so engrossed in getting the best video record ever of Mr. Ackles's handsome face (oh, were other people up there as well?) that it took her a few minutes to notice that he was staring down the lens of her camera and making odd little jerking motions of his head to the right, where Eric Kripke was answering a question. The unspoken message was clear: "I'm not even talking—he's talking! Point the camera at him!"

Kathy, embarrassed on Lynn's behalf, nudged her shoulder none too gently. Boundaries, Lynn! Don't be so obvious! But the visual record shows a consistent shift back to the camera's original focus, over and over. Both Kathy and Jensen gave up on correcting Lynn and just ignored her. Lynn wasn't the only one wielding a video camera. In keeping with what Neil Gaiman referred to at Comic Con that year as the striking immediacy of the Internet (even in 2007, before the Time of Twitter), the entire SPN panel was up on YouTube almost immediately.

When the panel was over, the members were whisked downstairs for the signing. We were used to lines by this point, but we were not prepared for chaos. We were surprised by the cluelessness of TPTB when it comes to fandom. They certainly didn't know what to do with the throngs of *Supernatural* fans clamoring for an autograph! Perhaps they just didn't think that demand for the signing would be so great. Perhaps they thought that the show just didn't garner that much attention. Perhaps they weren't paying any attention at all to the panel itself or to the long line of disappointed fans who could not get in the room. Or perhaps they just didn't care. Whatever the reason, TPTB wound up doing everything they could to thwart the very people that they were there to court that day. They originally said that no tickets for the signing would be given out ahead of time—and then gave out tickets ahead of time, *during* the panel upstairs. So the most determined SPN fans were all attending the panel and arrived to find that *Supernatural* signing tickets were already gone. What?? Hundreds of distraught fans milled about, confused and disappointed.

Lynn, still repeating her "No Regrets" mantra, went into strategy mode. The network was currently handing out tickets for the next signing, this one for television show *Smallville*, which of course added to the chaos. Lynn had arrived at just the right time to grab a *Smallville* autograph ticket, hastily formulating a plan to trade her *Smallville* ticket for a *Supernatural* one. She scoped out the crowd, easily identifying a guy who was a professional autograph collector instead of a fan. *Smallville*, Lynn reasoned, was a lot more popular than *Supernatural*. Perhaps he'd be willing to make a trade. He was. Lynn waved her SPN signing ticket in the air triumphantly in Kathy's direction and got in line. Once she was actually on her way to achieving that long-awaited goal of meeting Jensen Ackles, she immediately got cold feet. What would she say to him? Would she be able to speak at all? She had barely been able to say hello to the guy's girlfriend, so how much more terrifying would it be to talk to him?

By the time the signing finally got underway, a HUGE crowd (as in call the fire marshals) surrounded the little Warner Brothers booth, by that point heavily guarded by the usual pushing, crushing, yelling burly men who obviously had poor relationships with their mothers and knew no pity. Eventually things calmed down and something like order was restored. The people getting autographs filed by in one direction, while the people taking

pictures filed by in the opposite direction, thus allowing people to get really, really good pictures of the backs of strangers' heads. By the time it was
Lynn's turn, she had managed to pull herself together. The person ahead of
her in line got into some sort of disagreement with the security guy, which
gave Lynn some extra time to chat. She told Eric Kripke how much she loved
his show. She told Sera Gamble and Ben Edlund how much she admired
their writing. And then there she was, face to face with Jensen Ackles. Miraculously, Lynn started talking. She told Jensen how much we'd enjoyed
Ten Inch Hero and how nice it was to meet his talented girlfriend at the
after-party. He thanked her and told her that he wished he could have been
there (not as much as we wished it, Lynn thought silently). Jensen signed
the *Ten Inch Hero* poster that she'd brought with her, thanked her again,
and then graced her with a dazzling smile. Lynn remained admirably composed, smiled back, and went on her way. Of course, Jensen actually *talking*
to her and smiling at her rendered Lynn all but incoherent for the next
hour. Such is the power of the long-anticipated face-to-face encounter—not
surprisingly.

What did surprise us, then and on so many occasions afterward, was
how taken the other side is with *us*. Not TPTB who inadvertently created
such chaos, but the people who actually make the show. At this point in our
journey, we didn't realize that those two groups—although both were on
the other side of the fence from us—could not have been more different.
Jensen and Eric both whipped out their own cameras to take pictures of the
crowd, looking a bit blown away by all the attention. Not quite as blown away
as Lynn was at that moment, of course. Once she recovered from the euphoria of chatting with Jensen, we spent the rest of the day partaking of the
many joys of Comic Con, with visits to Artists Alley to peruse the amazing
variety of fanart and comics, a few non-*Supernatural*-related panels, and just
hanging out with other fans. The night ended with another endless line,
this one for the traditional Buffy singalong to the beloved episode "Once
More with Feeling." We left Comic Con deprived of sleep but full of fannish
satisfaction and already looking forward to coming back the next year. No
fannish regret this time.

The next day, while we were stuck in Detroit's airport for several hours,
Lynn wandered into the General Motors Collection store looking for souvenirs for her car-enthusiast son and came back with two miniature black

Impalas instead, one for each of us. The little hoods go up and the little doors open, so we gleefully reenacted a bit from one of the gag reels where Jared and Jensen have to shut the doors simultaneously. We did this over and over. And over. If the other stranded passengers were staring at us, we didn't really care. We were getting better at that.

FIVE

. . . . .

Fear and Loathing in Vancouver

We are not optimists by nature or conditioning. Kathy quietly moves through life on the assumption that nothing will work out and that complete happiness is a media construct, something that happens in films and Jane Austen novels but never in real life. Lynn is right there with her for the most part, though perhaps less quiet in her assurance that doom lurks behind doors number one, two, *and* three. There are no safe options and no sure bets.

So we returned from California encouraged by our informal discussions with Betsy Morris and our brief chats with Jared and Danneel and Jensen, but we had no expectation that this kind of luck would continue.

"Why would it?" would have been Kathy's first question. There really is never a good answer (incontrovertible proof will never present itself), which only proved her point.

Lynn would open her mouth to offer up an answer, stay like that for a moment, and then sink back into silence.

We're also introverts. Kathy is painfully shy and avoids most situations that require her to talk to people she is unfamiliar with or to speak in public. The irony that her job requires just that of her on an ongoing basis is not lost on her. For her part, Lynn has learned to talk enough to mislead anyone into thinking that she's the life of the party. Add to this the fear we all have of talking to anyone who's on the celebrity side of the fence and you have two anxious, pessimistic women whose every instinct told them not to reach out to people and never, ever to hope that they might reach back.

So when Lynn summoned every ounce of courage she had and emailed Adam Malin, the co-owner of Creation Entertainment, described our book, and asked if he'd be available for an interview at the upcoming *Supernatural* convention, at first she didn't even bother to tell Kathy she'd done it, so sure was she that it would come to nothing.

"I did something," Lynn said one weekend, when Kathy was visiting.

Of course Kathy's mind immediately went to the darkest places it could go. Bodies in the backyard? Sex tapes on the Internet? Answering one of those emails from Nigerian businessmen?

"I didn't want to tell you until I knew what would happen." Lynn waited a beat to let the anticipation build (as any good fanfic writer would) and then spilled. Adam had responded immediately and thought that our book sounded exciting. We would interview him in Chicago.

The research began in earnest.

We spent a week at the beach (nominally on a joint family vacation) joined at the hip, scouring the show's online fan communities, learning as much as we could about the (at that time still short) history of the fandom. If we were going to start interviewing people, we needed to know what we were talking about. We found out that the first *Supernatural* fan fiction community was created well before the pilot aired (based on Comic Con buzz from the previous year) and that the first Wincest fanfic was posted within twenty-four hours of the pilot airing. The first No-Wincest community was started shortly thereafter. Our family members occasionally rolled their eyes, wondering how much more of our lives was going to be taken up by this "fan thing" and silently contemplating an intervention. Perhaps those theories of fan psychology that viewed being a fan as an addiction really were onto something after all. At the time, we didn't see it that way.

"What are you reading?" Lynn's son asked as we all spread our towels and beach chairs out on the sun-warmed sand.

"*Theorizing Fandom*," Lynn replied enthusiastically, with a highlighter between her teeth.

Jeffrey rolled his eyes. "Good beach book."

"Stop reading!" Lynn's daughter ordered. "Come play Frisbee with us."

"She loves fandom more," Jeffrey observed, only half joking. Meanwhile, Kathy's nose was buried in *Convergence Culture*.

"Work at the beach?" her daughter sighed, somewhere between accusation and capitulation. Kathy wasn't sure that her daughter bought that this was actually "work" either.

We weren't entirely unsociable. We did pause at the appropriate times

to eat because our families made us and because you can't go to the East-
ern Shore of Maryland without ripping open a dozen or so crabs at regular intervals, but then we would go right back to work. Children watched
television. Partners eventually wandered off to bed. Alone. Our significant
others were struggling to understand our sudden obsession with all things
fandom. We made matters worse by taking a fangirl detour to go see one of
our favorite bands, Placebo, in concert. Lynn's partner Doug, a fan of music
if not of this band, came along. It was a chance for Lynn to include him in
her fan life for a change, and she hoped that it would help him understand
why expressing her fangirl side was so rewarding. Afterward the band did
a rare signing. We lined up to say hello and get an autograph, while Doug
stood to the side to immortalize the moment in photos.

Lynn and Kathy had both been fans of many things over the years. Lynn
admittedly had done some questionable things as a teenager to get up
close and personal with the performers she fanned. When she was twelve,
she chased the car that was rumored to be transporting heartthrob David
Cassidy away from the concert he'd just performed, tossing her purse to her
bewildered father/chauffeur as she ran down the street. When she was six-
teen, she slept on the sidewalk to get front row standing room only at a Rod
Stewart concert, only to be nearly crushed to death when the thousands of
people crowding the civic center rushed the stage. When she was seventeen,
she and her best friend managed to talk their way into one of David Bowie's
suites of hotel rooms. Once inside the coveted space, they took one look at
what was clearly the expectation of participation and had a change of heart.
"Oops, my boyfriend is on his way to pick us up, I forgot" was probably the
lamest excuse ever, but it got Lynn and her friend out the door and back to
some semblance of sanity.

So while Lynn might have demonstrated some questionable fannish decision making in the past, nothing unseemly had ever actually happened to
either of us on any of our fannish excursions. Doug, however, was not so
sure about this. So when Placebo lead singer Brian Molko leaned up for
a better look at Lynn's T-shirt (which featured a lovely photo of him), pronounced himself "quite fetching," and then offered with an eager grin to
sign her chest instead of the poster she was carrying, Doug was not happy.
While Lynn leaned over and giggled, Doug seethed. This is what happens
when Lynn and Kathy go on fannish road trips? He was so angry, in fact,

that he and Lynn ended up in a shouting match on the sidewalk in front of the restaurant where we all went for dinner.

"An autograph is an exception to the 'other guys aren't allowed to touch me' rule," Lynn insisted, trying and failing to keep her voice down.

"There ARE no exceptions to that rule!" Doug yelled back, emphasizing the gravity of his statement by waving his finger in her face.

Despite Lynn's dramatic eyerolls, no explanation of why Brian Molko would never be a threat to their relationship in real life (or remotely interested in Lynn) seemed convincing. Doug and Lynn eventually agreed to disagree before dinner got cold.

"Good thing he doesn't come along on *Supernatural* excursions," Kathy whispered as we said our good-byes later that night.

For Doug and Lynn, it was the first big fight about fandom—but it wouldn't be the last. Fandom was changing us for the better in some ways, but it was also taking a toll on our real-life relationships—we just didn't realize it yet.

As it happened, our next *Supernatural* excursion came a lot sooner than we had expected, which didn't exactly make our families any less cranky. Early that fall, Betsy Morris clued us in to yet another upcoming convention: a fans-only con being held in Vancouver. They were going to screen *Ten Inch Hero* there as part of the convention and were hoping to invite the cast and crew of *Supernatural*. We already had our tickets for the Creation con in Chicago in November, so the decision to go to Vancouver just a few weeks before felt particularly reckless, but it also seemed like too sweet an opportunity to pass up. This was Vancouver—Mecca, the place where the show was filmed, where the boys were! We broke the news to kids and significant others with no small amount of trepidation, which turned out to be well founded.

"Another convention?" was quickly followed by raised eyebrows and incredulous expressions. "In Canada??"

We nodded. That's where the research subjects were, after all. We had no choice!

Fresh from our success in arranging an interview with Adam Malin and wholly invested in our research, we decided to email the organizer of the all-fan convention and request an interview with her as well. Sharon Vernon of Fans First emailed back with yet another "I'd be happy to." We set up a meeting with her for the day before the convention. With two successes under our belts, Lynn decided to gather her courage once again and make a few phone calls. We were going to be in Vancouver, which might be the only opportunity we would ever have to visit the *Supernatural* set where the magic was made. Lynn knew that she would regret it if she didn't at least try. She wrote out a little blurb about who we were and what we were writing, hoping to convince TPTB that we were (a) serious scholars and (b) not stalkers. Lynn was so nervous that her hands shook, but she managed to get through by phone to the publicity contact person and made her pitch, reading from her homemade cue card.

"We're university professors and we're writing a book about *Supernatural* and fans," she told him, hoping that her voice wasn't shaking.

"You're writing a book about this show?" he asked, sounding incredulous.

"About the show and its fans, yes. And it would be really helpful if we could come to the set while we'll be in Vancouver and interview some of the producers or actors. Maybe [director] Kim Manners?"

The publicity guy paused. Lynn chewed on her pen, trying not to get her hopes up.

"Interesting project," he said finally. "But we don't allow anyone on set, sorry. Good luck with it though."

Damn.

Lynn wasn't surprised, but the disappointment was still hard to swallow. She crossed that option off her list. Then she tried the next one—Jensen's manager.

"We're university professors and we're writing a book about *Supernatural* and fans," Lynn said to the person who answered the agency's phone. "Can you put me in touch with Mr. Ackles's manager or her assistant?"

The assistant was pleasant and attentive. "Huh," she said when Lynn finished her spiel. "Can you put it in an email?"

Again a tiny bit of hope blossomed as Lynn typed furiously and hit "send." It lasted for a whole twenty-four hours until the reply came—from the manager herself: "Interesting project, but sorry, he's not interested."

Braver in email than on the phone, Lynn replied with a few more reasons why it would be a good idea for Ackles to participate in our little project. You know, for his own good. She didn't expect a reply, but a one-line email came the next day.

"Answer is still no," the manager said. "But I admire your perseverance."
Damn.

Maybe third time's the charm? Next Lynn emailed a plea to series creator and showrunner Eric Kripke, again explaining the book and why he might want to be interviewed for it. Of course, we didn't have Mr. Kripke's actual email address, so we sent it to his manager. This time there was no reply.

Discouraged, we confided our frustration to Betsy Morris, who as a fellow writer had been supportive of our book and was by this time a good email-friend. Betsy knew us as professors and researchers. Although she knew we were also fans, we hadn't divulged the details of just how we participated in fandom—that is, she had no idea that we wrote racy *Supernatural* fanfiction. At least, that's what we thought until we got an email saying that she'd put two and two together and connected our online selves to our real-life selves. We panicked. Pretty ironic, really. Here we were extolling the virtues of fanfic and the liberating value of fandom, only to be struck (painfully) with the reality that we were far from immune to shame ourselves. Our panic turned out to be misplaced. Betsy, a writer herself, could have cared less. (Of course, if we were writing fanfiction about her, she might have been less comfortable with the situation.)

"Hey, your fanfiction is actually good," Betsy reassured us. "It even has some deep psychological insights." She offered to put us in touch with David Mackay, the director of *Ten Inch Hero*. In stark contrast to Lynn's striking lack of success with cold calling, Mackay immediately agreed to an interview while we were in Vancouver. Success!

Our failures were easier to accept than our few successes. We were still having a hard time feeling anything close to legitimate, continuing to think of ourselves internally as fans while externally presenting ourselves as academics. But even as academics, it was hard to understand why anyone—let alone a film director—would want to talk to us.

Despite all this we went to Vancouver full of something like hope. Betsy had also put us in touch with Joanne, one of the con organizers. Joanne was an enthusiastic *Supernatural* fan and a Vancouver native. She'd worked as an extra on the show and knew some of the local crew and production assistants (PAs). She was also particularly talented when it came to finding the show's filming locations. We had no illusions that we could just stroll up and chat with Jared and Jensen, but we thought that we might be able to talk to some PAs or crew as part of our research. And if we just happened to catch a glimpse of "the boys" while they were filming, it would in no way distract us from the important work we were doing. Joanne agreed to help us out.

As if all this wasn't good enough, David Mackay offered us an introduction to Jensen (resulting in a few hours of hyperventilating on our part) provided that he was going to be in town but let us know that we probably wouldn't know until the last minute. That was okay, we thought. Last minute was okay. Breathe. We could do last minute. Breathe. No problem.

We arrived in Vancouver with everything going our way. Even the weather was glorious, crisp with the coming fall but not cold and not a cloud in sight. And everyone was so damned nice to us, from the immigration official who stamped our passports to the helpful man who shuttled us over to the car rental office, that it exceeded all the stereotypes of polite Canadians and threatened to slide over into caricature. Surely we were going to pay for this.

As soon as we arrived, we sat down with con organizer Sharon, who gave us our first lesson in the role that conventions play in contemporary fandom.

"A convention is an amazing experience," Sharon said. "I went to a convention in Germany to head up their volunteer events and was running the autograph line. There was this one woman, and she got to the bottom of the ramp as she was walking away and just leapt into the air with such a look of elation and joy and literally hopped away like a rabbit. That right there makes it all worth it. A con can make people happy for a year—or a lifetime."

We agreed. We'd already experienced some of that power ourselves.

For the rest of the weekend, we were introduced to the attendees as the "ladies who are writing a book on fandom," immediately set apart and above. This was exactly what we did not want. Or at least we kept saying this, even though we enjoyed the perks of our position. We were invited to dinner with the convention volunteers and listened as they planned the weekend. We didn't mind excusing ourselves after the screening of *Ten Inch Hero* to set up the details of our interview with its director David Mackay and driving off the next morning to meet David for brunch. At that small convention, in our very limited capacity, we were important.

And suspect.

Always viewed as researchers in the eyes of the people we were talking to, we found that we had to establish our fan cred with them even as we were trying to establish our academic cred with everyone else. We drank at the bar and swapped fan stories, watched episodes and discussed whether or not John Winchester was a good father, debated the relative merits of the assets of Jensen Ackles and Jared Padalecki, physical and otherwise. A scheduled costume party (common for many fandoms but not as common in the *Supernatural* world) was really just an excuse to drink and hang out. Eventually, over a few drinks, we ended up talking to several women who divulged their LJ names and turned out to be on our friends list and fans of our fanfic! Small world—and an uncomfortable moment for us. Should we "come out" as fanfic writers or stay in academic mode? After all, these people knew our real names, our actual universities. Could we also tell them that we wrote not quite G-rated fanfiction online as entirely different personas?

We opted to keep the secret in part because we got a firsthand taste of just what some fans thought of slash. One of the fans we joined for dinner was Ann, who had traveled from Australia to come to the Something Wicked con.

"Live Journal scares me," she confided from across the table. Our ears perked up immediately. LJ scary? The safe space? How could that be?

"I went on there the other day," Ann continued, "to read a write-up of Jensen's play, *A Few Good Men*. But then I scrolled down and there was a story about Jared and Jensen. *Together.* Disgusting! Why would someone write that?"

Ann made a face, apparently feeling nauseated just thinking about it. Across the table from her, we felt equally sick. Both the write-up and the fanfic she read were written by one of us. We stalled for time, playing with our food and taking a few giant gulps of our drinks while Ann waited for us to explain the pathology of slash-writers.

"Uh, well, probably lots of reasons," Lynn hedged, while Ann scowled, no doubt imagining what those reasons might be and definitely not enjoying the images. We were saved by the entrance of a few other fans who were eager to share their stories of finding *Supernatural* filming locations, so we never did have to give Ann an answer—or out ourselves.

Different ways of "doing" fandom have existed as long as there have been fans. Long before fandom took to the Internet, "circles" of fans gathered together at conventions or at friends' houses to discuss their love of a film, book, or television show. Each circle attracted like-minded fans who valued the same things in a fannish object. Some *Star Trek* fans produced or collected fanart; others wanted to discuss plot and characterization and the science fiction universe; still others wanted to write and share fanfiction. These fans produced fanzines full of early fanfiction and fanart, mimeographed and sent through the postal service to a mailing list of fellow fans. The lists were kept secret, and new fans who wanted to join a fan community were carefully vetted and then gradually indoctrinated into a specific group. Those who wanted to read and write fanfiction that stayed close to the characterizations and relationships seen onscreen (known as canon) did not tend to mix with those who wanted to expand those relationships into something sexual—especially when it was something homosexual. From the beginning, slash fans haven't always mixed comfortably with other fans. The rampant popularity and publicity surrounding *Fifty Shades of Grey* has brought fanfiction out of the closet—even NC-17 rated fanfiction with naughty bdsm themes. But *Fifty Shades* is still premised on a male/female relationship, which even today seems more acceptable to the mainstream reader than a male/male one. The higher levels of shame and secrecy surrounding slash communities persist, as they do in the fan communities who write hurt/comfort fic. Neither of these genres is well understood by outsiders, including other fans.

We did out ourselves to a few of the Something Wicked fans who were also fanfic writers—not at the con, but by email in the following weeks. Mara and Charlie were already on our friends list and tended to run in the same "LJ circles" as we do, so it seemed dishonest not to let them know who we really were. We asked them to keep our LJ identities confidential, however, rationalizing the shame-inspired decision by telling ourselves that knowing too much about who we were on LJ would tend to contaminate interviews. Better to be a blank slate and have people share themselves honestly.

We met David Mackay the next morning for brunch, thrilled to be getting our first pieces of insider information and equally thrilled to be treated as professionals by someone on the creative side of the fan/celebrity fence. David was remarkably candid, talking openly about his struggles with TPTB in making *Ten Inch Hero* what he and Betsy wanted it to be. It was a labor of love for both of them, but inevitably that labor of love had to pass muster with the corporate side of filmmaking as well—whose perspective did not necessarily agree with their creative vision. Betsy and David wanted to tell a story that was gritty and real—about things we don't talk about very much in our culture. Many of those things were the same stories that we wanted to tell in our book, the things women talked about in fandom but not anywhere else. The struggle to be real and take off our fake identities. The longing for community with other women, where we can talk openly about the real stuff. Like sex. *Ten Inch Hero* talked about the things women weren't "supposed" to—the things we talked about in fandom too. TPTB wanted David to take those things out. Women having sex? Talking openly about masturbation? Supporting and validating each other as they learned about themselves and their own sexuality? Heresy! And far too likely to snag the film a hard-to-market NC-17 rating.

"I made the film this way for a reason," David said adamantly.

I just like to keep things as real as possible. You don't always believe what you hear, but you believe what you see. If someone talks about having sex all the time, and you never see them do it, I don't know if I really believe it as much. You can intellectually understand that this character is sex obsessed because she talks about it, but one hour and five minutes into the movie, when she's riding the guy, you realize immediately, okay, she maybe really is, it consumes her, it's self-destructive. You have to see that to appreciate it, and it makes you feel more for the character. That's why I want it that way, I did what I thought would feel real.

David was fighting with TPTB to find someone who would pick up the film as it was instead of a watered-down version.

"I hope *Ten Inch Hero* succeeds financially, of course, but it is a little bit more of a message movie and a passion project, therefore a piece of art, and also something you want people to like. It's unconventional and different from what's out there right now, and I like that."

It was a passion project for Jensen too, David said.

He was really enthusiastic, wanted the part more than anyone else who'd read it. I wanted someone who was gung-ho and enthusiastic. Jensen loves the film. I wish management was more supportive. Those people just jump on the bandwagon once there's a bandwagon to jump on. If we get picked up theatrically, they'll be at the premiere, but if it's now and I say hey, please come to a screening for possible distributors, no one will show up. People are going to love this movie, and it's hard to become a household name—you'd think the managers would realize that.

David's insights into TPTB and their disconnect from the creative force behind a film or television show were completely novel to us. Our own creative vision lined up with David and Betsy's—we naïvely assumed that TPTB would be lined up as well. Apparently not so much. David had, in desperation, made end runs around managers and agents on multiple occasions just to get the project done. It didn't matter that an actor was on board—actors weren't the ones calling the shots. Neither was a director. TPTB, we slowly realized, were aptly named. They had all the power—and no idea how to wield it.

While we were talking with David, the rest of the fans were taking a bus tour of Vancouver, stopping to take photos of past *Supernatural* filming locations. Vancouver is an increasingly popular destination for fan pilgrimages, with popular films like *Watchmen* and *Twilight* and many television shows filmed there. Fans go to walk in the footsteps of their favorite actors, perhaps to get a glimpse of filming, and generally to geek out. Vancouver, in other words, is our Graceland. The studio was inexplicably nervous about a busload of fans being right in their backyard, however: security guards greeted the bus not with smiles and gratitude but with a surly "move along" when fans tried to get off and take pictures. What sort of threat the security staff thought twenty grown women with cameras might pose is unclear, but it left a bad taste in the mouths of the fans.

Since we missed all that excitement, Sharon had arranged a late night location scouting adventure for a small group of us. We traversed Vancouver and its suburbs as the last of the sunlight faded, taking barely visible in the moonlight photos of alleyways and overpasses, bridges and bars, gas stations and storefronts that we recognized from episodes. Were we being ridiculous? After all, these are *past* filming locations—nothing but a bridge or a bar or a beat-up gas station. No way.

A growing body of literature examines pilgrimages to filming locations, childhood homes, significant places in an actor, singer, or writer's life, and the gravesites where they rest. If you are a Beatles fan you might want to go to the Cavern in Liverpool or the hotel in Montreal where John and Yoko staged their bed-in for peace. For some, a trip to Paris is not complete without a stop at the Père Lachaise cemetery to pause in front of the graves of Jim Morrison or Oscar Wilde. This is not a new phenomenon, of course, and is not confined to modern media fandom. If you go to the temple of Poseidon in Greece, a helpful guard will automatically point you to the column where Lord Byron carved his name as he was passing through, a testament to the frequency with which pilgrims come in search of traces of the poet's life. Pilgrimages have always been connected with a spiritual journey, leading to catharsis or enlightenment. Perhaps modern media pilgrimages fill the gap left by our declining participation in organized religion or the fact that we live in an increasingly fragmented world. Shared popular culture narratives bring us the fulfillment that we can no longer find through traditional channels. As Roger Aden (*Popular Stories and Promised Lands: Fan Cultures and Symbolic Pilgrimages*) puts it, "The kind of escape popular stories promote is a ritualistic journey of the mind to spiritually powerful places where a vantage point that is anything but mundane affords us a reassuring view of an imagined promised land."

Once that promised land has been imagined, the logical next step is a physical escape to the place that has taken on so much meaning. Thus the rise of tour packages to New Zealand as the stand-in for Middle Earth in the *Lord of the Rings* or the bus tours that take avid fans on a *Sex in the City* tour of Manhattan or a *Doctor Who* walk through Cardiff. And the emotional impact of the fan pilgrimage is often just as strong and meaningful as a trip to Lourdes or Medjugorje or Varanasi. Kathy's own unexpected experience entering the Cavern Club in Liverpool attests to this. She went expecting to buy the mandatory souvenirs of the place and promptly burst into tears, overcome by a wave of emotion that combined nostalgia, sadness, and the memories of a score of significant moments in her own life that are inextricably intertwined with the lyrics of Beatles songs.

For *Supernatural* fans, every place where the boys have walked and run and fought demons—their own inner variety or the ones literally threatening to kill them—offers the possibility of entering the "liminal world where the ideal is felt to be real" (Victor and Edith Turner, *Image and Pilgrimage in Christian Culture*). These places have meaning precisely because they represent a different world order (where good consistently defeats evil, where family is the bedrock of our lives) or offer us an emotional connection back to our own lives. We visited the gas station from the episode "Home," scene of Dean's quietly desperate phone call to his missing father, and the park in which Dean tries to connect with a young boy traumatized by witnessing the death of his father, both powerfully moving moments in the character's life. The last place we were determined to find was the distinctive fence along the river where a pivotal scene takes place—Dean grudgingly confides to Sam their father's warning that Dean might have to kill his brother if he can't save him. Because this scene is one of the most intense emotional moments between the boys, and one of the rare moments in the early seasons of the show in which Dean opens up to Sam, the spot is particularly meaningful. As night fell, we took two not quite watertight ferries (which have since been closed and used as SPN filming locations themselves) then hiked down a wooded trail at midnight (without flashlights), whooping with glee when we finally found the spot.

Predictably, that's when the local police showed up.

Officer (who did have a flashlight): Is there a problem?

Us: Uh, no officer, no problem.

Officer (understandably skeptical and very good at stating the obvious): It's late.

Us: Yes, officer, we were just leaving.

Officer: What are you doing here?

Lynn: Well, we wanted to find this fence—

Kathy: From a television show—

Lynn: Where something happened—

Officer (holstering his big flashlight with a put-upon sigh): Oh. Fans.

In Vancouver, they were used to this sort of thing. The policeman drove away shaking his head, no doubt thinking that we were nuts but harmless.

We breathed a sigh of relief.

The convention ended with a planned group discussion of the show and

Sam and Dean get serious at the fence we risked our lives to find. Totally worth it.
Courtesy of Warner Brothers Television.

its appeal to fans. Clara told us one of the most touching stories we've heard
about what the fandom and the show meant to her:

Back in February 2007, I was having a very hard time personally. One of my
dearest friends, Diane, was dying a slow and horrific death from cancer. My
life was just filled with so much upset. I was trying to cope with everything
and I remember just thinking about *Supernatural* and Thursday night's episode. I typed in Sam and Dean and *Supernatural* in the search engine and a
fanfiction site popped up. I logged on and started reading and knew, from
the very bottom of my heart, that I had found my people, fellow fans who got
it, and I was hooked. I set up my account and started writing and writing and
writing. It helped get me through the very hard times when Diane was suffering so, so badly. One of the last things Diane ever said to me was that I should
go to see Jensen in Texas [in *A Few Good Men*]. She died in May 2007. I was
holding her hand when she died. As I watched Diane take her last breath I
got on my knees and said my prayers for her. The whole time in the back of
mind was the disbelief that this could even be happening, I mean, my God,
was this it, a life lived and then a very horrific and agonizing death? I thought
then and there that I would never ever again, save things for good, I'd pull

everything I was saving in my hope chest and start using them and no matter what, I was going to Texas to see Jensen. My tickets for Casa Mañana arrived on the day of Diane's funeral. I feel her with me on all my *Supernatural* trips. It's a very wonderful feeling.

The next day, full of love for the show and determination to find where they were filming it, we set out for the *Supernatural* studios in Burnaby with our volunteer tour guide, Joanne. We'd gotten the message loud and clear from our failed phone entreaties that we couldn't speak to the actors, but we figured that nobody would mind if we talked to some of the crew. Surely they had some interesting stories about fans!

There were no trailers in the studio parking lot, which meant location shooting that day. So off we went to track them down, following the not-so-subtle hot pink arrows all over Vancouver directing crew to the correct location. Good plan, wrong set. Apparently we're not that good at following hot pink arrows. Undaunted, we snagged a crew member there, explained that we "had to" get over to the *Supernatural* set, and asked if he could tell us where it was. And he did! We drove across town to the hospital where they were filming the episode "Dream a Little Dream of Me," then lurked in what we hoped was an inconspicuous fashion in the hallways and parking lot, acting as if we didn't know or care that they were there, waiting for the right moment for a brazen ambush of crew members with our questions. From our point of view, we were polite, naïve, middle-aged women who innocently asked for information and assumed that everything was fine because we were given that information. We had broken no rules. We were, after all, in a public space where anyone could be. We were getting in no one's way. And we weren't asking to talk to "the boys." We shook off the uncomfortable feeling that we were somewhere we shouldn't be (which of course we were) and looked for someone to interview. Joanne eventually spotted a PA she knew and introduced us with a description of the book we were researching. We asked if any crew members would be interested in being interviewed.

Mandy, one of the PAs, came out a few minutes later and said sure, she'd be happy to speak to us. We gave her a business card, described the book, and requested permission to record the interview, which she pronounced just fine. They were on a break from filming for lunch, so our timing was apparently impeccable. All went well until Lynn asked the unexpectedly loaded question "Have you ever had anything weird happen with fans?"

We were looking for funny stories, but instead we got a gasp and a vehement reply: "Yeah, we've got this one girl. I don't know if you guys have heard of her through researching *Supernatural*, but she offers free stalker tours. Her name is Jan or Jean or—Joanne! That's it, Joanne!"

"Really?" we asked with some trepidation. "Can you tell us about her?" Mandy was all too ready to talk.

So, she has a mole somewhere. Someone on the crew, someone that tells her where we are going to be and when. So she is sometimes in contact with us, and will show up on set with a group of fans that she has brought for the free stalker tour. And she'll give them a lowdown on what to say—really gives them this whole spiel on set etiquette. So when they are on the set, they are not asked to leave. But, this last weekend, she had a big convention where she actually flew in forty fans from various parts of the world, and they watched the episode and then toured all the *Supernatural* sets. So their plan was to come to the actual set. Luckily we were in studio, but yeah, that's the main girl we have to worry about. She's quite crazy.

Imagine our horror, knowing that we were two of those fans and that the person she was talking about was standing right beside us. Back at the car, Joanne was visibly shaken by what she'd just heard. From her perspective, she had always been polite while watching filming, never getting in the way or asking for anything. As a matter of fact, whenever she did bring other fans to the set, she made sure to lay down the rules of engagement before they left and assured potential visitors that they would have to leave if they didn't abide by her rules. How could her image of herself align so poorly with the way she was perceived? Joanne was dumbfounded and upset, and we were all eager to get away from Mandy. We headed over to the crew parking to see if we could talk to some crew members there. Seemed like a good idea at the time.

As we pulled into the parking lot, an SUV was pulling out. The tinted glass and the stern-looking driver told us that this was the boys on their way back to the set. Okay, we thought, at least no one will accuse us of stalking them if we're here and they're not. Stalkers follow their prey, right? Our reasoning seemed sound at the time so we went on with our business, snagging a crew member tidying up the area to ask her about fans. She was happy to talk. About the fans, about the actors on shows she had worked on previously. About anything. She was just about to share a bit of gossipy, behind-the-scenes information about the star of another show also filming in Vancouver when her walkie-talkie crackled. She listened, nodded, and turned to us, all thoughts of sharing now gone.

"Uh, they're coming down to talk to you," she informed us.

Idiots that we were, we actually thought that someone was coming down to offer another interview. How exciting!

Instead a large authoritative man appeared and told us to leave. Immediately.

"Oh, and don't speak to anyone on your way out," he warned. He watched as we slunk off to our car, red-faced and humiliated, though we had no idea exactly why we'd been banished like naughty children. Now we were just as mortified and ashamed as Joanne had been earlier. They didn't need to ask us to leave—we just wanted to get the hell out of there. As we walked back to the car, a man on a bike passed us, pedaled into the parking lot, and then circled as we got into the car. Even then, we didn't realize that he was security until he followed us out of the lot and down the road, as if expecting us to make a clandestine U-turn and sneak back. Obviously this guy didn't know the power of shame.

Only much later did we understand that our well-intentioned request to interview crew or PAs, assuming that permission was only required for interviews with actors or directors, inadvertently ignored multiple layers of authority. The entire incident was painful, both for us and for the hapless Joanne, who had tried so hard over the years to be respectful of the show she loved and make sure that the fans she helped watch filming were always respectful too. Hearing herself characterized as a crazy stalker by the very people of whom she was protective made her question her involvement in fandom, as she confided in a heartbreaking email to us:

I'm still reeling from Monday's news. I've been wracking my brain to think if I've done anything crazy but I can't think of anything. The best I can come up with is that they probably think I actually do have an insider and am handing out location info, when the truth is that I've never shared a live location with a fan I didn't already know personally. Everyone else has to settle for their own little tour of past locations. Anyway, I really hope my involvement hasn't had a negative effect on your book. If so, I'm truly sorry. If I had any idea at all that they would react in that way I never would have suggested we go.

Later that week, at Joanne's request, TPTB helpfully defined the term "stalker" for her. The actual definition of stalking behavior is "the willful and repeated following and/or harassing of another person with unwanted obsessive attention and intimidation." The studio's definition was a bit different.

As it turns out, all one needs to do to be considered a stalker is to show up to watch them film more than once. (!?!) If I had known this before it would have had a huge impact on my actions over the past year, but I always thought I was a good little fan who stayed out of the way and presented a positive voice online. Shows how much I know! lol. Apparently I'm public enemy #1 and the most feared fan in all the world! It's funny, but the more I think about it, the more angry I get. Nobody on set has ever said or done anything at all to make me feel that I wasn't welcome to watch. In fact, they have always been really nice and took the time to chat between takes and share information on the technical side of things, which is basically the reason I go to watch. I'm fascinated with set dressing and design, and I want to be there while they're filming because that way I can compare the dressed set that day with the un-dressed set at a later date. Does that make me a crazy stalker??? Then I think about all the times I had the opportunity to act like a crazy fangirl but didn't. Like a couple of weeks ago when one of my online friends was up from LA and we went down to watch. A crew member pointed out the boys' trailers and told us to go hang out by the doors in case they came out. We said no way were we going to do that because it would show a lack of respect for their privacy, and we went the other direction. There are hundreds of fans out there that would have taken the suggestion and stood outside their doors. Doesn't the fact that we said no say something good about us? Sorry about the rant, but like I said, it just makes me angry. Anyway I'm going to mail a letter of apology to the whole crew early next week. As for me, I'm fine but still feeling like a dog that got swatted with a newspaper. It bugs me, but I'll get over it. I haven't been banned from set or anything like that, but I assume if I go back it will only make things worse. I keep thinking about what you said about

men and sports. If I were a sports fan, would I be considered a stalker if I
went to the practice games? I mean geez, what kind of a crazy person would
be interested in seeing a preview of the action before all the regular fans?

Our humiliating experience at the location shoot was our first clue that
what we'd been calling the "creative side" is far from a homogeneous entity. The *Supernatural* crew members, as Joanne already knew firsthand,
are friendly and welcoming and grateful for fans' support. They're as passionate about making the show as we are about watching it and generally
welcome the opportunity to share their contributions with fans. The cast,
while most aren't as accessible as crew members, are similarly welcoming.
In fact, by the time *Supernatural* had been on the air for seven seasons, the
cast and crew were so welcoming of fans who camped out to watch them
film that director Phil Sgriccia turned the cameras on the fans at the end
of a long night of shooting, while the cast and crew applauded them. But
TPTB—the studio suits that we had been lumping in with the rest of the
"creative side"—are anything but welcoming. They are also where most of
the power actually resides. We just didn't know that yet.

We took Joanne out to dinner that night, still trying to shake off the awful
feeling of being viewed as the stereotypical stalker fangirl and still confused
about what we—and Joanne—had done wrong. If we felt this ashamed,
surely we had done *something* wrong. At the airport the next day, the United
States immigration officer asked us why we had been in Canada. We certainly weren't feeling the need to own up to being fangirls, so Kathy said
"business." Wrong answer.

"What kind of business?"

"We're researching a book."

"On?"

"Fans."

This was followed by the inevitable explanation of what we meant by fans.
No, not the things that go round and round. Fans of television shows or
music or—

"Oh—you mean crazy stalker chicks!"

"Yeah," we both replied glumly, as we scooped up our passports. "Crazy
stalker chicks."

It seemed like an appropriate end to the weekend.

Don't Ask, Don't Tell

Our experience in Vancouver changed us. The suspicion, stigma, and shame that we'd encountered confirmed Kathy's desire to differentiate herself from "fangirls." She never wanted to be looked at that way again. Even Lynn's fannish enthusiasm was dampened. By the time we arrived at the first Creation convention featuring *Supernatural* in Chicago in November 2007, however, the sting of Vancouver had worn off a bit. Our friends Lana and Kate joined us in Chicago, and we had a girls' weekend planned. Lana had put aside her resentment at being left out in Fort Worth, or at least was trying to, and Kate had come along partly out of a fondness for *Supernatural* and partly just to spend some time together. The four of us had been friends for years, sometimes sharing fandoms and sometimes not. Chicago was a chance to renew our friendship.

Easier said than done. Our original plans to squeeze some Chicago sightseeing in between guest appearances proved misguided on two counts: we weren't actually in Chicago (unless a distant and inconvenient suburb counts) and there is *never* any time between guests. One short foray into the city left us $75 poorer (cab fare from nowhere to somewhere is never cheap) and considerably grumpier than when we started. We weren't having fun yet. Back at the hotel, we indulged in several "purple nurples," a drink referenced in the *Supernatural* episode "Hell House." The bar was serving them all weekend in conjunction with the convention. We had no idea what was in them, but it didn't matter. They were purple, alcoholic, and went a long way toward (temporarily) diffusing some of the tension—until we ditched our friends to go interview Creation co-owner Adam Malin.

Adam and his partner Gary Berman have been in the business of putting on conventions since they were kids. Adam's first experience of a convention changed his life in much the same way that finding an online community of fellow fans had changed ours. "It was an unbelievable revelation to me," he told us. "I felt so empowered." Beyond the similarity of our shared response to finding fandom, we were also interested in how Adam and Gary got started in the business. Adam said:

> We've always been fairly fearless about things. We're not really afraid to talk to people. We would go down to the corner drugstore, to the pay phone that was outside, and we would just call up whoever . . . We didn't know the meaning of fear. We were kids who would travel into Manhattan from Long Island to seek out comic books in the backs of what were essentially pornography shops. These were peep show shops in the 1960s. We had to walk through these guys standing at these old machines and in the back of these places were rooms with comics that we would prospect.

Given our own fears and hesitations about the project we were undertaking, this functioned as a timely bit of advice. Be fearless! Okay, we could do that. Maybe.

Lana and Kate wandered by several times as we sat with Adam in the closed hotel bar, casting pointed glances in our direction. We didn't look back—or offer to make introductions. By the time we finished the interview, Kate and Lana were hungry, envious, and just plain pissed off. With good reason. We were not only ignoring our friends in favor of interviewing the con organizer but also stepping on Lana's toes in a big way. Creation, after all, was Lana's thing. We had never been to a Creation convention (unless you count Lynn and her husband taking their far-too-young children to an early *Star Trek* con). Lana, in contrast, was a Creation con veteran. It was Lana who shepherded us through the stressful process of stalking the online website in order to get the best seats the moment tickets went on sale. It was Lana who reminded us to buy photo ops with the boys early, before they sold out. She warned us about the endlessly long lines and the necessity of taking time out for things like food and sleep, even when your fangirl priorities are leaning more toward just staring at your favorite actors. Lana had been to so many Creation cons that the volunteers and the con photographer knew her; at her last con, when she'd been about to miss her plane, they had allowed her to jump to the front of the line for her photo op. We were impressed; Lana felt special. Now here we were sitting with Creation's owner at the hotel bar.

At the time, we didn't stop to think about how Lana might have felt about this. We were too caught up in the excitement of interviewing Adam and the anticipation of the very first *Supernatural* Creation con. It was most American fans' first opportunity to meet the stars of their favorite television show in person, and everyone was giddy with the prospect. Unaware that we had just damaged our relationship with Lana even further, and angered Kate as well, we joined them for dinner, where we probably made things worse by sharing some of the inside information we'd heard from Adam. We chattered excitedly. Kate nodded politely. Lana changed the subject.

The next day we experienced firsthand the phenomenon that is a Creation convention. The guest appearances began at noon, with autograph lines and photo ops and auctions sandwiched in between. We'd had plenty of practice with long lines at Comic Con, but we didn't expect them here. Once again we were being herded and barked at and getting confused. One thing was clear though. Enormous amounts of money were being thrown around, from the cost of the seats (several hundred dollars for the premium spots) to the photo-op tickets (hundreds more, depending on how determined a fan was to get her picture taken with all or just some of the guests) and auction bids of over a thousand dollars for things like giant banners of the boys, too large by far to hang in any home except an enormous castle.

The day was topped off by a "dessert party," a strange mix of alcohol and ice cream sundaes for fans who had purchased a gold ticket (the most expensive option). We all want to get up close and personal with the celebrities: Creation makes that happen—in two-minute intervals. In this highly choreographed opportunity to be spontaneous, each celebrity was escorted by a con volunteer with a stopwatch, who told the celebrity when to sit down and when to get up and move to the next table. The two minutes allotted for "conversation" made for some terribly awkward stammering and staring. It usually took the awestruck fans almost that long to get their voices working again. By the time they did, time was up! When you're a fan who has paid a lot of money for such moments of access, however, the artificiality can be a small price to pay for the sheer thrill of the moment. Some celebrities have mastered the art of making all fans at the table feel as if they've gotten at least a few minutes of personal contact. Matt Cohen, who plays young John

Just what every house needs: Creation auctions off some Winchester wall décor.
Courtesy of Elizabeth Sisson.

Winchester on *Supernatural*, makes it a point to hug each and every fan.
The illusion of informal cocktail party conversation is just that, however—
while you're chatting, the ever-present stopwatch ticks away above the celebrity's head, counting off the minutes until the boundary between fan and
actor is reinstated and the celebrity is whisked away. Kathy coined the term
"speed dating with the stars" to describe the weird artificial intimacy of this
convention tradition, which made us vaguely uncomfortable. We could only
assume that it made the stars uncomfortable too. After all, they were the
dogs and ponies in this particular dog and pony show.

   At the Chicago con, the celebrity guests were as mystified by the dessert
party as the fans were—some jumped up and ran as soon as the volunteer
tapped them on the shoulder, while others seemed uncomfortable with the
transition and tried apologizing for exits so abrupt that they seemed almost
rude. Some just ignored the tap on the shoulder and kept talking. Samantha Ferris was the first guest at our table that night. She may have had a
drink or two to steel herself against this experience (a logical preparation for
something this uncomfortable—for fans or celebrity guests). In fact, she
confided to a table of captivated women her plans for the rest of the evening,

which centered around the hot guy waiting patiently for her in their hotel room. So much for boundaries!

The dessert party ended at about 2 A.M. The next day was already starting. The boys were making their first appearance at the con at breakfast, another special event just for gold patrons. This meant more jockeying for position, with all of us heading for the same coveted tables in the front of the room and trying to get as up close and personal as we could. Some enterprising fans were already lining up. We grabbed a few hours of sleep before staggering down to join the line. One of the rules of conventions is that anticipation will always trump exhaustion. The fans who actually had the audacity to get more than an hour or two of sleep started to stumble downstairs at 5:00 A.M., astonished and dismayed to see the already long line, which by this time snaked up the stairs and through the lobby. Despite some disappointment, however, the mood at the convention is always different on Sundays. This is the day when the boys are there, and every single person knows it.

While we were waiting, we passed the time talking about the show and sharing fandom news and looking at photos of Jared and Jensen on laptops, stopping every now and then to check the time impatiently. Finally, we were let into the room at 8:30. Fans rushed to get the best locations, trying to secure tables that were as close as possible to the small stage. Our long night in the hotel hallway paid off—we were right up front. Time for caffeine. We grabbed a relatively good spot. Then we waited some more and ate. And waited some more, pushing our cooling eggs around on the plate, fidgeting, adjusting our chairs for optimum viewing pleasure, checking cameras. We stared at the two microphones set up side by side on the stage as if staring would make the boys materialize. We watched the doors, looking for some telltale sign that they were about to burst through them. A person on the other side of the room got overly excited and began to clap, setting off an entire room of gasps and heads whipping around. People picked up and then abruptly dropped threads of conversation that were going nowhere. We all readjusted our chairs repeatedly, as though it was theoretically possible for three hundred people all to have an unrestricted line of sight to the stage. At 9:02 a table somewhere off in the corner began a muted stamping of feet and clinking of glasses. You got the feeling that we would all be holding up lighters soon.

Finally four burly men in suits, sans necks (hereafter referred to as MWNN

[Men with No Necks]), appeared at the four corners of the stage. We clearly
needed four of them to be certain that a roomful of adult women didn't
suddenly lose their minds and try to take down a couple of pretty damn fit
actors over six feet tall. Creation owner Adam Malin took the stage, teasing
the audience with a quiz about countries of origin while we all waited, rolling our eyes and thinking "Who cares?? Where are the boys???" Australia,
Singapore, Japan, Israel, Sweden, Germany, Britain, Canada—we'd come
from all over the world just to be here, in this moment. And then—finally—
Jared and Jensen took the stage, and the room and the crowd erupted in
applause. Lost sleep and long lines were forgotten as cameras flashed from
all sides. The boys were back in town!

Jared and Jensen together are not only overwhelmingly gorgeous but
also hysterically funny. And they have enough chemistry together to power
a small country. As soon as the applause died down and the cameras
stopped blinding them, they started teasing each other about the gigantic
appropriate-for-your-castle banners of them looking sexy that were hanging
all over the room. From their point of view it must have been disconcert-
ing to be confronted with these images of themselves, but they also clearly
knew what the fangirls wanted, playing up their "epic love" masterfully.
They could easily do this for a living—the J2 Comedy Hour.

The brotherly affection that the two stars have for each other is by all
accounts genuine, but the awareness of fans' appreciation for what the
website afterelton.com calls slashwink is something new and of increasing importance to TPTB. "Slash fans," an article on the website explained,
"can be a pretty intense breed, but for film and television projects looking
for a dedicated and highly involved fanbase, the kind of audience that will
explode a project's social media footprint, the fangirls and fanboys who ob-
sess over slash are a valuable market to court, and Hollywood might just be
waking up to slash's potential."

Slash is a subset of shipping, which is a fan's keen interest in the pairing of two characters—straight, gay, platonic, romantic, bromantic, whatever ("shipper" is short for "relationshipper"). If you are on TeamJacob or
TeamEdward, you're a shipper. If you want Castle to get it on with Beckett,
you're a shipper. If you watched *Moonlighting* back in the day, you were almost certainly a shipper. Slash fans ship two same-sex (usually male) characters who are generally not an actual couple in canon—or, in the case of

Jensen and Jared (a pairing known as J2 or J-Squared), two real people who aren't together in real life. Shippers base their fantasies on a subtextual relationship, using their keen observation skills to uncover every bit of insinuating dialogue, every long look, every casual touch or extra-warm smile—or out of practically nothing at all. Film and television shows are increasingly wise to the audience's love of slashy subtext and will sometimes encourage the slash shippers with a "slashwink," a nod to the slash relationship within the show. It's subtle instead of overt, often in the form of a joke, so that the more conservative audience members won't take offense (or even notice) but the eagle-eyed slashers will, and the show will benefit from the subsequent social media chatter. Some shows have released official promos that play up the fans' favorite slash couples to court fans, most recently *Hawaii Five-O* and *Teen Wolf*, whose showrunner began to write the show itself in a slashy direction when he became aware of the popularity of "Sterek," the slash pairing of sidekick Stiles and alpha wolf Derek. The *Teen Wolf* actors have engaged in slashwinks of their own, exchanging suggestive tweets on Twitter and filming a video which overtly suggests that they have just woken up from a bit of afternoon delight in order to court votes for the Teen Choice Awards.

Jared and Jensen hadn't exactly jumped on the slashwink bandwagon. But long before the networks were even aware of the possibility, their natural boyish enthusiasm and affection for each other resulted in plenty of fodder for fans who wanted to "ship" them. And they'd certainly done nothing to discourage it. Whether interpreted as bromance or romance, "J2" is good business. For example, the Twizzler Incident occurred around this time. Jared is giving an interview. As the camera rolls, Jensen helpfully distracts him. With a Twizzler in his mouth. He pokes Jared with a stiff red stick candy that he's holding in his mouth. The Freudian implications were not lost on the fans. The Hershey factory struggled to keep up with the sudden increased popularity of one of its candy products. Next came the Buddy TV interview that leaked the news that the boys were in fact living together. Fandom responded with an incredulous HUH? and then a collective OMG SQUEE!! heard all over the Internet. This was followed closely by Jared's video clip interview in which he confided that Jensen was "into me" and then described Jensen's morning routine: "He basically rolls his little pretty ass outta bed and gets in the shower." During their charity appearance at the

Redbull Soapbox Derby, J2 donned matching team shirts, folded their six-foot-plus selves into tiny little race cars, and acted like giggling six-year-olds. They also spent the day joined at the hip. For a fandom already in heaven over the prospect of the boys living together, the charity appearance was like crack to an addict. Then there was the unfortunate, possibly Freudian, slip made by a CW Network captioner, who helpfully supplied the name of the actor being interviewed as "Jensen Padalecki." "J2 Gay Married in Canada, Jensen Takes Jared's Name!" proclaimed post after post on LJ.

The show itself provides a wealth of subtext that fans have used to ship sibling characters Sam and Dean—thus the popularity of Wincest. In later seasons, slash fans split between those who shipped Wincest and those who shipped Dean with the (male) angel Castiel, a pairing known by the portmanteau of Destiel. In both cases, subtext was available in abundance.

As we've mentioned, the issue of whether or not it's okay to write fanfiction about real people, especially whether it's okay to "slash" two guys who identify as straight in real life, creates a great deal of controversy. But there are at least as many *Supernatural* fans who like to fantasize about the two lead actors getting it on as there are fans who are scandalized by that sort of fantasy. The former are known as "tinhats" or "hats," a tongue-in-cheek reference to how "crazy" it is to imagine such things. The latter are sometimes known as "hets," because they like to fantasize about the relationships the guys have with women who may or may not be their significant others.

Whether fans chose to view Jared and Jensen's affectionate banter at the convention as a continuation of the homoerotic subtext of the show or as the epic real-life J2 bromance, Ackles and Padalecki gave us plenty of fantasy fodder at the con. The story of the Eyelash Incident was an instant fan favorite. Jared explained (and reenacted) a tender scene at a Vancouver restaurant in which Jensen reached over to brush an eyelash from Jared's face then recoiled in horror with an "Oh my God, what am I doing?" Too late, apparently, they both realized that while they're used to being this intimate in the "enclosed environment" of the set (whatever that means—use your imagination), unfortunately they were in public. Jensen attempted to recover with the time-honored save-your-macho tactic of telling Jared "Quick, chug your beer, chug your beer!" Fangirls all over the room spontaneously combusted. The boys blushed endearingly and grinned at each other. Reality? Fan service? Who cares. It was adorable.

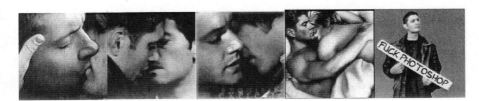

Slashwink, subtext, and Wincest, oh my!

And then came "the hug." To understand its significance you also have to understand how fervently many fans are invested in the certainty that Jared and Jensen are in fact a couple. This is not to suggest that we actually believe it but rather that we want to. We want them to act out our fanfiction, to validate our fantasies and give us a reason to write yet more of the stuff. The hug, a spontaneous bit of fooling around, provided that reason and more, and we managed to capture it. Our photo would later appear on hundreds of fan icons. Once again, we felt special. We posted the breakfast wrap-up in our LJ and comments immediately started pouring in. Lana gave us her clandestinely taken vids to post on YouTube (videotaping at the cons is technically not allowed and is policed diligently by overzealous volunteers, which makes no sense because it's the thing that sells most fans on actually going to them) and had five thousand comments in two hours. This, amazingly, was before the Time of Twitter, which has taken immediacy to a whole new level for fans.

After the breakfast, it was time for another convention staple: photo ops with the celebrity guests. This meant that Kathy and Lynn parted ways for a little while. Kathy is determined that no photographic record of her existence will ever surface and was certainly not going to pay money to be photographed, no matter how hot the actors were. Lynn, in contrast, believes wholeheartedly that opportunities to bump shoulders with Jensen and Jared just shouldn't be squandered. Photo ops, we soon realized, are weird things. You wait in a very long line, holding the tickets that prove you've paid the requisite (and substantial) fee, hand over your purse to an unknown security person (at least you hope it's a security person), and are then instructed precisely when to step up and stand next to the celebrity already posed for the camera. The whole process is generally over in under a minute. We couldn't help but wonder how it felt to the actors as they sat there and gamely attempted grin after sleepy grin. Smile, perhaps bump shoulders with the celebrity, and then you're herded out the exit door, usually still in a somewhat dazed state and thus quite malleable. But that's not to say that the experience isn't worth it. Oh hell yes, it's worth it for that one moment when the person you are a fan of is actually seeing you. Maybe even smiling at you.

Often it's not even about having the photo, it's about being up close and personal with the celebrity, to say hello, perhaps to bump elbows. Photo ops

Fangasm! Jensen fangirls Jared. Courtesy of Christopher Schmelke.

can be enormously powerful moments for fans. One woman left her house for the first time in four years: her desire to be face to face with an actor was the most compelling reason she'd found to start recovering from her severe agoraphobia. It's about sharing space, not possessing a picture.

Chris Schmelke, Creation's photographer, told us: "I think people get

Fangasm! Jared fangirls Jensen. Courtesy of Christopher Schmelke.

addicted to the space that they're in for that short period of time—it's an escape, for that moment their problems are forgotten. It's not even about the picture—explain the person who had a [William] Shatner photo op in Vegas, and Missouri, and LA, and she never even claimed them. She never wanted the picture, she just wanted to be next to him."

We got it. It may sound odd, but for some people it's as much paying for the opportunity for a brief moment of physical connection as it is for the concrete evidence of that moment. Chris said:

I think it depends on the person. Someone who's getting a picture taken with William Shatner doesn't have the same interaction as they would with, say, someone like Samantha Ferris from *Supernatural.* Shatner is there to take the picture, and that's it. I'm using Shatner as an example because he doesn't have the personal interaction with the fans, whereas the boys [Padalecki and Ackles], they do. The worst thing for me is for someone to come there and want a photo and be told that there's a possibility for it to happen and then not being able to have one. It's one thing to know beforehand that it's not going to happen, it's another to come all that way and make an effort to be there—and if I have the power to deliver that, I'm going to do it. I was able to get to every single one in Chicago who was in the standby line.

Clearly Chris understood how important photo ops are to fans. He's widely beloved for his ability to make a photo op a satisfying experience, even in under a minute.

I take a lot of pride in it. Some convention photographers just use a tripod and basically have it set up and just hit the button and don't do anything. For me, it's not so much just getting a photo, but trying to get the emotion of the photo. It could be 10 or 15 seconds, but if a fan is having a conversation with the guest, who am I to butt in and interrupt that person's moment? I know what I'm capable of in a certain amount of time—and okay, out of three hundred fans, there might be one who will take advantage of that. But if you make it into an experience, this part of the con has the ability to be either the highlight or the lowlight. It's the most one-on-one interaction the fans will have with the guests, and if I'm in a position to make it a highlight, I will. I take a lot of pride in these photos, I look at every single one. If someone blinks, I'll generally have people retake them. And from what I hear from fans, that's something that isn't done at other shows. I'm just not going to give someone shitty photos. For me, I'm going to try to capture the best possible moment of this best possible moment, not just Hi! Bye! It makes it robotic for me, and I don't enjoy that. I would take fifteen minutes to set up the lighting for each fan, but we don't have that kind of time.

Chris, unlike some other photographers hired to shoot conventions, takes his responsibility seriously—because he gets it. "The first Creation show I worked was the *Star Wars* 10th anniversary show. I was still young enough to be playing with the toys, and I got to meet George Lucas himself, and I got a picture taken with him. If I were to go to a convention myself, it would be for *Twin Peaks*. I have all the soundtracks, I listen to them all the time. So I have a different point of view than some people—that I won't look down on anyone who would go to something like this."

Once through the Jensen line, it was time to do it all over again for Jared, who didn't care at all for the "no hugs" rule that the convention had put into place. Lynn was completely unprepared for Jared's long arm snaking around her when she stepped up beside him, so she ended up falling into him with a striking lack of grace. Kathy laughed at her from her vantage point safely outside the room.

The boys continued what to many of the women in the audience was clearly innuendo-filled banter during their Q&A sessions. Many of us were determined to read any and all comments and actions as flirty, no matter how innocent. When Ackles entertained the fans by twisting the plastic water bottle he'd been holding between his thighs until the pressure built up so far that it blew its top and shot off with a dramatic pop, fangirls spontaneously combusted. The fanfiction was writing itself! Padalecki rolled his eyes indulgently.

And then we had to get in line again, this time for autographs. Lines are an integral part of conventions, as they are at most entertainment venues. You go to Disney World, you wait two hours for the thrill of Tower of Terror. You go to a *Supernatural* con, you wait two hours for the thrill of asking a celebrity a question. Nobody likes the lines or the subtle condescension that seems to go along with them. "Stand there, move there, keep going, not too fast, not too slow, up against the wall." We half expected the next instructions to be "eyes forward, heads down" or to be frisked for hidden weapons. A disturbing depersonalization occurs when an entire group is herded from one place to another, though the alternative—lack of organization—is even worse. Still, we couldn't help but feel a nagging sense of shame and inferiority as we allowed ourselves to be moved along from line to line, with our admission passes looped around our necks and plastic color-coded bracelets around our wrists.

Fans line up to wait for their moment with the boys. Courtesy of Karen Cooke.

You might think that all this relentless organization left a bad taste in our mouths. Did we give up on cons after our experience in Chicago? HELL NO! The combination of an entire hotel full of fellow fans and the opportunity (however constrained) to interact with Jared, Jensen, and the other SPN celebrities left us wanting to do it all again. As soon as possible.

We were still determined to see fandom as one big happy place where everyone played nicely, even if we already had evidence to the contrary. It was only much later that we saw the potential for misunderstanding and real hurt. Even being told point blank at the time did nothing to shake our faith in the healing powers of fandom. And we *were* told—by someone who had every reason to know. Our friend and fellow fangirl Charlie overheard us about to reveal to someone our online identities along with our real-life researcher ones. She grabbed us before we could finish our sentence and admonished us: "Don't tell! Never tell." She had learned the hard way.

"Fandom can be very vicious and small-minded as a group. I ran a fansite for an actor from another television show which also filmed in Vancouver. A group of BNFs approached me because they wanted to set up a fundraising outfit to promote the actor, and they wanted me to be involved because I'm

right there and had ready access to him. I'd already met him through some
volunteer work we both did, and he didn't see me as a threat. I mean, hell,
would you?"

This was a rhetorical question for us, because we knew Charlie quite well
by then. But for those of you following along at home, Charlie is a professional woman in her fifties, married with grown children, smart, articulate,
accomplished and caring. Threatening? Not so much.

> So we set up this charity, but then one of the people involved (let's call her "J"
> for jealous) decided that I was too close to the actor, and that I needed to be
> neutralized so she could take over. He was filming a movie at the time and I
> was welcomed at the shoot with some others from the fansite, and he invited
> us down to another location shoot the next day. Sometime that afternoon,
> apparently, J handed him a printout of one of my very explicit slash stories
> about him and told him that we were planning to do something—I'm not
> really sure what she said, that we were going to kidnap him or something!
> When we went down to the location shoot the next day, we were turned away.
> As of that day, we were locked out of the fansite and it kept going without us.
> I was very hurt, and it confirmed my feelings that too much trust is a very
> bad thing. It happens again and again. If someone is perceived to be a BNF
> in fandom, they suddenly become the target of people who want to be that
> BNF but can't. I'm happy not to be one.

We paled. Is this what would happen if other fans pegged us as the kind
of fans who wanted to be "special," to gain access to the celebrity side, to be
set apart in some way? Is that in fact who we were? And if so, were we any
different than everyone else? We kept quiet, though we felt as duplicitous as
the woman behind us in line, who confided that she had lied to her husband
about where she was going in order to sneak off to this convention.

"He thinks I'm visiting a friend," she told us with a shrug. "He has no
idea I'm in Chicago."

Such is both the allure of fandom and the danger. The pressure to keep
quiet—whether it's to hide your emotional investment from a significant
other or to avoid the maligned tag of "BNF" and the consequent resentment—is as much a part of fandom as the joy of finding like-minded others
to celebrate with. Our fear of being the targets of wank kept us quiet and

convinced us to keep our fan sides completely separate from our researcher sides. It was awkward but apparently necessary.

Facing up to the wank that is as much a part of fandom as its sense of community gave us a lot to think about over the holidays. We even felt a bit of kinship with the show itself as the beleaguered Season 3 finally resumed in early spring after the writer's strike ended, bringing accusations of misogyny, racism, and homophobia in the show—a different kind of fandom wank. Fans may love to excess, but they're far from mindless, nonjudgmental consumers. Online fandom exploded with intellectual discussion (known as meta) about whether *Supernatural*'s Dean Winchester hurled words like "slut" and "skank" around because the show was carelessly misogynistic or because the character is flawed and the objectionable words fit with his flaws. The wank about homophobia in SPN was an especially unexpected one for us—this is, after all, a show that attracts as many queer women as straight women, as well as some gay men. The main characters' relationship (and that of the actors who play them) is often read with a homoerotic subtext, so clearly viewers didn't fall for the show because it came off as homophobic!

Creator Eric Kripke took on the accusations of homophobia in an episode featuring a gay character. The character's feelings weren't reciprocated but weren't ridiculed either, and in the end he was the one who saved the day. Unfortunately, he also died, thus evoking the same argument made by fans about the show's perceived misogyny and racism: women and minorities on *Supernatural* rarely survive an episode. (Never mind that most of the white male guest stars don't either.) We followed the wank with interest and decided to try to get an interview with the only person who could really address the accusations of misogyny, racism, and homophobia in *Supernatural*—Eric Kripke himself.

Our experience at the con fanned our obsession with the show, our love affair with fandom, and our desire to keep writing about both. Unfortunately, it didn't have nearly as positive an effect on our friendship with Lana and Kate. The con was supposed to be a time to celebrate our shared love of *Supernatural*, to kick back and ogle Ackles and Padalecki, to have a few drinks and some good food and forget the stresses of everyday life. Instead, the fence we were straddling between being fangirls like our friends and trying to do research (which, let's face it, was about being an insider as much as writing a book) led to yet more problems in Chicago. Kate and Lana were thoroughly disgusted with us—and who could blame them? Amazingly, we could and did at the time, feeling indignant and wronged that they didn't understand how important our research was. This was relatively easy to cling to, because there was certainly some truth to it—both our university jobs hinged on writing and publishing. But where we thought we had been practical and discreet, we were insufferable, putting our own agenda before our friendship at every opportunity.

Once we got home, we resumed our quest to gain access to the "creative side" of *Supernatural* in earnest. We had failed to reach Kripke but managed to find an email address for *Supernatural* writer and producer (later show-runner) Sera Gamble and sent her an email describing our research. To our surprise, Gamble replied immediately and agreed to do an email interview. This resulted in us once again having repetitive phone conversations that mostly consisted of "ohmygod, can you believe it, ohmygod?!"

Our email exchange with Gamble was our first bit of inside information about *Supernatural* itself. It was also one of our first moments of affirma-tion from the "other side." When we mentioned to her that entire fanfiction communities were devoted to torturing Dean, for instance, she immedi-ately understood the attraction.

I didn't know about this at all! People are writing fiction to torture Dean? Now that I'm thinking about it, I'm not surprised. We torture him on purpose. It makes for good drama. And action heroes are there to be beat up—they're not nearly as heroic if they don't pay mightily for their selflessness. On our staff, no one enjoys torturing the boys more than I do. Or, at least, no one else sits in the writers' room giggling their head off about it. It's because I'm turned on by the same thing those fiction writers are. I think brave, tortured heroes are sexy. Somewhere in my gooey center, underneath my eye rolling and cynicism and my collegiate intellectualizing of story, I have a taste for the romantic. So I feel it in my gut when we get it right. Self-sacrifice for the one you love is romantic. Tough guy getting beaten to shit and having a hilarious attitude about it to cover up the pain is romantic. So it's not an intellectual process for me—my inner girly girl just lights up and goes, "Tell that story! I am so not changing the channel while his lip is bleeding!"

Gamble was also aware of "how into the boys' relationship everyone is. And of course we're aware of the subtext, or the perceived subtext. I think it happens on lots of shows with male leads who are very intimate."

She assured us, however, that she never reads fanfic. Not because it might not be fun to read, but because Gamble knew the world of the Winchesters so well that she feared she might be annoyed if someone got it "wrong." And she wouldn't want to steal someone else's story idea by accident. Though we could think of a few fanfic plots we wouldn't mind seeing on our TV screens, come to think of it . . .

Heartened by this success, we put aside the sting of Vancouver and began to strategize again. How were we going to get to the actors?

Be fearless!!

In our case, being fearless meant that Kathy found the phone number for actress Samantha Ferris's agent and then made Lynn call. Again to our utter amazement, she responded. We were on to do a phone interview with her the following week. Kathy drove to Philadelphia.

Our first interview with an actor wound up setting the tone for most of the ones that followed. They involved technical difficulties, severe illness, and near death. At best we were a sort of slapstick comedy act. One thing going wrong cascaded into the next calamity, and so on until the end of the scene. Our downfall that day was phones, or more precisely how to work the conference call feature on Lynn's home phone. Once we figured out that the phone didn't *have* a speaker, we raced to Lynn's university office to use one of the phones there. Half an hour, three tries, and much hand wringing later, we finally placed the (now significantly late) call, with Lynn holding the audio recorder right on top of the little plastic speaker and Kathy kneeling beside the desk so that she could both talk and hear.

Samantha was eager to talk about how female fans reacted to her character. Already, as an actor on the show and someone who had interacted with fans online and at conventions, she understood the fans better than TPTB ever would. "I'm not a threat," she said. "Look at most of the women they brought in—they're a threat [to the fantasy that female fans have about Sam and Dean], but I never was. I'm a mother figure to these guys. With their dad gone, I can be a shoulder to cry on. I'm never a threat to the fangirls."

Samantha was right. She also endeared herself to us by promising to buy our book. Little did we know that she'd have to wait another five years. That spring, buoyed by our success, we shored up our determination to find a way to get to Eric Kripke. Creation had scheduled another convention for March, this time solely for *Supernatural*, which had apparently now proven itself able to attract enough people to make a con worthwhile. Even Kathy didn't hesitate to sign up for this one, though none of our children were any happier about us flying off to LA than they'd been about us flying off to Chicago or Canada. Since the con was being held in LA, Eric Kripke was scheduled to appear, along with Jared and Jensen. This would be the perfect time, we thought, to speak to him in person. But how?

We asked Sera Gamble for advice on how to contact Kripke. To our surprise (yes, we really were constantly surprised), Sera put us through to Kripke's assistant, who routed us through the "proper channels" to TPTB (i.e., Warner Brothers). Just like that, we were set up for an interview. Such is the power of TPTB. Lesson one: it's who you know. We also had the distinct advantage of being the only people out there at the time interested enough in their little-known show to want to write a book about it. TPTB knew an opportunity when they saw one. We were literally bouncing (Lynn bounced; Kathy watched) with anticipation at the news. We would actually have the chance to speak to Eric Kripke, the creator. Because of his time constraints after the writers' strike, he wouldn't have time to do the interview in person at the convention. Instead, he agreed to a phone interview afterward. (Great. Back to the phones. We're so good at that.)

We were headed to LA for the convention anyway, so we also pursued an interview with *Supernatural* guest actor Jim Beaver. Jim was not appearing at the convention, but he lives in LA. Kathy found his agent's email address, sent a respectful request, and waited to be ignored. Instead, she found an email from Jim himself sitting in her inbox the next day. At first she thought it was a joke. Of course it wasn't Jim. Of course he wasn't emailing her directly. She sat for a while, mouse hovering over the entry, wanting to click on it but half afraid it would explode.

Kathy called Lynn instead. "I got an email from Jim Beaver."

"What?? What does it say???"

"Don't know. I haven't opened it yet."

"What do you mean you haven't opened it yet?! How do you know it's from him?"

"You know—it has his name on it," Kathy answered, a bit annoyed at what to her seemed like a ridiculous question.

"Well, OPEN IT!!"

Buoyed by Lynn's support/screaming at her, Kathy did open the email. We were on for an interview. Jim Beaver would call us when we got to LA.

Right.

We thought about posting the good news on LJ and realized that was probably a very bad idea. We were, after all, spies in the house of fandom. Our double life had begun in earnest.

SEVEN

Coming Out in LA

"Ladies and gentlemen, we're having a slight problem with the left engine. Someone should be here shortly to fix it, and then we'll get underway to Los Angeles," our pilot informed us before takeoff.

Kathy, a white-knuckle flier under the best of circumstances, did not take the news well. As always in these situations she imagined wrench-wielding gremlins perched on the wing of the plane. (She had watched a lot of *Twilight Zone* as a kid.) She grew paler and paler the longer we sat on the tarmac.

"We're going to die" suddenly became her new mantra, repeated over and over with the inevitability of her own imminent demise.

Lynn, who tends to think everything is either "awesome" or a disaster of epic proportions, was more worried that we'd get to LA late and thus that none of our interviews would happen, increasingly convinced that the entire trip was unraveling even before we'd left the gate.

"We're never gonna get there in time," Lynn whined, impatiently staring down the flight attendants as though they could somehow hurry things up. "And we'll probably never get the chance to interview anyone ever again, ever. EVER."

Kathy took a deep breath and attempted a smile; it looked more like a grimace. "Yes we will," she said curtly, more to shut Lynn up than to assuage her fears.

Lynn was not encouraged.

Both Kathy and the plane managed to hold themselves together for the duration of the trip. Once we landed—almost exactly on time—Lynn reverted to "everything is awesome," ecstatic at being able to sunbathe poolside in March. Kathy was far less thrilled. Her attitude toward sun can be summed up succinctly: "It burns, it blinds, it causes cancer." Did anything more really need to be said? Apparently yes. Almost as soon as we dropped our bags in the hotel room, Lynn was poolside while Kathy sat sullenly in the shade in her usual black jeans and black T-shirt and black Doc Martens. It's a good thing we have *Supernatural* in common.

Once the sun went down and Lynn could be dragged away from the pool, we headed out on the first fangirl excursion of the trip, bound for Hollywood and the Hotel Café to see Steve Carlson play. We'd planned a meet up with fellow fangirls Julia and Sabrina. We had stayed in touch with them since Comic Con. It should have been a fun plan, which should have put us in a good mood. But we weren't in California just to have fun—we had interviews to worry about. No longer distracted by the California sun, Lynn slipped quickly back into catastrophizing. We had arranged to interview Jim Beaver the next day, but we had no firm plans. Lynn was increasingly convinced that the interview wasn't going to happen.

"He's not going to call," Lynn grumbled, obsessively checking her cell phone.

Kathy ignored her, navigating our rental car through LA traffic with single-minded concentration. In addition to the fear of flying and the fear of being photographed, Kathy also hated feeling lost. In the days before GPS devices, all she had to rely on were Mapquest directions and Lynn's navigational skills. They were doomed.

"We didn't even set up a time and place," Lynn continued, more and more upset. "Why didn't we set up a time or place? How stupid of us!"

That was enough to prompt Kathy out of her silence. "Calm down and read me the damn directions!"

Lynn took a deep breath, wondered at Kathy's priorities, and pulled out the scrap of paper on which we'd written down Julia's detailed directions to Hotel Café. We'd already found the right block—or at least we thought we had. "Turn into the alley," Lynn dutifully read.

"What alley?" Kathy asked. And yes, her voice had become somewhat shrill.

"The alley," Lynn helpfully repeated, shrugging when Kathy glared at her.

There was indeed an alley to our right, and Kathy did what she was told, turning abruptly into what was unfortunately the wrong alley and a very narrow one. After a harrowing three-point turn (actually more like eight points, all done under the amused eye of someone whose job apparently entailed standing around and laughing at people who make wrong turns into his employer's alley), we were finally pointed in the right direction. We were about to emerge back out onto the street when Lynn's phone rang.

Lynn looked down. The caller ID said "Jim Beaver."

"STOP!" Lynn screamed at the top of her lungs.

"WHAT?" Kathy shrieked, her mounting fear that they were now lost in LA and about to enact the nightmare scenario from a hundred bad movies about being lost in strange cities threatening to overwhelm her entirely.

"Don't move," Lynn dictated as she pushed the green button on her phone.

Was Lynn serious? Was this really the time for a chat?

We blocked the alley for five minutes while Lynn talked with Jim Beaver and Kathy tried to piece together the gist of the conversation, waving a hand in Lynn's direction to try to get her to indicate what was going on. Then it was Lynn's turn to make the frenzied universal gesture for paper and something to write on. A mad scramble ensued. Lynn's purse was upended, makeup and brushes and loose change tumbling out. Kathy's purse followed: recorder and camera and batteries (Kathy had learned over the past year never to go anywhere without batteries) added to the debris on the floor of the car. Finally Kathy triumphantly held out a note pad and a pen, and Lynn scribbled one word: "HOUSE!"

Apparently we were going to meet with Jim after all. The next day in fact. At his *house*. Kathy's first reaction was "Is he crazy?" The academic in her wanted to keep him safe from the fangirl threat, even if that fangirl was her. Her next reaction was to wonder at her first reaction. There would be a lot of that over the next few days.

Lynn was feeling pretty pleased with herself when we finally joined Sabrina and Julia and the rest of their "gang" of fangirls. Kathy was just glad not to be driving anymore. Sabrina, Julia, and their friends occupied an interesting in-between niche themselves, somewhere between fangirl and neighbor to the actors and musicians who also live in Studio City and West Hollywood. They were fans at conventions, laughing through photo ops because the boys recognized them as neighbors, and just fellow music lovers at the local concert venues, hanging out with Jensen and Danneel while they listened to Steve Carlson or Jason Manns. Jason had been known to play practice sets in Julia's living room. The girls were keenly aware of their hybrid positions in the highly stratified environment of fandom and the potential for other fans to be envious—or worse. At times, the fangirls were more aware than the actors of the lines that they so carefully straddled.

Sabrina told us a story about actor and musician Riley Smith, a friend of Ackles and Carlson.

"One night a couple of fans came up to Riley at a show and were fangirling all over him," she confided. "They thought we were too, and Riley was like 'these are not fangirls, these are our friends,' and it was like oh my God! To hear that was this great feeling—they don't see us as fans that they *have* to be nice to. They *like* to see us."

We smiled right back, though our smiles might have been a bit tight. Once again it seemed like being a fangirl was something to move away from, not something to aspire to. We'd started out feeling euphoric about being fans, about being part of a seemingly egalitarian fan community. And more and more we were jumping at the chance to set ourselves apart, as researchers rather than fans.

Julia was well aware of the lure of being treated differently by someone "famous." At the same time, she recognized that the preferential treatment did not, at the end of the day, make them more than fans—an illusion that most people, ourselves included, find it hard to let go.

"It is a little awkward," Julia admitted, "because everyone likes to feel like they're special. It starts to feel like you're social acquaintances, and they're talking to you like that. You need to take a step back and remind the actors that you are in the fan box, and that they know damn well that they are famous."

And you—no matter how friendly people on the other side might be to you at times—are not.

This hybrid identity had also made Julia and the girls protective, both of the celebrities/neighbors and of sustaining their privileged position. The bits of inside information that they got from informal chats at bars over drinks are exactly what fans most want to hear. This is the currency that a fan uses to achieve BNF status, and it's hard as hell not to plaster it all over the Internet: "Hey, listen to what Jensen Ackles told me last night!" Yet, paradoxically, sharing the inside information would leave them in a less privileged position. It would also make them targets of fandom envy and wank, as other fans tried to knock them off their BNF pedestal. So mostly the girls kept their moments of behind-the-scenes access to themselves. None of this made us feel any better about our own hybrid position or, to put a less charitable spin on it, our own duplicity. We were becoming aware of the same risks and reacting with the same secrecy. At the very least, as Julia pointed out, "It increases the number of filters you have to have, and it's hard to negotiate them all."

It's hard not to get caught up in the moment, though. When we were introduced to Carlson and his band members we were generally made to feel like long lost members of an elite tribe. And we liked it. We even liked the envious glares of others who watched the introductions. Having experienced that sort of fannish envy ourselves, we were grateful to be on the other side and spared little energy considering the potential costs. Once you've crossed over and are looked at as a BNF (with a fair amount of derision), can you ever go back? The irony was not lost on us, but we approached it as we might another academic question—from a distance. What we initially loved about fandom was the sense of belonging, that feeling of being "in this together" with like-minded people. And yet, almost as soon as we'd happily immersed ourselves in *Supernatural* fandom, we'd tried to set ourselves apart.

The next morning we left the convention hotel to set ourselves apart a bit more. Lynn was too nervous to eat breakfast, fretting that LA traffic would make us late. She checked the directions obsessively then checked to be sure that we had our audio recorder and notepad and pens. Then checked again. Lynn's insistence that we leave ourselves "plenty of time to get there" meant that we were almost an hour early for the interview. We spent the extra time sipping coffee at a café near Jim's house, going over notes, bouncing ideas off each other, and working up a head of intellectual steam that felt good, right, even relaxing. One last obsessive check for the recorder and extra batteries and we were on our way to Jim's. A few minutes later we were settled into his living room.

Almost four hours later we were still there.

Jim was particularly interested in our book.

Long before I got involved in this show or anything like it, I've always had a fascination with what makes people get caught up in things like this. For years I've been working on a book of my own on the life of George Reeves. I was a big fan of *Superman* and the comics, and my fascination with him as a person grew. I never met him, but I've met hundreds of people who knew him and I feel very close to him as a person. And my interaction with the small but extremely devoted fandom for him constantly surprises me. It's almost like fandom is a subset of the species. People who don't quite function the same way that people who aren't in that subset do.

Jim had been in a similar position to the one we were attempting. He was a fan who became a researcher, which then complicated his position as a fan.

I was the historical, biographical consultant on the movie *Hollywood Land*. And I was really taken aback by how many dyed-in-the-wool Reeves reacted negatively to that movie, because we worked very hard to make a real-life human being out of that character, and a lot of people didn't want that. I still get emails from people asking how did you get away without including the charity part of his life, and I was like . . . it's just a movie? A fully accurate movie about that man's life would have been forty-five years, four months, and three days long! It was a real revelation to me that like John Ford said, when the legend becomes fact, print the legend. They don't want everyone to have feet of clay.

No, they don't. Except when they do. That's how difficult it is to figure out what fans want and try to give it to them—just ask any network. They want their fannish objects up on pedestals so they can be adored and viewed as perfect, yet they can't wait to watch *Keeping Up with the Kardashians* to tear them down and laugh when they fall. The intensity of fans' emotions about their favorite celebrities is striking, whether it's love or hate. Fans of Michael Jackson filed a class-action lawsuit after the singer's personal physician was accused of his murder, claiming that Jackson's death caused them "emotional distress" and comparing the loss of their idol to losing a childhood friend in a car accident. Predictably, comments ranged from "Get a life, you strange lonely people!" to calling fans "obsessive saddos." But fans really DO feel that strongly about their fannish objects.

Even with some understanding of how invested fans are, however, Jim was genuinely surprised at fans' strong reaction to his character on *Supernatural*, Bobby Singer, giving us some insight into how unexpected being put on a pedestal can be to a "celebrity." Jim had been acting all his life, but this was the first time he'd had passionate fans of his own.

"Frankly I'm dumbstruck about any of this attention to Bobby," Jim said. "Okay yeah, he's a nice guy, and these boys need a nice smart guy in their lives in a caring way, but I mean, golly doesn't every show have one of those?"

We shook our heads. "Not like Bobby!"

Jim confessed that every once in a while he Googles his character to see what pops up. "I was struck by how many times people would get into conversations about the tiniest little details, about 'what does that mean?' I remember there was something about the charms that I gave the boys so they wouldn't get possessed, and somebody said, 'Did you see the look on Bobby's face when he handed those charms to them, it looked to me like he had something he wasn't saying, something he was keeping back.'"

"What was it?" we asked, intrigued.

Jim laughed. "What I was keeping back was that I had no idea what I was talking about!"

We laughed too, but we also got it—when you're fannish about something, you pick it apart and study it like a museum specimen, trying to figure out what makes it tick so you can enjoy it even more.

"It's interesting to see how invested people are. Not just in the show and the characters, but in the minutiae of it," Jim said. Later in our conversation, Jim turned the tables. Having a "representative of the fandom" doing your interview was a handy way to figure out what exactly fans wanted. "What would be fans' favorite scene with Bobby?" Jim wondered. We had no trouble coming up with one—a powerful and tender scene when Bobby confronts Dean about bringing Sam back from the dead. The scene had only a few lines of dialogue, but the actors nailed the emotions with the looks on their faces and the way Bobby's hand cups Dean's face, half wanting to smack him and half wanting to comfort.

Jim wasn't surprised. "Up until then, half of what I'd done on the show was in Latin or they'd been 'smart Alec' comments. Especially in a genre show like this, you don't always get a chance to touch on real emotions other than the big surface ones like scary or sad—you don't always get to play with the nuances. I don't know about Jensen, but when I got the script, I could tell that scene was going to go well."

It did. Fandom is all about the emotional scenes—most fans we know watch more for the complicated, angsty, sometimes heartbreaking relationships between the characters than for the monster of the week mystery.

"The fans really like Bobby," we told Jim. He agreed:

I like Bobby. He's fun to play. He seems like he'd be a good guy, the kind of guy I wouldn't mind being. Somebody did a YouTube tribute to Bobby and I was looking at it last night. I watched the clips fade and I knew exactly what scene it was—it was a look I gave Jared when I was working on a gun. I was saying 'and it's gonna take me as long as it takes me.' And he asked if it was ready and I just gave this *look*. That kind of stuff is delicious . . . I've always thought the best actors know something you don't know. Like they've got a secret, and it may never get revealed. The best people I've seen act, there's something underneath too, and it makes me want to watch and figure it out. Just to convey that there's something going on other than just the words.

We nodded. "In other words, subtext—something fans adore." (And the basis for thousands upon thousands of fanfiction stories.)

Jim agreed with us:

I love to find bits of subtext that didn't occur to me before. Subtext is great! My favorite movie in the world is John Ford's *The Searchers*. The driving force is John Wayne's love for his brother's wife and vice versa. It's the thing that drives virtually everything that happens to the main characters. And there is not one bit of dialogue actually relating that. You see the looks between the characters, you see his reaction when she dies, you *see*, but nobody says a word about it.

This is precisely what fan vidders rely on when they mash up or remix clips from their favorite shows, sometimes with music to play up the emotional interchange, sometimes with bits of remixed dialogue. In *Super-*

natural, the emotion-filled intense looks often exchanged between Sam and Dean are the backdrop for Wincest, and similarly intense looks between Castiel and Dean are the basis of the pairing known as Destiel.

Jim said:

> It wouldn't work if these guys weren't good actors. I think you could do an episode of *Supernatural* without a single word of dialogue with this bunch. Not for the gimmick value, but because the crew on this show is capable of doing an awful lot of expression nonverbally, and making people really think deeply about what is being conveyed with no words. I did an episode of *Melrose Place*, and I wouldn't want to do an episode with no dialog with them.

Though that did have the potential to be hilarious. Perhaps not intentionally though.

> But on this show, we feed off each other pretty well. The fact that we all like each other is helpful, but it's also the fact that Jared, Jensen, and I must be very similar actors. We all three are the kind that can be joking around, and then they say action, and we are *in it*. None of us are the kind of guy that has to sit in a corner for an hour to get ready. Nothing wrong with that, but we're just very attuned to the same kind of work. We just kind of relate to each other in ways that work well, and fit well. That the boys are good buddies and enjoy each other's company, that too is not all that common. Sometimes magic hits . . . And to a certain extent, you can't fake that chemistry. I feel pretty lucky to be a part of it.

That chemistry between Jared and Jensen is the basis for most of the romantic slash fanfiction that we and other fans have written. Of course, Jim didn't know that. Right?

Jim poured us some refills of home-brewed iced tea while we tried to decide whether or not to break the First Rule of Fandom and ask him. Before we could work up the courage, Jim beat us to it.

"The first time somebody online mentioned that they had read a piece of fanfiction about Bobby, I was dumbstruck," he said casually, thereby solving our dilemma. We were, we admit, a little caught off guard.

"Oh, so you know about that, huh?"

Jim smirked. "I was actually reading some *Supernatural* fanfiction the other night. I've only read three or four, but both in fanfiction and to an extent at the conventions it seems like there's a role-playing kind of engagement with the characters. I think that applies to a lot of the fantasy-slash-supernatural-slash-science fiction."

He paused, with a mischievous look on his face, then went on. "And I don't mean 'slash' in the way of fanfiction."

No way could we stop the gobsmacked look on our faces that time. "Wait, you know about slash?!"

At our surprised expressions, Jim remarked dryly, "My vocabulary is expanding."

We knew that these were the things we weren't supposed to talk about. The First Rule of Random is tell no one about fandom, and right underneath that is an even bigger red-lettered prohibition that says "Tell no one about slash!" But what were we going to do? Jim had already brought up both. So we did what any good interviewers would do. We took notes and asked more questions. And gave Jim a little more secret information.

"A lot of fans write slash because of the subtext they see between Dean and Sam," Lynn explained. "The long looks, the standing too close together, the casual touches—which they interpret as the same kind of repressed sexual tension that made *The Searchers* so compelling."

Jim pondered that information for a minute. "Freud would probably go along with that," he admitted, "though Jared and Jensen might pick a bone with it. I'm sure they are aware of it. I'm kind of amused, but the fact is you can draw those sorts of connections and parallels to almost any aspect of life if you pull apart at them long enough."

Probably true. And fans are better at pulling apart the things they love than just about anyone. Television, with its propensity for extreme close-ups and bromance-y buddy relationships, provides a lot to pull from.

Jim was still confused, though. "But this is the thing I'm mystified by. When I first started hearing about Wincest, it didn't jive with my idea of who the fans were. Now, my image of who the fans are might be widely skewed, but my impression is that the majority of *Supernatural* fans are women between twenty-eight and fifty. That doesn't seem to me the kind of group that would gravitate toward that interpretation."

Wait, he not only knows about fanfiction—and slash—but he even knows the word for Wincest? It took us a minute to compose ourselves enough to answer.

"That's because fans would never admit it to you—even if it's true!" Kathy finally said. She added, "It's not all fans, though."

"I'm not thinking about the brother part," Jim said, still confused. "Just the homosexual part! I had no idea we had so many gay fans."

This was our cue to give Jim Beaver a "brief history of slash," going back to the days of Kirk/Spock, including the fact that it's mostly written by women and, perhaps more importantly, *for* women—straight women, queer women, bisexual women, all kinds of women. Of course, we didn't mention that we were two of them.

"This is bewildering," Jim said, clearly surprised. "I would have bet the farm that romantic/erotic fan fiction for this show would have involved one or the other of the guys and a damsel in distress. This gives me a clearer notion—it really helps me understand a little more the negative response to Ruby and Bela. It makes sense, especially since it seems the majority of fans are women."

"Some fans do like that sort of fanfiction," Lynn explained. "But a lot of fans don't like anyone coming between the boys, whether you interpret their relationship as brotherly or more than that."

Jim pondered for a few minutes. "Maybe I'll jot one down," he said with a smile. "In fact, I need a T-shirt that says 'I Read John/Bobby'—I can wear it to the *Supernatural* convention next week!"

"I dare you," Lynn blurted out.

Jim grinned. "Now you're tempting me."

Our time with Jim was so pleasant that we had no idea how long we'd been in his living room. Unfortunately, Lynn had been far too nervous to eat before we drove to his house and was expecting only a half-hour interview. Three hours in, she had a raging migraine. The nausea was rising. She calmly asked for directions to the bathroom. Once there, she debated the pros and cons of vomiting in a celebrity's home. Meanwhile, Kathy, who had no idea that Lynn was sick and had even allowed herself to relax a little bit after three hours in Jim's house, was having a freak-out of her own. We're a team for a reason—Lynn tends to talk too much, and Kathy reins her in and slows her down and gets the interview back on track when Lynn has gone off on a tangent. Kathy is quieter and doesn't easily make small talk. Being left alone with an interviewee for twenty minutes was not the way things were supposed to go. She was a hair's breadth away from a cold sweat when Lynn came back, pale and slightly wild-eyed. Kathy could have cared less. She just darted her hateful "Where were you for so long??" look in Lynn's direction.

Lynn sank down on the sofa next to Kathy, asked one more question, then abruptly stood up.

"Well, okay, thanks for your time, we'd better get going."

Kathy and Jim looked confused but got up and headed toward the door. Jim paused to show Lynn a photo with Haley Joel Osment. Lynn knows him from her son filming *The Sixth Sense*. She looked at the photo, mumbled something in acknowledgment, and then darted for the door. Kathy, still confused, followed.

As soon as the car door closed, Lynn ordered, "Drive away and as soon as you can, just STOP."

Kathy got behind the wheel and grinned. "You wanna squee?"

Lynn turned a close-to-green glare at Kathy. "No, I wanna puke. Now drive!"

Kathy laughed. "Too much excitement, huh?"

"No—I really have to puke!!"

Kathy's grin slid sideways when she realized that Lynn was serious. She also realized it would not be cool to throw up in a rented car (Kathy is always the practical one). She drove back to the café where they had brainstormed, got Lynn a soda, and then followed her into the bathroom and waited with a wad of paper towels in one hand, drink in the other. Lynn emerged after a few harrowing minutes, thoroughly miserable, to find Kathy standing there with an outstretched hand and the symbols of comfort. That, Lynn thought, is a good friend. She managed a shaky smile, sipped at the soda, and gushed about how Kathy was the best friend in the world. Kathy admirably hid the fact that in her dark, dark heart she had been thinking about the car as much as about Lynn.

When we got back in the car, Lynn was still sick and of no use when it came to navigating. Kathy's repeated question "Which way does the map say to turn?" was met mostly with inarticulate moaning and Lynn banging her head against the window sobbing for someone to make it stop. This was not particularly helpful. So now Kathy's worst nightmares were reasserting themselves—she was lost in LA. And there was moaning. Her panic rose to nearly unbearable levels.

Time to randomly pick a direction. Miraculously, it worked.

By the time we got back to the hotel, Lynn looked less green and Kathy more so, stressed and drying out from a flop sweat and very much in need of a drink. Or two. Before the drinking commenced, however, we needed to get back into fan mode and register for the con. We intended to say nothing of our afternoon with Jim Beaver and definitely not to out ourselves as researchers to the con-goers who knew us as fangirls. Once again, the boundary proved difficult to sustain. Lynn walked up to the registration table and gave her name so that she could pick up her prepaid tickets and photo ops.

The volunteers frowned at her. "Nope, sorry, you're not registered."

Lynn had a moment of panic. Not registered = not seeing Jared and Jensen at the sold-out con.

"What?" she shrieked, trying to rein in her catastrophizing. "Yes I am!"

She surrendered her credit card, hoping that they could solve the mystery.

"Oh," said the volunteer, "Here you are. Your credit card says Dr. Lynn Zubernis, so you're under 'D.'"

Lynn nearly collapsed in relief.

"What sort of doctor are you?" the volunteer asked conversationally as she fastened a plastic wristband to Lynn's arm.

When Lynn answered that she was a psychologist, three or four people suggested that she write a book on fans, because "nobody understands us—even us!" Somehow, perhaps because the migraine had left her with little impulse control, Lynn blurted out, "Oh, actually I am."

Oops.

As Lynn was turning to leave, one of the convention photographers pulled her aside, confiding that she too had contributed to recent articles on fans. That was our first introduction to Lizz Sisson, a gifted photographer as well as a fellow *Supernatural* fan, who was taking professional photos at the con. As Lynn headed back to the ballroom, Lizz suddenly leaned in close and asked in a conspiratorial whisper, "Who are you on LJ?"

Crap! Lynn had just registered with her full name and even her credentials. The last thing she wanted to do was combine that with her fanfiction-writing alter ego! Going against most of her good instincts, and only because Lizz had played the "I'll tell you mine if you tell me yours" card (the similarity to childhood games and the flashing of forbidden body parts was not lost on her), Lynn spilled her secret identity. She then worried about it for the rest of the day.

The next day, Lynn had no time for worry—the con was in full swing. Actor Chad Lindberg, who played Ash across four seasons of *Supernatural*, related the crowd-pleasing tale of being actually naked when his character Ash (naked) met Sam and Dean (unfortunately not naked) for the first time. (Any story that involves nakedness, Sam, and Dean will invariably be crowd pleasing.) Fred Lehne, who played the first "big bad" on the show, the Yellow Eyed Demon, came out with guitar in hand to sing "Sympathy for the Devil" (music is also a crowd pleaser, though not nearly to the extent that naked stories are). In addition to the lineup of actors, this con was special for the gathered *Supernatural* fans, because series creator Eric Kripke appeared onstage to answer their questions. Eric proved himself exceptionally tuned in to his fans, acknowledging the problems with the two female characters recently added to the show (mostly at the clueless network's urging). He also endeared himself to the fans by offering to sign autographs for free for anyone who wanted one, sitting at a side table and patiently chatting with every fan who lined up.

We came over to introduce ourselves as the researchers who were scheduled to interview him in a few weeks. To our surprise, Eric knew immediately who we were. He apologized for not being able to do the interview with us in person but said how much he was looking forward to it. As we assured him that it was fine and that *we* were the ones who were grateful, he called after us to tell us how excited *he* was about our book. Lynn walked out of the ballroom grinning. The creator of the show was excited about our little book? Looking forward to being interviewed by us? In what universe could this possibly be happening? Lynn turned around to Kathy, expecting to see a matching ear-to-ear grin and sweep Kathy into a hug. Instead, Kathy burst into tears as soon as we got out of the room, even more overcome by the enthusiasm of the series creator than by the prospect of meeting the actors. Lynn was too dumbfounded to carry through with the hug. And what could Kathy say? She's a fan of writers. This was the woman who had a high school crush on Byron (the fact that he was long dead just made it all the more romantic—talk about doomed love!) and thinks Tom Stoppard is a god. So she cried.

Once Kathy had calmed down, we touched base with Creation owner

Supernatural's version of God: creator Eric Kripke. Courtesy of Elizabeth Sisson.

Adam Malin for a brief follow-up interview. He escorted us backstage for our chat, instantly setting us apart from the fans we'd been standing with. We definitely didn't mind.

For a straight guy, Adam was surprisingly well aware of the contribution of two men who look like Jared and Jensen to the show's popularity.

"I think that's part of the wink of the eye that this show does, and part of its charm," he said. "It's not that the boys are full of themselves, because clearly they're not. But Eric realizes how magnetic they are. You can't underestimate the animal instinct of the women attracted to the men of the show—there is an animal magnetism that Jared and Jensen have that women respond to. I think it only goes to prove that sex drives our society on some level."

We nodded sagely and wondered how many times Adam had poked around fanfiction sites.

Conventions are tests of stamina as much as anything. That night, it was time for yet another awkward dessert party. This one was made even more uncomfortable by a plot cooked up by a table of fangirls in the corner. They planned to ask Chad Lindberg to get up onto the table during his allotted two minutes, sprawling across the middle so that everyone could have equal access to him. To do, you know, whatever. They actually did manage to talk Chad into laying himself out on top of the round table to be petted.

When we interviewed Chad a few months later, we asked him what it was like. Was the objectification weird? Was it fun?

"It's all those things," Chad said. "I have my boundaries. There are certain things I won't do, but I love to make sure people have a memorable experience, and if I'm asked to get on the table and pose for them, I'll do it. Of course then there are the people that want to talk to you when you're going to the bathroom, and that's when it's not okay. You develop a thick skin."

Much later that night, we also ran into Fred Lehne, the Yellow-Eyed Demon, in the elevator. He was searching in vain for his lost car keys. We may have all been a little bit drunk by this time, so it seemed like a good idea to hit him up for an interview too. Why the hell not? He said yes, thus validating our "inebriation as research tool" approach. We may have been out of control, but then so was everyone else. We blended. To top it all off, we got a phone call from *Ten Inch Hero* director David Mackay saying that Danneel Harris had actually agreed to an interview too. This prompted some hyperventilating and a rush of euphoria that left us grinning like fools. Jensen Ackles's girlfriend was going to meet with us? Really? David had given Lynn's cell phone number to Danneel so that she could call us tomorrow, the same day the boys came back to town. This research gig was getting sweeter by the minute.

Given the pattern of the weekend so far—great things happening and then going horribly wrong—we should have known what was coming. Sunday morning we were 100 percent passionate fangirls, up at the dark side of dawn once again, needing to be first, front and center, there, right *there* to see and hear everything. The morning's first event was, and always is, Breakfast with the Boys. The early birds get the best table, at the feet (literally) of Jared and Jensen. Creation had attempted to bar fans from sleeping in the hallway all night, making them promise not to get there before 7:00 A.M.—if they were "good," they'd be let in early. The problem for fans in this situation, as with so many others, is that the definition of good is variable. Good fans don't always equate with good citizens. Certainly not when you're lining up for the J2 show.

Once inside, everyone made the obligatory mad dash for the best tables. We positioned ourselves front and center before the small stage where we knew the boys would be standing. Kathy tried to get cerebral, tried to analyze the situation from a purely academic point of view, tried to pull herself out of the moment to take in the bigger picture. And then she mentally bitch-slapped herself for doing what she's done a thousand times before—analyzing rather than experiencing. Her problem at the moment, as ever, was that she wanted to do both simultaneously, a clear recipe for disaster.

Meanwhile Lynn was obsessively checking her phone. "Noooo!!" she gasped. It was the plaintive moan of a beast in distress.

Kathy assumed that Lynn was passing a gallstone from the sound of it.

"No reception!" Lynn said, wide-eyed.

For Kathy, who hates phones (really, what doesn't Kathy hate?), this didn't seem like a big deal. The world really is too connected anyway. An hour out of cell phone reception seemed like a welcome respite, an opportunity just to enjoy the moment.

Lynn wasn't as philosophical. "What if Danneel calls?"

Kathy honestly didn't hold out much hope that this would actually happen—a yellow on the threat scale at most—so she wasn't concerned.

Lynn was taking up her slack by flailing around, banging buttons on her phone as if somehow this would jolt it into action. "How can there be no cell phone reception in LA??"

Lynn had a point. We're reasonably certain that there is cell phone reception in the Arctic Circle, but there was not a bar to be had in a hotel in LA. LA!! The town where everyone's people are calling everyone else's people, where iPhones are accessorized to coordinate with the day's outfits, where a missed call can ruin a career. Jared and Jensen distracted Lynn for the duration of their time onstage, but as soon as it was over Lynn made a bee line for Jared's girlfriend, Sandy (the woman sitting in front, wearing a hoodie so no one would recognize her—except Lynn, apparently). Lynn wildly explained our dilemma to the stunned and probably scared actress. It was a good thing the MWNN were only being paid to guard "the boys," or Lynn would have been face down on the carpet.

While Lynn was doing this Kathy was pretending that she did not know Lynn.

Sandy was sympathetic but didn't know if she'd even see Danneel. Lynn thanked her for the sympathy and moved on to the next person who might be able to help. She attempted to enlist convention photographer Lizz, to no avail, and finally Creation owner Adam.

"I'll try, Lynn," he said, sounding slightly exasperated. "But I'm kinda running an entire convention here."

Thwarted again, Lynn pulled out all the stops. During her Jensen photo op, she stopped everything to explain the situation to Jensen himself.

"Hi, Jensen," Lynn said, hoping that her voice wasn't sounding too shaky. "We have an interview set up with Danneel today for the book we're writing on fandom, and she's supposed to call us, but I don't have any reception on my phone, so I'm afraid she won't be able to."

The photo-op process screeched to a halt, and the room fell silent. Photo ops, you see, are not a place for conversation. They are highly valued by fans, who pay top dollar for the privilege of standing next to a celebrity, and they are relentlessly organized. The entire experience lasts about twenty seconds, and during that time you're expected to say hello to the celebrity, smile, perhaps get an arm around your back or lean into said celebrity's very firm bicep, and then move the hell out of the way and let the next person crowd in for the next picture. The photo ops allow no room for deviation.

So when deviation happens, no one is very happy. The photographer wasn't happy. The other fans weren't happy. And the MWNN looked ready to move into swift and potentially lethal action.

Not that any of this stopped Lynn. "Can you put us in touch with her?" she continued, oblivious to the threatening stares all around her.

"Oh right, the interview," Jensen said.

Lynn just nodded, though inside she was stuck on "OMG Jensen knows about our interview and our book, ohmygodohmygod."

"Maybe she can email you," Jensen continued. Then the conversation abruptly ended as Lynn was grabbed unceremoniously by the back of the neck and "escorted" from the photo-op room. Uh oh. She hadn't experienced that feeling since being a two-year-old caught trying to get away with her baby brother's coveted teddy bear. Lynn was most definitely in trouble—and even worse, she'd made no progress in getting in touch with Danneel, who didn't even have our email address!

Lynn, ever the intrepid researcher, was not deterred. She thanked the Man with No Neck for his assistance and got right back in line for her next photo op, the "sandwich" photo (as in sandwiched between Jared and Jensen, which is vaguely dirty and thus very popular). As Lynn walked up, Jensen immediately tried to continue their conversation.

"So do you want to . . ." he began, while Jared looked confused. After all, the celebrities know the no talking rule as well as the fans.

Lynn held up a hand defensively. "Shh, I'm not talking to you. I totally got in trouble for it before," she added, as the MWNN hovered threateningly.

Jensen laughed. "I got in trouble too," he protested.

We doubt the MWNN were involved.

"Can Danneel get us her email?" Lynn managed as she was once again "encouraged" to leave the room as quickly as possible.

There was no time for an answer. Damn. Thwarted again. We were disappointed, but Lynn was relieved that she wasn't escorted out of the entire con (the specter of the Flying Fangirl from Asylum still looms large at these events after all). We were still feeling like an interview with her had been too good to be true anyway, so we tried to swallow our sadness and settled in to watch some of the other guests. Midway through the next panel, Lizz the photographer came out into the audience and passed us a note—from Danneel. It just said, "Send me an email, love danneel" and included her email

Bad boys (J2 and bodyguard Clif Kosterman). Courtesy of Christopher Schmelke.

address. Being a bit clueless about the popularity of smartphones in 2008, we figured this meant that she wanted us to get in touch with her later for an email interview. We were disappointed that we wouldn't get to talk to her in person but incredibly excited—and feeling not a little bit special—that she'd given us her email address. We wandered back outside and tried not to be too miserable about the Danneel interview not happening that day. We were hanging out in the hallway chatting when Lizz suddenly appeared and yanked us away in the middle of a sentence with an exasperated, "Come with me!" She led us down a small side hall.

We still weren't entirely sure what was going on. Were we in trouble again? Had the MWNN decided to kick us out after all? Moments later, Danneel emerged from the side door, introducing herself with a smile. Somehow we managed to compose ourselves and smile back. Apparently

Jensen had facilitated the interview after all! Danneel suggested that we all grab some coffee, so we headed upstairs to the hotel's Starbucks, where Danneel insisted on treating. Even before we sat down and officially started the interview, Danneel was asking us questions about why the fans perceived her as they did. Why did they think that she was a bitch? We cringed on her behalf, already sure that was far from the truth.

Danneel told us that she was thinking of making her own T-shirt (what was it about celebrities and T-shirts that weekend?) with a shout-out to her chief nemesis on the IMDB message boards—an antifan who called herself merylthepearl. She planned to have it say merely "I Love Merylthepearl." A brilliant way to take the high road and send a message too. We snickered at the T-shirt idea and assured her that she should do it. Why not? We'd already told Jim Beaver that he should wear a T-shirt promoting slash at the next fan convention. It wasn't as if we had any boundaries ourselves anymore, was it?

Coffee in hand, we went back downstairs to start the interview. Danneel suggested that we go backstage to talk, and then came a weirdly symbolic moment. The very same Man with No Neck who had tossed Lynn unceremoniously out of the photo op for daring to speak to the talent now held back the curtain to the backstage area, solicitously helped Danneel and us step over the various wires and cables snaking across the floor, then closed the curtain behind us to seal our crossover. The irony wasn't lost on us. Nor were the stares of our fellow fangirls as they watched us walk through the autograph signing with Jensen Ackles's girlfriend. There is real danger, as a fan, in setting yourself apart in any way, and suddenly we couldn't avoid it. Of course, at the moment we didn't want to. Kathy whipped out her trusty voice recorder just as she had done for every other interview we've conducted, turned it on, and . . . nothing. We were interviewing Jensen Ackles's girlfriend and there was NOTHING. It wasn't the batteries, which had been checked and rechecked. Kathy tried to maintain some semblance of professionalism. She would quietly figure out what was wrong and then she would just as quietly fix it. Deep breaths. Okay, the recorder was FULL. Not to worry. She excused herself, leaving a confused Lynn to entertain Danneel.

First the cell phone, now the voice recorder. Sunday turned out to be the day technology failed us. This, for Lynn, is an everyday occurrence. For Kathy not so much. She loves technology. She embraced the Internet years before it got pretty, she used a "portable" PC to write her doctoral dissertation (portability is of course a relative designation—relative to muscle mass and stamina), and she gets gleeful over the prospect of using every new toy her university has to offer. So yes, technology was her friend. Until it wasn't.

While Kathy dashed upstairs to grab her laptop (wishing that she could grab a shot of tequila), Lynn attempted to keep up a conversation with Danneel without actually asking any of our carefully prepared interview questions. Without a recorder, there was no way she'd remember a damn thing that was said—so that left small talk as the only option. Luckily, Danneel and Lynn connected over their mutual love of writing, swapped college stories, and then Lynn (as always) managed to talk about her children. Danneel proved herself a great listener. Minutes went by—lots of them—and Lynn realized to her horror that Jensen and Jared were almost done with their autographs. After that, it was off to the airport—and we would lose our interviewee to her boyfriend as she left with Ackles. Where was Kathy???

Finally, shortly before Lynn had moved on to telling Danneel about her daughter's first steps, Kathy returned and hurriedly tried to download everything onto the laptop while time quickly ran out. Come on!! All Kathy could focus on was how long it was taking for everything to download. That and the rising nausea that threatened to overtake her. Lynn, in desperation, started asking the interview questions (which, since they weren't recorded, are lost to posterity—and to this book).

Suddenly Jared Padalecki walked by, meaning that autographs were over and people were getting ready to leave. We despaired of a recorded interview, heartbroken over the squandered opportunity. And then, quite unexpectedly, Jensen Ackles was standing there, smiling and saying hello. Even more improbably, he held a fluffy white dog in his arms. For a moment, Kathy was sure this was all part of the nightmare, because fandom at the time had no clue that Jensen even owned a dog. Icarus, however, was quite real—and quite fluffy. Icarus was almost as excited to see Jensen as we were—he'd apparently been whining backstage every time he heard his owner's voice during the Q&A. We hugged Icarus while Jensen hugged Danneel and tried to talk her into riding with him to the airport. All Kathy heard in those words was that it was too late—she'd blown it.

Danneel, however, had other ideas. She blew Jensen off. No wait. This part can't really be happening either. More of that dream? Kathy was contemplating poking herself with a sharp object, sticking her finger in a wall socket, anything to jar herself back into reality. This was surely just her own anxiety-ridden psyche toying with her. Must be. Who says good-bye to Jensen Ackles so that she can talk to US?? But Danneel really was excusing herself to say good-bye to Jensen, Icarus happily following, with assurances to us that she'd be right back to finish the interview. Kathy gathered together the few shreds of sanity she still had, sorted the problem, and figured out how to record directly onto the laptop.

Danneel returned, true to her word, and the interview finally began. We relocated to the "green room," the cloistered and heavily guarded room where the guests are confined between stage appearances. The green room, as we were well aware, is a private space—more or less a "No Fans Allowed" clubhouse for the celebrities. We immediately felt like imposters, occupying a space where we clearly shouldn't be. The room offered a small banquet of food, a bit of which we gratefully sampled, and a table stacked full of fans' gifts for "the boys." The coolest of these was a hairdryer that looked exactly like Dean Winchester's favorite gun—and yes, it actually worked!

Danneel, of course, was quite comfortable in the green room and turned out to be very good at making us comfortable as well. Lynn asked questions. Danneel answered. Kathy breathed. Everything was going to work out just fine. Somewhere the unicorns of fandom were neighing happily.

And then the laptop went dead.

Kathy again tried to be unobtrusive as she flailed around trying to find an outlet. No point in making a bigger fool of herself, right? Sooner or later, though, it became apparent that she was in need of assistance and everyone, including Danneel, was up and scouting for an outlet, crawling under tables and moving furniture to do so. Danneel, we decided, had the patience of a saint. She never lost her sense of humor either, shrugging off our apology for keeping her from accompanying Jensen to the airport by wryly noting that "Jared would have been in the limo anyway, it's not like we could have made out on the way to the airport" and jumping up to knock on wood when we asked her about the possibility of marriage.

In the midst of all the sitcom mishaps we did manage to carry on an interview. Since we were doing it in the middle of a *Supernatural* convention, we asked Danneel about her experience with the fans. When you're the girlfriend of a heartthrob, there are inevitably some people who would rather deny your existence, whether to fantasize themselves into the role better or to fantasize Jensen with his co-star instead. Danneel was aware of the variety of reactions, some of them less than positive.

"Some fans are nice," she said diplomatically. "It seems like it's a mix, probably half and half."

Danneel understood that her current onscreen character, the television show *One Tree Hill*'s resident bitch, was not helping her find acceptance with her boyfriend's fans.

"If I weren't an actress, I think they wouldn't be so mean. Because the character I'm known for is evil and mean, so they're like 'why would Jensen date someone like her?' And it's like well, because she's not like that in real life!"

Understatement. Danneel had already proven herself far to the extreme of nice, not to mention patient, by helping us through our repeated technical difficulties.

"The Internet is helping," she said. "When people see me in interviews, fans are like 'Oh! You're not mean, you're acting! You wouldn't really push someone off a cliff and watch them die.' And I'm like—NO!"

Danneel was also trying to expand her repertoire with some very different roles. "I'm doing two movies now, one I play a lesbian—and that should open up a whole new section! And the other one I'm playing is a really sweet role, a sweet girl who kind of goes south, but not in a mean way. I've been dying not to play the bitch!"

We wondered if it was hard for Danneel to stop herself from reading negative comments online, now that finding out (in excruciating detail) what fans think of a celebrity is both instant and everywhere.

"I should just keep off the message boards," she admitted. "Jared tells Sandy not to look at them, but Jensen is like, I'm not babying you, if you see another thing you don't like. It's mostly this one fan—she doesn't hurt my feelings anymore because it's just funny. It's like 'Why would Jensen date that self-obsessed drug head?' My character on *One Tree Hill* had a heroin overdose, and now I'm a druggie? I try not to go on those sites, but I have friends who do and say, 'Hey, listen to what they said about you.'"

Danneel had already been to a few *Supernatural* conventions. We wondered about how the infamous "Flying Fangirl" incident had impacted her; after all, it was her boyfriend being jumped.

"Flying fangirl, that's awesome!" she grinned. "I think I just found my Halloween costume."

Okay, that's one costume we would have paid good money to see. Though we have a feeling that Ackles's reaction to being tackled by Danneel might have been a bit different than it was at Asylum.

Danneel understands fans pretty well—she's a fan herself, and she's also pretty damn perceptive.

Going to the *Supernatural* conventions with Jensen, I just kind of stay out of the way. It's awkward for me because I don't really like to be in the room when he's signing stuff because people will look at me and wonder, or make it something about me, like they'll say I looked like I'm uncomfortable, and they'll write on the Internet like she is so weird. I like to stay out of the way, but I like watching him do his thing, because he has such a great personality. It's fun for me to watch. I'm a fan of Jensen's. We're fans of each other. I think he can do anything. When you watch the one you love being loved by all these people, it warms your heart.

Who could disagree with that?

EIGHT

. . . . .

Playing the Fame Game

No matter how sunny it had been in LA, it was cold and dark back in the mid-Atlantic a few weeks later. Kathy was tripping the light fantastic. These were the days she lived for. The day of our phone interview with Eric Kripke, Kathy was happily driving up I-95 toward Lynn's house, with her favorite Finnish Goth band providing appropriate accompaniment as the clouds gathered and snow began dusting the roads. Could life get better, she thought?

Perhaps not, but it could get a whole hell of a lot worse. The interview itself came off without our usual technical difficulties. Eric was as interested in the fandom as we were in him.

"We do pay attention to the fandom," he said. "With certain restrictions. We actually welcome the arguments. I think we're equally unhappy when everyone loves something. We're happiest when there's debate. Part of the job is that you're supposed to drive the fans crazy. They'd be far more disappointed if they were satisfied every week with every character conflict."

Well, we thought to ourselves, Eric and company must be pretty damn happy most of the time—because fandom is rarely across-the-board happy!

As soon as you give the fans what they want, they're irritated that they're getting what they want. I have the core story I'm telling, and I've never deviated from that story . . . that true evil is within all of us and true good is within all of us, and it's about the choices you make. [But] we're open to self-reflection, if there's a subplot that everybody hates, and even the writers can pick out the flaws, I have no problem dropping it. I think the majority of shows have this attitude like we know better—and we don't.

Eric had recently listened to nearly unanimous fan opinion and dropped the character of Bela, who seemed to be a network insert to up the "tits and ass" quotient of the show.

"It started to feel ridiculous every time she showed up in an episode," Eric said, agreeing with fandom. "She started to seem a little artificial and inorganic. If there's ongoing drama between Sam and Dean that is driving fans crazy, it's [that] they love to hate things, so you have to separate that from if they just really hate something." Like Bela.

Eric is a fanboy himself, starting with membership in the ET fan club as a kid. He gets how fans think—the importance of continuity and consistency and noticing small details that nonfans wouldn't.

"There's that fanboy in me," he said, "that tries hard to develop that consistent universe. If there is any fight I get into frequently among studio and network, it's when I say you can't do that because in Season 1 this or that thing happened, and they'll say, why does that matter? And I'll say, it matters."

It does. Ask any fan.

"We're the red-headed stepchild on the network. We wear it as a point of pride."

Eric seemed happy to talk with us about a whole range of potentially controversial subjects—including fans' accusations of homophobia in the show. We had sent him the questions beforehand, so he'd had plenty of time to think about it.

"Do you see any evidence of that?" Kathy asked as we listened intently to Eric via (a miraculously working) speakerphone.

"I think in my mind we had one line that went too far," Eric answered. "It was in [the episode] 'Bedtime Stories,' and Sam is pointing out a reference to Cinderella, and Dean said 'Could you be any more gay?' I think that went too far . . . but this is the way young men talk—there is no malice behind it, but when you get guys together, there is some tone that gets taken on. It's in the DNA of stupid men, and it's a reflection of our culture. I think we made up for it in the episode 'Ghostfacers.' The core of that story is how love supersedes anything."

"That's what we took from it," Lynn agreed. "And what most fans took from it too. There are plenty of fan-made icons online that quote the episode's message: Gay love can pierce through the veil of death and save the day."

"Right," Kripke went on, "and just because there happens to be a gay character that ends up being [dead], people say it's homophobic, and I don't get that because the hero is a gay man, and the other character is someone who comes to realize the power of love."

And speaking of the power of love, Eric was already well aware of *Supernatural* fanfiction.

> I was aware of slash fiction between the boys. I think people read into the fact that there are two good-looking guys on the road and you can't avoid going there. I take it as a compliment, because what we set out in the beginning to create is a really self-contained, self-functioning universe. And as a fan myself, there's nothing I love more than a universe in which fans can come and go, and the rules are consistent. So just as in all good universes, you can find new ways to expand and explore other corners of that universe. The fact that fans are doing that is a good sign. I love it and I welcome it. I wanted to create a universe where we welcome others to come and play.

Well, that was validating. The builder of the sandbox was glad we were playing there.

"I see you guys mention that someone wrote me in fanfiction," Eric went on, "and I was not aware of that."

In fact, we'd run across a few. Some that used Eric as a background character, along with Sera Gamble and Kim Manners. And one that cast Eric as the main character.

"In ways that you undoubtedly have never considered," Kathy confirmed, rather ominously.

"That is very, very disturbing," Eric said, pondering.

Lynn felt that a warning was in order. "You would actually not like to direct your mother to some of these stories."

On the other end of the phone line, Eric's voice went from disturbed to gleeful. "Wait, am I in porn fan fiction? You HAVE to send me that!"

So we were sending porn to Eric.

Right.

Never mind that we carefully removed all evidence of where it was posted and who posted it. This was a boundary violation that dwarfed our earlier timid crossings, shattering the rule that says "tell no one about slash." Especially the celebrities who star in it!

If we were worried about Eric's reaction, there was no need.

"No, don't worry," he emailed after he'd read them.

I'm not traumatized in the slightest. I found it all very amusing . . . a bit strange, true, but interesting and entertaining. And illuminating . . . upon reading, my first reaction was to laugh at how dead wrong the writers got it. I mean, beyond the obvious . . . All the characterizations of me, Kim, and Sera are so off the mark. (Kim and Sera barely know each other outside of conference calls, etc.) But then it occurred to me, I've written all sorts of things about real people during the course of the show (Thomas Edison, Samuel Colt, etc.) and never once worried about getting my facts straight, it was all artistic license. So it's interesting to be on the "receiving end" of that artistic license. So I see how it doesn't matter whether it's accurate . . . even though the character is nominally "me," I have no ownership over it, it belongs to the writer. So, yes, very surreal in a funhouse mirror kind of way to have a writer use you as one of their chess pieces. Or at least use a plastic facade of you . . . because underneath, it's all them.

A few weeks later Jim Beaver announced to fans—quite dramatically—that he had no real problem with slash either. At a convention in Florida (one of the few we did not go to), Jim walked out onstage to thunderous applause and even louder gasps. He was wearing a T-shirt that proclaimed: "I Read John/Bobby."

The one we dared him to wear.

Some fans loved it, taking it as validation. Others were horrified—did he know? OMG, had he actually *read* it?

We were horrified in our own way, wondering if somehow fandom would find out that this was ALL OUR FAULT. Jim's cover story ("A fan gave me the T-shirt. I have no idea what it means!") deflected attention, but we were still worried. And at the same time we were pretty damn impressed with ourselves for having had this kind of influence over our fandom and dying to share our insider knowledge of what really happened. We didn't, but we wanted to.

Our next convention was in Dallas, just a few months later. By now our frequent travels and the stress of negotiating fan, family, and researcher identities were starting to take a toll. We were struggling to write the book, while at the same time trying to justify our fannish excursions as research. We were also starting to get on each other's nerves after a year of traveling together, vacationing together, and writing together. As is probably clear by now, we have very different personalities. We had also begun to develop different ways of coping with our fangirl guilt—and thus different ways of "doing" fandom. Lynn had vowed to grab hold of whatever opportunities she could find to indulge her fangirl side, even if she was resolutely couching it in terms of the necessity for research. Kathy, in contrast, was coping by denying that she *had* a fangirl side—or at least not the stereotypical fangirl one. And because she was going ever deeper underground with her own fannishness, she found herself judging Lynn just as she had judged the fangirls in that Fort Worth theater lobby. She was not that extreme. She had perspective. In fact, she even worried that Lynn might have become too invested, too emotionally attached. Was Lynn "doing it wrong"?

Lynn was thinking the same thing about Kathy. Why was Kathy so determined to stay in research mode even when we were sitting at the feet of Jared and Jensen? Where was her partner in crime, the giddy passionate fangirl? Why was Kathy suddenly doing it wrong? Lynn wanted her fellow fangirl back, to share the squee and the adventure. Both of us wanted the validation from each other that we were, in fact, doing it right. This sort of "you're doing it wrong" accusation runs through fandom, creating all kinds of nasty infighting. It's the source of a lot of the wank that we were so disappointed to discover is as common in fandom as the sense of belonging.

Why did we care so much? Why do most fans? The answer lies partly in the psychological processes that make us all want to belong. Fandom is a group. As in all groups, members tend to define themselves and others in terms of in-groups and out-groups. It's important because this is how we establish our own identities. In-groups are "like me," and being surrounded by the in-group makes us feel good about ourselves—that we're doing it right. Out-groups are perceived as "not like me" and tend to be looked at as threats to self-esteem. This is all well and good if the in-group is the rest of fandom and the out-group is TPTB trying to police our playground—then the in-group members band together against the external threat and feel even better about themselves. The problem comes when someone within

fandom is "not like me." Maybe they read Wincest and you prefer to fantasize about Sam Winchester courting Madison the werewolf/woman. Maybe
you're a big fan of Castiel and they wish he'd fly off to some other show.
Maybe they stick to watching the show and posting comments on the official site and you want to "do" fandom by scraping together your pennies
and traveling to conventions. Any time there's a difference, the potential for
wank exists.

Add to this the passion that fans feel and their constant fear that the rest
of the world is judging them for it, and you've got a powerful brew of emotions. Any fan who's perceived as not doing it right poses a threat to other
fans' positive identity. "I'm not weird, I'm not a crazy stalker—she is!" Or
the related "Get out of my fandom, you make my fandom look stupid!"
Thus the swift and lethal ostracizing of the Flying Fangirl and any other fan
who is perceived as outside the norms. In research terms, Social Identity
Theory holds that people become vulnerable when they are "out of role" and
are then fair game to be attacked by the rest of the group. That could mean
being a Sam!Girl instead of a Dean!Girl or a slash fan instead of a gen fan.
It often comes down to simply "If you like something I don't like, you're
wrong. If you don't like something I like, you're wrong. If you disagree with
me about some point of whatever we both like, you're *really* wrong."

That's precisely what was happening to us. We had developed vastly different coping strategies when it came to fandom—and we were both convinced that the other person was doing it wrong. Very wrong. Because we
were women, however, we didn't tell each other. Steeped in the "good girl
code" that we'd both grown up with, we instead swallowed our annoyance.
God forbid that we would take a chance on losing a friendship that was of
great importance to both of us just to communicate some petty grievances,
right? Of course, not telling each other was a very bad idea.

Inevitably, our annoyance with each other came out in other ways. "Pillow fight!" Kathy announced the moment we got into our hotel room in
Dallas and she sized up the mound of pillows heaped on the beds.

Lynn rolled her eyes. "What are you, like six?"

Kathy thought "Yes!" and began hitting Lynn. It felt good.

After the pillow fight (Lynn didn't put up any resistance, so it was over
quickly), Lynn was hungry and eager to have some fun in the Texas sun;
Kathy, as we've established, does not do sun. Luckily she does do beer, bi-

son burgers, and six-foot-four Texas boys. We decided to head out to a place called Sammy's, the sole reason being that we could relate it to the show. As fans do. Any restaurant named after Sam Winchester was clearly going to be excellent. Lynn was hungry and cranky by this time and not much use navigating, so we got lost in downtown Dallas. This of course made Kathy cranky because she does not like being lost and because Lynn actually had us literally driving in circles on the same street. We gave up on Sammy's, deciding that it didn't actually exist, and began looking for someplace, any-place, that seemed to be offering food. But we were hungry and cranky with a double dose of frustration and unvoiced anger to boot, so we eventually screeched the car to a halt, got out, and decided to stand on a street corner and yell at each other for a while.

"What about that place over there?" Lynn barked, gesturing to a restau-rant on the far corner.

"No. Too expensive," Kathy said through gritted teeth.

"How can you tell from here?"

"I just can! What about that one down there?" Kathy pointed down the block.

"Fine!"

"Fine!!"

And then we just stood there. Glaring.

Eventually we climbed back into the car and drove over to the restaurant. It was closed.

Lynn may have sobbed. If she did, Kathy was determined not to hear it. We drove on.

"PULL IN NOW!" Lynn ordered at the next place with a parking lot. An open restaurant. Good enough. And, coincidentally, it was named Jake's (for the non–SPN addicted, a pivotal guest character). So the *Supernatural* tie-in was there after all. Once we had menus in our hands we started to re-lax, feeling that maybe this was a sign. Then we looked across the street: at the top of a big building was a giant lit-up actual sign that just read "Dean." That was it. The fangirl switch flipped. Our frayed nerves were temporarily repaired. We giggled across our beers and grinned at each other, accusa-tions of directional impairment and faulty driving skills forgotten. And to sweeten the deal, the guy playing guitar while we were eating played a Led Zeppelin riff (often used in *Supernatural*, which is known for its 1980s cock rock soundtrack) to close out his set. Obviously this was where we were meant to be.

We had come with no interviews set up and no work planned, but if we were going to explain to family and co-workers why we absolutely *had* to travel to Dallas (and if we were going to justify the cost of hotel, flight, and con ticket) we needed to do something to rationalize our trip. More access didn't hurt. But so far we'd had no luck arranging anything. Our luck began to turn when we got back to our hotel room and checked our emails. When we had run into Fred Lehne in the hallway a few months before and he had scribbled his email on a scrap of paper, we had a sneaking suspicion that it was one of those "how to get an unwanted stalker to leave you alone by giving them the number of the local zoo when they ask for your phone number" situations. Especially when Fred didn't answer our email asking to schedule the interview in Dallas. But in our inbox there was an amusing message:

Subject: RE: Interview request—Dallas
Hello ladies,

Don't know what prompted me to cruise thru my bulk/spam inbox, but there you were. Guess that's what prompted it. I am free on Saturday until 3 P.M.—my cell is xxx-xxx-xxxx (I trust you'll hold that # in confidence—or I'll have to hurt you). Call me Saturday morning and we'll get together. Fred

Needless to say, we kept it in confidence. Nobody wants to piss off the guy who so convincingly played the Yellow Eyed Demon. We had an interview—the Dallas convention was officially a research trip.

Apparently demons don't sleep in. We met Fred Lehne for breakfast at the hotel restaurant, not completely awake but ready for unlimited refills of coffee. Fred in real life was closer to sweet than devilish. When Lynn wished out loud that the buffet included grits, Fred disappeared for a few minutes without explanation. A short while later our waiter appeared with a big bowl of buttered grits just for us. We asked Lehne, in between spoonfuls of grits and gulps of coffee, how conventions for a show like *Supernatural* compared to cons for the television show *Lost*, which he had also attended as a celebrity guest.

"There's some overlap, but I think the superficial impression is that the *Lost* fans are a little more quiet and sophisticated, whereas the *Supernatural* fans are a little more 'yeah, dude!' A little more rock and roll. And the chick to guy ratio is heavier on SPN for obvious reasons. Like the boys' bodies."

Really? Jensen and Jared have hot bodies? We hadn't noticed. We're pretty sure that Fred didn't buy it.

Like all of us, Fred had some stereotypes about fans before he actually started meeting them.

> I had no idea what to expect. In America, a good percentage of my peers in the entertainment industry think fans are loonies. Everyone saw William Shatner on *Saturday Night Live* make fun of *Star Trek* fans and tell them to get a life. And I think he's kind of an asshole for saying that, kind of a slap in the face to your fans, you jerk. I guess I was wary of that, coming to conventions and interacting with fans. What I've found in life is that there are people who are passionate/obsessed about everything. They go to a hockey game, and that's positive—just like when these people get together, they meet like-minded folks and they revel in it. It's good, there's nothing wrong with it. There are crazy people every once in a while, and I'm not Jared or Jensen, but I'm talking to someone every now and then and realize they're fucking crazy, but really these people are good people, they're passionate.

"Yes, exactly," we said excitedly. "That's what we want to write about! That passionate doesn't equal pathological. Though every once in a while, a few people do have a bit of trouble separating the actor from the character."

"When I did a season of *Dallas*," Fred said, "I was with a friend in some car lot, and this woman came up to me and hit me with her purse because I'd been mean to Charlene on the show. I started laughing, but then I realized she wasn't kidding."

Purse attacks aside, some perks come with being recognized. Fred told us:

> A person can't help but like walking into a room full of people who like you. And if for some reason people walk up to me in a photo op and the person is trembling, I like to settle them down and be like "I'm glad to meet you too, and there's nothing special about me." I take pleasure in letting them know I'm just a person, and if I can make their day a little better, it makes both of us better people. I'm a fan too—of baseball players. I collect cards, I go to games, and I'm thrilled to meet them. I've had some be exceedingly gracious,

but you can catch any human being at a bad time. People write on IMDB that they met someone in an elevator and he's a prick. And maybe that person just got some bad news about their sixteen-year-old or something, you really don't know, so I cut everyone slack.

We thought about Andie's experience running into Danneel Harris in the bathroom of the theater in Fort Worth and imagined what sort of constant vigilance it must take to be a celebrity being scrutinized (and perhaps mis-interpreted) at every turn. Most of the celebrities could relate to the experi-ence of being a fan since they'd been fans too. They understood the nerves, the anticipation, the fumbling awkwardness of wanting to say something significant and instead only managing to stammer out something stupid. But the constant pressure to be entertaining and to uphold the image the fans have of a celebrity—to maintain the persona—was a source of anxiety for most of the "famous" people.

Fred admitted that he was nervous coming out onstage at the con and singing "Sympathy for the Devil."

"I went to the sound check in the morning with Adam [Malin], and said, 'Is this going to fly? Is this at all good?' And he said, 'Do you know how bad you'd have to be for this to lose?'"

Well seriously, who's going to throw rotten tomatoes at the Yellow Eyed Demon? But Adam—and Fred—also recognized that fans will cut you a lot of slack if you're already a fan favorite. He didn't need to sing well, he just had to play the part of the character fans knew and loved.

The next time we caught up with Fred, at a different con six months later, he was a bit more cautious about how much he put out there at an event like a *Supernatural* convention.

"I have found that one has to be a little more vigilant as to how open you are, because some people can take advantage of that. It would be nice if you could be accessible, but some people go straight to way too personal, and they don't know where the boundaries are," Fred said. "If you confide in them with not so much statements and words but emotional accessibil-ity, they take advantage of that. People try to outdo others with how much inside knowledge they have. It's not going to put me off, but it will make me smarter about what people hear and see."

Fred's girlfriend Ginger joined us, and we asked what cons were like for her.

"It's weird, you almost become a celebrity yourself while you're here, because fans look at you as an extension of Fred. I try not to say too much. One day a girl at the pool was asking me all this stuff . . ."

Fred looked a bit concerned. "What was she asking you?"

"About our relationship and if this is what you want."

Okay, so fans don't *always* ask totally appropriate questions.

As we left the restaurant with Fred, we overheard one of the fans we knew whisper excitedly to her table of friends, "I know those women he was sitting with."

Oh yeah! We were famous. Well, okay, we were having breakfast with someone who was a little famous. At the time, it was enough. Feeling optimistic about our interview abilities, we called Jim Beaver, who was also appearing at the con, and arranged to meet him at the hotel bar for a follow-up interview.

"Is it safe for me to come down?" Jim wanted to know. He had been warned by convention security against walking around unescorted. We looked around the bar and didn't see anything that looked particularly dangerous, unless you count fangirls consuming purple nurples. We dutifully informed Jim of the potential risk. He joined us anyway.

Perhaps the security people had a point. Every fan in the place quickly went from "Hey, Jim Beaver's in the bar!" to "Let's go say hello," so there was a steady stream of fans attempting to talk to Jim as he attempted to eat his dinner. We were well aware that we would most likely have been part of that steady stream ourselves if we hadn't already been sitting there with him. Jim was gracious, but we were increasingly uncomfortable with the hateful looks being cast our way. Who are those two women monopolizing Jim's time? Didn't we see them in the audience a while ago? Jim was oblivious to the daggers we were getting, though one fan actually came right out and asked: "Who are you two? How do you know Jim?" When we told her that we were writing a book, she seemed placated. As long as we weren't "just fans" our presence there was acceptable, if not welcomed. Jim confided that he was still a little freaked out by the sudden attention he was getting.

Why me, why does anyone care? And then I realized, it's not even about me. It's got nothing to do with me, in the purest sense, because whoever played Bobby Singer in a way people liked would be the guy of the moment. I want to be very respectful of the fans because I do respect them. Talking about the rock star syndrome—it seems like an easy thing to take advantage of. If I want to get to know someone, I can get to know anyone I want to if they are *Supernatural* fans, in any variety of ways, the doors are open. If I want a rich, rewarding, lifelong relationship with someone, it would be easy to find a *Supernatural* fan, but it might not be so easy to find someone that I would have a rich, rewarding, lifelong relationship with. Because they would not be coming to it because of who I was.

It's true. Once people know you as a "celebrity," they can never know you as just the real-life person you are, simply because they can't "unknow" the celebrity awareness. No wonder so many of the truly famous pair up with other similarly famous people and value the friendships that they made before they were famous so highly. It's too anxiety-provoking to have to wonder on a daily basis whether someone just wants to hang out with you because you're on *Supernatural*.

"Are you speaking from personal experience?" we wanted to know.

Jim nodded. "It's interesting, I met a fan in Orlando and we kept up an email conversation and it was kind of intriguing and then at some point I was like okay, I would like it if you started talking to me about things that didn't have anything to do with the show."

Asked if he'd ever felt unsafe around fans, Jim shook his head. "Granted, there are crazy people out there. But it strikes me that at a fan convention is the least likely place you'll find one."

"Yes!" we agreed emphatically.

"Even that woman who jumped on Jensen at Asylum, she just wanted to be on him. The only remotely inappropriate thing anyone has done is a young woman popped me on the ass at one of those things," Jim said. "As a general rule, I don't mind that, but it was a little like, I got a little taste of being a woman. One night after a show at the Dallas Shakespeare Convention, half the cast went to drink at a gay bar, and a guy came up to me and did that, and I remember having a vaguely similar response, Uh . . . who said he could do that? And kind of . . . hey! I basically found it flattering."

We raised eyebrows. Jim joked, "I wish more women would do that."

Jim was still surprised that he actually had the ability to make some fans nervous enough that they couldn't think of a single thing to say.

Kathy nodded. "Yeah, that pretty much describes me. If I don't have anything intelligent to say, I just say nothing."

"How about 'Hey, I forked over forty bucks to sit in line for four hours!'" Jim countered.

Anything that makes this [the con experience] impersonal for me is disappointing. One of the reasons it took me so long to get the autographs done was because I wanted to talk to people . . . I was there to make sure everyone got what they paid for. I remember this one woman, I thought she was going to collapse, she was so nervous. I still find that confusing because I know that sort of thing happens with big stars, but it's almost like they must be another species, whereas I feel like I'm Joe Average—I'm shy a lot of the time with people I don't know. Why anyone would quiver rather than say "Hi, how are you"—I can see them doing that to Harrison Ford, but not me!

But that's the thing about being a fan. *Supernatural* is important. So Bobby Singer—and by extension Jim Beaver—is important too. Once again, our chat with Jim was too interesting to cut short. Eventually we continued the interview in his hotel room.

Ultimately it seems these conventions are about realizing or confirming a sense of both self-meaning and connection. Just watching somebody on TV can be really interesting and rewarding depending on the show and level of the work, but if you've invested a great deal of yourself in that process, it seems to me that going to one of these things and meeting the person and having them not spit on you is a way of almost saying yeah, I am part of this equation.

"Exactly," we said. Being acknowledged by the stars of your favorite show—maybe even hugged or graced with a few words or a smile—confers a validation. It's the feeling that we're all in this together, fans and producers, consumers and creators. That feeling is a big part of why fans crave interaction with the creative side, whether it's face to face at a convention or online through Twitter or Facebook.

Jim confided that several fans had asked him about the infamous "I Read

John/Bobby" T-shirt that he'd worn to the con. The one we had dared him to make. Now that we were alone in Jim's hotel room, he could drop the innocent act.

"I came this close to telling them I had made the shirt," he said. "These three women who were talking about it, they were unanimous that they didn't care for slash. One of them said that she writes fanfiction and they were all like God, no! The one who writes fanfiction said basically what you said to me, that it's women who read and write it, and it was almost exactly what you said to me in my house, but from her, she said it's because there's no complication in the relationship."

We nodded, and Jim turned a mock threatening glare on us, with an evil glint in his eye: "A lot of people want to know who gave me that idea."

We paled. "But hey, you knew about slash even before we told you about it!"

"I knew about it, but I didn't know enough to know the details or extent of it. The one I read, it was the two brothers. Wincest. This was before I talked to you guys and I thought we had a lot of gay fans. Now I know it's mostly written by women. Which brings up an interesting scenario. Even the people who write that, I wonder what they'd think if Eric popped out an episode that dealt with the same issues."

Write Wincest into canon? Fast forward another six months and guess what? Kripke did just that, when he gave us Becky the fanfiction-writing superfan. Jim was already pretty savvy as to what the fans want.

"I've discovered if there is anything that pleases the fans, it's if they can feel like they have embarrassed me in a fun way, and you know, I'm fully capable of playing that," Jim said. "When the gasping was winding down after I showed the T-shirt at Eyecon, I was like, what? What does it mean? The more worried I got about what it meant, the more they loved it."

Jim intended the shirt to say something a bit different.

"Actually, I screwed up the shirt. It was supposed to say 'I *Write* John/Bobby Slash.' I looked at the shirt and was like 'read?!' It's supposed to be 'write!'"

"Maybe your next shirt should say 'I write Wincest,'" Lynn suggested.

"How about Bob-cest?" Jim quipped.

"Well, Bobby is kind of part of the family now," Lynn shot back. We all grinned. Jim's grin was evil.

We talked a bit about fame with Jim too, and how it can be a double-edged sword. Fame gets people to line up and pay money for your autograph and gets you invited to conventions and makes people care about the T-shirts you wear. But it's a bit like winning the lottery—everyone wants something from you once you have it.

Every once in a while there is someone that wants me to do something for them. There's someone at this convention who's been emailing me wanting me to have Jared and Jensen make a recording for someone's birthday. It's easy once or twice, but forty times a month? That book, *When I Say No I Feel Guilty* . . . that was written for me. I had a little trouble at first because it was like I wanted to say yes to everyone. There was someone in Germany, her best friend was a fanatic, and her birthday was coming up, so she wanted to arrange for her friend to visit the set. I went to the production office and asked, what do you do if someone wants to see the set? And they were like, "You say no—it's a warehouse, not a Universal Studios tour!"

Another challenge of fame is getting used to being interviewed. Not just by nobodies like us but by people whose articles are widely read and circulated among fans. In an interview after *Supernatural*'s Season 3 finale, Jim mentioned Jensen "crying" on the set (where he had to be suspended in a harness for hours to simulate hanging on meat hooks in *Supernatural*'s version of Hell), not realizing how provocative such an offhand comment would be to a fandom that's fiercely protective of its boys.
Jim rolled his eyes.

People completely misconstrued what I said—I was just ripping on Jensen . . . I remember the very first interview I ever did was in college, I was doing a play, and a guy from the newspaper interviewed me. I was playing the title role, and he said what's the toughest part about playing this role, and I said, "Submerging my own personal altruism," but it came off without the smiley face. That was my first interview and my first lesson that in print is not the same as in person. Jensen had said that was the hardest day he ever had on the show, it was physically draining. There was one point when he told me he was in make up for about three hours and he was all urghhh I had to get here at 5 A.M., and I told him the story about my wife [Cecily, also an actress] who had to come in for *Star Trek* at 2 A.M. and they didn't use her until midnight.

And she couldn't lie down or eat or hear because everything was all covered [by masks and makeup], and I'm telling him all this, and of course it's the last thing he wanted to hear. But he was talking about the actual hanging in the harness—one of the buckles had gotten turned around and it was digging into him and almost cutting through the skin. He decided that if he made them let him down, it'd be another two hours to fix it, but he said, "Man, I was hanging there and tears were in my eyes, it hurt so bad and I couldn't do anything about it."

I took that and said in the interview, "I can't tell you what happens in the last episode, but I can tell you Jensen cried like a baby!" And I remember telling someone, "Wait, no he didn't, I was just ragging him!" But it was too late. You've got to be careful what you say because someone down the line will take it literally. At the wrap party this year, I was asking about the rumor that we maybe were coming back early to do additional episodes, and someone said, "The only thing we know we are going to do is that hot tub scene with the two lesbians." But put that in print, all of a sudden it's not joshing.

Wait, what happened to the hot tub scene? Can we have one with Sam and Dean too??

Fame, as addictive as it is, can be—and almost always is—fleeting. Celebrities are acutely aware of that fact. Once you have fame, you're always worried about losing it.

Jim had already thought about it.

I am not going to be the guy sitting there at a convention signing hoping someone comes along and remembers who he is. Unless it's the difference between my kid eating or not. I don't want to be sitting there at some table with a sign in front of me, to remind everyone of who I am. If I've got a weak point, it's my fear of the day when everything that everyone thinks is cool now is forgotten. It comes, almost without fail, so I just don't want to get to the position when I am clinging to that. I did a telethon years ago in LA and they announced that there was going to be a song by Hoyt Axton, and he sat down and they had a bunch of little kids around him, and I remember he said, "That's right. kids, I'm the guy who wrote Jeremiah Was a Bullfrog." They didn't care, they didn't know him, that song was twenty years old when they were born! I thought, please don't ever let me be someplace where I am (a) presuming people who have no reason to know me know me and (b) I feel like I have to tell them. I'm not going to do these [conventions] forever.

Being an actor looks pretty glamorous from the outside, but rarely does the glamour last—and what comes after can be far from pretty. Jim knew this all too well.

A few years ago I'm going through airport security and recognized an actor from some network series when I was a kid, and being a buff, I knew exactly who this guy was. I guarantee you, he had not worked more than a day or so in twenty-five–thirty years, and he was working the security line, that was his job. I said wow, I'm a big fan and just wanted to say hi. So I basically looked at him and said, "You used to be on TV, and now you're working security." And he was embarrassed. So I learned. The night before last, I was walking out of a restaurant and I saw an actor I knew that I had worked with, and he was waiting tables, and I just walked out. We were actors together—he didn't want me to see him like this.

The emotional costs—and the rates of depression, addiction, and suicide, from Marilyn Monroe to Michael Jackson—weren't lost on Jim. "That's why I get nervous when my daughter says she wants to be in a play. She'd love it and I would love for her to love it. The actors who are good who don't get careers, it's because they gave up, and they gave up for the most part because they couldn't handle how much they are rejected."

The experience of being "famous" while at a *Supernatural* convention, Jim realized, was an exception to real life. A rarefied space in which he was temporarily famous.

At Asylum, there were 1,400 people screaming. I stood out in the lobby and when my van came there were 100 people on the side of the road waiting for me. The next day I get up and am walking around the town, just sightseeing. I'm heading back to my hotel, and I looked down this alley toward Leicester Square, and there are thousands of people crammed in there, screaming and lifting their cameras up over the crowd. It was the *Sex and the City* premiere. So I walked down through this crowd and nobody paid any attention to me—no one knew who I was. I didn't look any different than the day before.

A similar thing happened when Jim was a regular on the television show *Deadwood*.

> At the end of the first season, they flew me out to be the Grand Marshal of a parade there—I got a free trip to a place I've never been, and was treated kind of cool, and we ride down this street in Deadwood, probably less than a mile long. And you know, there are a lot of people cheering and taking my picture. And we get to the end of the street and the guy driving the buggy says, "Well I can take you back to the staging area, or you can get off here since you're right in town." So I got out and walked back through the street—the same street—and NOBODY knew who I was. It's the same people. Nobody. I thought the same thing both times. That story George C. Scott told in *Patton*—in ancient times, when they returned in triumph and had a parade, Caesar would have a slave stand behind him in the chariot as they went through the thronging crowd and this slave's job was to lean in and whisper in his ear that all fame was fleeting. It's very balancing, though it's also a little irritating, like how can I be famous over here but not over there? On this side of the street, though, I can go to dinner and actually eat it.

Those of us who aren't famous sometimes forget that there's a cost to fame and a benefit to not being famous.

> When I called Creation here to ask if there would be a problem if I went to the restaurant to meet you guys, it was the first time I thought, "Oh my God, what if I can't go down there?" It was the first time I thought that this is the tiniest tip of what that cost is. You know, it's an interesting conundrum whether or not one would willingly accept the disadvantages that come with that if one actually knew the experiences up front.

Some of us will never have to make that decision. We eventually said good night to Jim, grabbed a few hours of sleep, then got up to be fangirls the next morning. The Dallas con also had another surprise guest—Papa Winchester's truck, affectionately nicknamed Truckzilla, which the studio had recently sold to a fan. Johnny, who takes care of the vehicles on the show, drove it down to meet her, and the fan then drove it all the way to Dallas. Fans gleefully lined up to get their photo taken while pretending to be Jeffrey Dean Morgan (John Winchester). Lynn, giddily back in full fangirl mode, took her turn, opening the driver's side door and then staring up and up and up with an awed expression. Truckzilla was so gigantic that Kathy had to give Lynn a not-quite-graceful heave up so that she could get behind the wheel, explaining its nickname. Kathy wisely declined her turn after watching Lynn's ungainly scramble.

We like to complain that a room full of mostly grown women at a convention should not have to have their questions vetted. This con, however, stretched the boundaries of our conviction in fandom's good judgment. The most asked question—because the same person asked it of *every single guest*—was: "You've just been kidnapped. You wake up with your junk stapled to a table. Your kidnappers set the room on fire. Do you rip and run or stay and burn?" Mixed answers to this one. Fred said he'd just take the table with him, which seemed the most sensible solution.

It was that kind of con.

As soon as we left, we wanted more.

A few months later, with the new semester about to start, piles of work to be done, and several children between us starting new semesters of their own, another con was announced. This was a bad time to be taking off for another fan convention. We wavered. Then we got an email, out of the blue, from actor Chad Lindberg. He had never responded to our query about an interview (as often happened, alas), but he sent us a sweetly apologetic message and asked if we wanted to meet up at this convention, called Eyecon. Now we had an interview lined up, so we figured what the hell.

Our families figured we'd lost our minds.

In a rather transparent effort to make it seem like the trip was too productive to pass up, we quickly tossed out a few more interview queries and lined up a chat with musician Jason Manns and a follow-up with Fred Lehne. The con organizers, Kenny and Voni, also agreed to an interview. This was all suddenly starting to come too easily.

We met Chad for coffee shortly after we arrived at the hotel. Instead of starting the interview by answering our questions, he turned the tables and asked about us, wanting to know all about the book and how we came to be writing it. Once we'd said our piece, Chad put his coffee down emphatically. "You have to meet Tony."

Tony, it turned out, was Tony Zierra, the filmmaker behind a powerful documentary about the price of fame, *My Big Break*, which starred Chad Lindberg, Brad Rowe, Greg Fawcett, and Wes Bentley and was screening at Eyecon. Chad introduced us to Tony and the film's producer, Elizabeth Yoffe. The similarity of our book and their film was striking.

"You're trying to understand the relationship between the fans and the stars, and here comes along in your journey this movie that deals with that very same topic. Kind of like fate," Tony observed, and we knew we were going to like these people very much. Tony began filming his actor roommates as they all struggled to get work and keep afloat in Hollywood. Of the four actors living in the house at the time of filming, three got their "big breaks" and suffered the highs and lows of sudden fame. What we found even more compelling was Tony's own journey, also chronicled in the film. At the time, we intended to write a book that was mostly research. That's what we were used to doing, and we felt safe and comfortable doing it that way. We would set the record straight about the awesomeness of fandom— without ever really outing ourselves as fans. Just as we initially wanted to remain invisible in this book, reporting on what we saw without the risk of putting ourselves out there, Tony did not appear in the first version of his film, *Carving Out Our Names.*

"I didn't want to be known," Tony admitted. Then there was a moment that changed things, when actor Wes Bentley turned the camera on Tony and wouldn't take no for an answer. And Wes was right. He and the other "famous" people were the ones who were "out there," while Tony (and we ourselves) remained safe, no matter what happened in the course of the book or the film. Tony and Elizabeth challenged us to write ourselves back into the picture, even though some of the pictures were bound to be embarrassing. They also encouraged us to tell the truth, to expose both the people we were writing about and ourselves.

"If you gloss it, nothing will be seen, people won't see anything real in the book or in the movie," Tony told us. "It will look like everyone gets along, everyone is friends, everyone is perfect. There's no substance. The more you put in, the more it will explode—so put everything in there and let them [TPTB] say take it out. They don't know what you know about this world. You might open their eyes to something they've never seen. They might be like, this is controversial, but it will bring people in."

Our friend Night said the same thing. "Here you are, two really intelligent women, and all of a sudden you find yourself on the couch with a bag of Doritos waiting for the next episode of *Supernatural* to come on and it's like, how did I get here? That's the book you need to write!"

We thought about it, though at the time we were still leaning toward a comfortably academic book. But inspired by Tony and Night's challenge not to play it safe, we started to focus our interviews even more on the kinds of things actual journalists didn't talk about—but the kinds of things fandom did. The next morning, we joined Jason Manns in the autograph room for our planned interview. Jason had led off his duet with Jensen at the Asylum convention with a strangely slashy introduction ("No pictures with little innuendos, we're sharing a microphone, completely platonic—just be sensitive"). We asked him why.

Jason laughed. "I'd just been made aware of those, what do you call them?"

"Icons?" we suggested.

"Icons, yeah—somebody was like, this is pretty funny, check this out, and I think it was of Chris [Kane]," Jason said. "It was all pictures of him and some other guy, and there's that moment when you lean in to talk and if you take a picture it looks like you're going to kiss or something. It had some sort of word at the bottom like 'love' or 'the kiss' and I was just thinking wow, somebody spent a lot of time on that. For some reason, that just popped into my mind. It just came out, it wasn't planned."

Hey, we get it. Half of Lynn's questions come out that way too.

"Thankfully, we tried to keep our distance. Another funny aspect of that too was at the last convention when Steve [Carlson] brought me up on stage and we sang that medley of 'Let's Get It On,'" Jason said. "So I'm singing in harmony with Steve to Lionel Richie, and you have to watch someone to sync your words up to theirs, and apparently I was staring at Steve, and it's a love song . . . So I got an email and someone said, there's a video and it looks just like that. But I don't think anyone *really* thought that."

Oh no. Of course not. Tinhats optional.

Our interview stopped and started as fans came up to ask for an autograph from Jason or bought a CD. One woman had a stack of zines, the predecessor of online fanfiction. Before the days of the worldwide web, fans still wrote fanfiction, passing it around from fan to fan at conventions and eventually via snail mail. This fan's zines prompted a discussion of fanfiction, as we continued our don't-play-it-safe rule. How did Jason feel about sometimes being in it?

"I'm in it?" he asked, surprised. "I got an email pretty recently actually with a link to Live Journal, and I was like, this isn't for me, and just didn't read too much. It's just a private expression for the fans, and it's not something for me. I kind of let fandom be fandom."

Good boundaries, Mr. Manns.

Saturday evening presented us with not one but two opportunities to interact awkwardly with celebrities, first at the Platinum Banquet where a celebrity guest sat at each table and fans picked whose table they would run to. This provided a chance to relive all the fun of a middle school dance (choose a celebrity partner and spend an hour making desperate stabs at conversation). Then there was the Platinum Cocktail Party, where we got to watch celebrity guests get shitfaced and play Guitar Hero. It was more fun than the dinner by far, because conversation was most definitely optional. After both of these events, we joined a group of friends in the hotel bar. We drank, swapped con stories, drank some more. One fan began talking about fanfiction.

"What's that?" another fan, Jane, asked.

As it turned out, Jane was the lone newbie at a table full of fanfic writers. We all jumped in to explain, and eventually someone said the "S" word.

"Then there's slash."

"As in killing them?" Jane asked.

Not quite.

"It's about putting them into a relationship with each other," Clara explained.

Jane looked upset, which probably should have stopped the conversation in its tracks. Unfortunately, everyone was pretty far from sober at that point, so on it went.

"But they're brothers," she protested, frowning.

"Doesn't matter," the rest of us said in unison. The conversation turned to the ethics of fanfiction in an attempt to make Jane understand that it was all right, they were just fictional characters. It wasn't working. Kathy glanced over and saw Jane's eyes welling up. She pulled her aside to try to explain in a way that was more academic and less lascivious than the explanations currently going around the table. It might have worked if someone hadn't brought up RPS.

"I prefer Jared/Jensen," one fan happily declared.

Jane burst into tears.

If we'd been less drunk, we might have remembered that everyone does fandom differently. As fans, we were happily immersed in *Supernatural's* edgier fan communities. As researchers, we needed to remember that not everyone made those communities their homes—and in fact some were not all that happy to know they even existed. Unfortunately, cooler heads were not prevailing that evening. As we sat at the bar trying to comfort Jane, across the hotel lobby Jim Beaver was attempting to get into an elevator as a fangirl tried to get into his pants. He seemed to be trying to leave, but the girl kept following him. This was too much for Jane, whose moral code had been violated one too many times that night. She put down her drink in disgust.

"I'm going over there to rescue him," she said with determination. It's unclear whether Jim actually needed rescuing. What was clear was that the fans at the bar strongly disapproved of the woman who was trying to break some of the boundaries between fans and the famous. Whether out of jealousy or disgust, the other fans weren't about to let it happen. And whether it did or not—and hey, everyone there was an adult—the resentment and jockeying for position and the name-calling and shaming (of the female fan) that resulted were far from fandom as a supportive, safe place.

The night went downhill from there. Free beer and hard liquor were available in the infamous "game room" after hours, which made Eyecon more like a gigantic frat party than a fan convention, complete with unscrupulous guys just waiting to take advantage of a bunch of women who'd had too much to drink. Several men loosely connected to the convention (or at least claiming to be) did just that, impressing young female fans with "I know someone who knows someone" and then using their influence to gain sexual favors that left several fangirls waking up the next morning traumatized. Literally. The dark side of fandom that we hadn't wanted to see was starting to make itself very clear.

We were confronted by more fan-on-fan nastiness the next day. Eyecon headliner Jared Padalecki appeared at the convention on Sunday. Lynda, one of the fans we knew, had paid a jaw-dropping price for a private breakfast for six with Mr. Padalecki. For us, this was a good thing, as we were able to squeeze in some pseudo-interview questions without emptying our wallets by merely giving them to Lynda. She'd ask Jared, and then we'd meet up with her for lunch and debrief her over burgers. The auction for the breakfast was held over eBay, so the price should have remained confidential. Of course, that's not how fandom works. We overheard a group of fans discussing the price tag in Starbucks. "What's wrong with those fans," they demanded, "to pay that much money for a lunch?" One fan complained that she didn't make that much money in six months. Another grumbled that the money could have gone to a charitable cause. (We wisely refrained from bringing up the glaring fact that this same fan's convention ticket and flight expense could have as well.) One person did defend the unknown fans, saying that if they made enough money to spend that amount on Jared Padalecki, then more power to them. The other fans rolled their eyes and continued their shaming. The definition of an obsessed fan? Apparently anyone to the left of exactly where *you* are on the fan continuum.

For Lynda, the price tag was clearly worth it.

"He was wonderful at breakfast, I can't even tell you," she said. "It was an experience of a lifetime, and I'll remember it to my dying day."

Lynda was concerned about the "cost" of such an experience, but not the financial one. Instead, she worried about one of the similarities of fandom and addiction—once you've had a euphoric experience, you want more. How can you top something like breakfast with Jared?

"For me, having a private breakfast with Jared was the con experience of a lifetime, and I'm at the point where I should almost drop out of this fandom after this. After all the conventions I've been to, Jared was the best. Once you've done this, where do you go?" Lynda asked.

Good question. And one of the reasons fandom is so addictive. You have an incredible time at a con, you want to have an equally incredible time at the next one—or ideally an even more incredible one. You come home with the perfect photo op, you want the better-than-perfect one next time. You buy one season of DVDs, you want all of them. Lynda did manage to ask Jared a few of our questions while they shared breakfast. The two stars of *Supernatural* had just moved in together, making fandom very happy indeed, so we had asked her to get some info on how that happened.

"Jared said that Jensen's apartment had been sold out from under him. And he had to get his stuff out and find another place. He was supposed to be looking for another place but really didn't have the time, so Jared said to him, just store your stuff in my basement," Lynda related. "So Jensen stored his stuff in the basement, and they're supposed to be out there looking for an apartment for Jensen, but neither has the time to do it. Jensen, in the meantime, is sleeping on the air mattress in the basement, so Jared finally said, why don't you just stay? They unpacked his stuff and he took over the basement."

Fans who enjoyed fantasizing about Jared and Jensen being more than friends were ecstatic, and in this case fans who just enjoyed their friendship agreed.

On the last night of the convention, we attended the screening of *My Big Break*. The film hit us hard. It was a raw and often uncomfortable picture of what can happen when a person is suddenly confronted with fame—the heady allure of it (and who doesn't want it) and what happens when you get too much, too easily, too quickly. Equally powerful was the depiction of Tony's encounters with TPTB, who first courted him and then told him what could not be in his film, lest it show his friends (now bankable actors) in a less than flattering light. It was a cautionary tale that we only half heeded at the time. We wondered how the film was hitting the rest of the fans, many of whom now knew that actor Chad Lindberg had been crashing on a friend's couch when he appeared at the last con. The contrast certainly wasn't lost on Chad himself, as he told us afterward.

I thought the screening went exceedingly well. It's great because people expected to come see a movie I was in, and I don't think they were expecting to be affected. I think it took them out of the *Supernatural* perspective they were in, and I even heard a few people say that they changed their perspectives as far as us, the actors, and how they react to us at conventions. I think it also bothered some people, because they want to know and yet they don't want to know, that there is all this crap, because it kind of ruins the illusion for the fans almost. They don't want to know actors are broke, they just want to see the fun. But all those things that happened to me are necessary in order to be humble and appreciate what you have, and to grow. I'm just lucky to be able to continue to work and do these things.

Meanwhile, rumors were swarming around fandom (as they always are) that Season 4 would be the last for *Supernatural*, that Eric Kripke was already winding things down. The rumor was fueled by Jared's own uncertainty as to whether they would be back next year, since there had not yet been an official pickup. Fans—including us—were understandably upset by this news and began letter-writing campaigns to WB and the CW Network before the convention even ended. We figured we needed to hear it from the horse's mouth, so we emailed Eric and asked him. He emailed back, reassuring us that they were in fact already working on Season 5 and were feeling pretty optimistic. Phew! There are definite benefits to being able to email the man making the decisions. Of course, we told no one, privileging our researcher identities over our fangirl ones. Again.

NINE

. . . . .

Stuck in the Middle (with You)

As we moved back and forth between our identities as fans and as researchers, we began to occupy a strange middle ground, which carried with it both the thrill of being an insider and the risk of alienating the community of fans that we valued being a part of. Everyone who's straddled the line has had to negotiate a balance. When we weren't trying to wangle our way into celebrity interviews, we sought out the others who had successfully found that middle ground.

Creation convention owner Adam Malin, the fanboy-turned-entrepreneur, seemed to relish his position as middleman between fans and celebrities. Creation keeps the lines of demarcation between the two sides fairly thick, with relentless organization and a slew of volunteer security in addition to the MWNN. They offer access, to be sure, but it's a carefully proscribed and not entirely spontaneous access. This has the benefit of making sure that all fans get their turn and get what they paid for and the down side of being more choreographed than fans might wish. At Eyecon, we met with con organizers Kenny and Voni, who were trying to create a different model of fan convention where fans got more open access to the celebrities. They weren't exactly what we expected—everyone had told us how "cool" they were, how fan-oriented and down to earth. We were more struck by how *young* they were and wondered how such a laid-back organization was going to work out, more used to the well-oiled machine of a Creation con. We described our book and how we were trying to cover the fandom from both sides, the creative perspective and fan perspective. Kenny nodded. "Just like us—we're right in the middle."

Kenny started out (if that's the appropriate term for an operation that was all of six months old) running conventions for other shows, until Voni convinced him to have one for the show that she was a fan of—*Supernatural*. At first, Kenny was reluctant. Voni was his significant other.

> Kenny: "I was too jealous of Jared and Jensen."
> Voni: "Finally he was like fine, I'll bring Jensen for you."
> Kenny: "I've since then accepted Jensen's hotness."

As have we all, Kenny, as have we all.

He'd been impressed with the *Supernatural* fans. "My expectations now are that every fandom is like this. They are so intelligent, picking apart the episodes and talking about what it means. I've seen people break down the cinematography and I'm like yeah, those colors. And Kim Manners is popular because he's a *director*."

We couldn't resist asking if either of them were in the room at the last Eyecon when Jim Beaver came out wearing the infamous "I Read John/Bobby" T-shirt.

Kenny, entrepreneur that he is, was immediately enthusiastic. "That was awesome! My position is that we look for anything that is going to get blogged about—when he did that it's like cha-ching! Anytime someone says your name, it's better for you. But it's still funny."

At least someone was happy about our T-shirt dare, if only because he stood to gain from it. Ultimately, Kenny and Voni's model of conventions ended up failing, perhaps because some of the boundaries they sought to break down are actually needed. Not the ones that require four giant security guards to police a room full of grown women, but the ones that keep an eye on both sides to be sure neither is taking advantage of the other. Voni, as a fangirl herself, understood what fans wanted—and Kenny tried to give that to them (and to Voni as well). Perhaps their own emotional investment at times clouded their judgment of just what that should be. Or maybe they were just too young and inexperienced. For whatever reason, the next scheduled Eyecons were canceled.

We also talked with Wayne, the organizer of Asylum, that UK con that we were so upset to have missed out on. If we thought Kenny and Voni were young, we were really shocked by Wayne. He looked younger than some of our own children.

Lynn: "You look very young."
Wayne: "I'm twenty-four."
Lynn (a bit wide-eyed): "You *are* very young."

Wayne gave us his perspective on the convention we only got to follow from afar. "The opening ceremony starts and there are eight hundred people standing up and the emcee announces Jensen Ackles and we had police coming in from the streets because of all the screaming. I don't think anyone realized how big *Supernatural* was going to be. It was like, this is nuts! None of my crew slept for four entire days. We had people from six to sixty-five, little kids running around, people dressed as Sam and Dean."

Why did he call the convention "Asylum"? The answer was a bit anti-climactic, after all our thoughtful academic theorizing about the multiple meanings of the word.

"Believe it or not," Wayne answered, "I just went through episode names and thought oh, that looks quite cool, done. For me, it was never going to be repeated, I was just going to move on. But 100 tickets sold the first day with no guests even announced, and the next year 300 sold the first day, so I said fine, we'll do another."

From his position in the middle, Wayne definitely understood the impact of the Flying Fangirl and the part that fan shame played in fans' reactions.

The first time I met *Supernatural* fans, they actually tried to jump Jensen. And then the other fans were all coming up to me and saying we are so sorry. All of them thought, oh no, what's going to happen, and they were panicking and apologizing. Like all of them did wrong if one did wrong, and they all felt guilty. We were all in the green room afterwards, and Jason said to Jensen, "Dude, you were jumped by one of the prettiest girls in the convention, like what's that about?" But now when you think about it, it's quite scary. I mean, it's like a holiday in the UK, this convention!

Apparently some fans got a little overly excited at the next Asylum too. "We had two people go into labor. Travis Wester [one of the show's popular Ghostfacers] said hello to her and her water broke just like that, and then the other's water broke just from the excitement. It's frightening what a buzz we have around this show, because to me, I think it's just a normal show."

Wayne may not quite get the appeal of Jared and Jensen (or the power of *Supernatural* to induce unexpected births), but he was savvy enough to keep a good read on who has caught the attention of the fandom. In fact, he'd already put in a call to Misha Collins after only two appearances on the show. And of course Wayne would like to have both boys: "I keep getting phone calls, asking can you give us Winchester sandwiches?"

Yum. That, of course, means a lot more money. "Every penny goes into the event. Asylum costs half a million dollars and there isn't money coming out, it all gets pumped back into the show."

Creation convention photographer Chris Schmelke is also a "man in the middle," which gives him a unique perspective. He's witnessed the interaction of fans and celebrities at countless fan conventions for everything from *Star Trek* to *Supernatural*. Like all fans, we think our fandom is the best. But even Chris told us he saw the *Supernatural* fandom as special.

> At *Supernatural* conventions, I see the most interaction between the fans, meeting and introducing themselves to each other. I think it comes from the fact that this fandom started on the Internet. This isn't just a show you watch, it's a show you watch and then everyone wants to talk about. The fandom grew up based around social interaction, whereas a fandom like *Star Trek*, people were watching by themselves. Fans here are more like "I've got your back." I saw two girls just standing in one spot for like six hours straight, just talking. And the energy here is unlike anything else. At the first *Supernatural* convention in Chicago, you could feel it in the air, there was just something. I'd say of all the groups I've worked with, the *Supernatural* fans are probably the most down to earth, grounded, and intelligent.

Chris also has the opportunity to see things from the celebrity's perspective.

> I think some get more out of it than others. Someone who's more likely to treat it as an opportunity to get to know people is gonna enjoy it more; whereas someone looking at it like these people are a bit freakish coming here to just stand next to me won't. Generally the celebrities are very down to earth and appreciative. They don't have to do this, but the fact that they do shows they get some kind of joy out of this experience too, I think. In Chicago, Jared was very hands on, whereas Jensen had had a bad experience

[referring to the Flying Fangirl], so he was a bit more standoffish. You saw the difference in the fans' faces when they went to Jared, whereas Jensen was just sitting quietly. And I knew Jensen had had that bad experience the first time, and I also knew that he takes pictures too, so we talked about that. I always make it a point to talk and be social with the guests and not just start working, get a rapport going and make people more comfortable. If the stars are comfortable, the fans will be too, and the photos will be better and that's ultimately my goal. At the next show Jensen was much different, like he did a 360. And Jared and Jensen do seem to remember the fans more than any other show I've worked with. I think that leads into the show and people saying how much they appreciate them and how they're not over the top. I've heard both of them numerous times saying we remember you from Chicago, or even remembering their names, and the fans go ballistic.

Fans went ballistic once again that summer at Comic Con, where both we and *Supernatural* returned in July of 2008. The year before, we had spent the long weekend flying our geek flag high and celebrating the bliss of being among fellow fans. By the time we returned a year later, our identities were split down the middle. Half the time, we were those same squeeful fangirls, clutching cameras and bags of fan swag. The other half, we were academics clutching briefcases and business cards.

We had spent the last year trying, and at first failing, to gain some access to the people associated with *Supernatural*. Eventually, with the age-old method of connecting with someone who knows someone who knows someone, we'd had some success. People on the creative side—actors, directors, writers—seemed genuinely eager to contribute. We had also connected with the other people "in the middle," including a few mainstream journalists who were recognizing *Supernatural* at the time—they too were excited to meet someone else who was writing about the little-known show. While we were in San Diego for Comic Con, we had dinner with *Ten Inch Hero*'s Betsy Morris, finally meeting the woman we'd been emailing with for a year. We had breakfast with Karla Peterson, the entertainment editor of the *San Diego Union Tribune*. Conversation on both counts included, unsurprisingly, the subject of Jensen Ackles. With Betsy, that meant a few behind the scenes *Ten Inch Hero* tidbits about Ackles's creative decision to wear a kilt and how much he could relate to a character who was judged by how he looks. With Karla that meant a whole lot of "holy hell the man is pretty" closely followed by "holy hell the show is amazing."

By this time, our inroads into the *Supernatural* creative side had also brought us and our little project to the attention of TPTB. Nobody was writing about *Supernatural* in *TV Guide* or *Entertainment Weekly* then, and even most online entertainment blogs didn't know it existed. The show was struggling to stay alive and needed a publicity boost to do it. And there we were—right place, right time, right credentials. After being brushed aside for the past year, we found that the studio was suddenly very interested in our book—so interested, in fact, that they wanted to publish the book themselves!! This unexpected news resulted in the same amount of hyperventilating as securing actor interviews had produced. Really?? We were now working with TPTB? We were official?

This was a turn of events that we'd never remotely considered. Almost immediately, we gained a whole new kind of access—one that didn't require us to make phone calls or send emails or do anything else other than show up at the appointed time and ask questions. As long as they were the *right* questions. After talking with Tony Zierra, we should have seen where this was going, but we were far too overjoyed at being on the "inside" to quibble about what sort of questions we should be asking. We were more than happy to sit back and allow TPTB to pleasure us for a while. Especially when the first pleasure that came our way was a follow-up interview with Eric Kripke, in person this time, at Comic Con—in the very same Warner Brothers booth where the year before we were among the huddled masses, yearning for a glimpse of the actors and writers. And, icing on the cake, we were also set up to meet with two of the editorial staff from DC Comics to discuss publication possibilities.

TPTB also introduced us to the other fans-turned-journalists who were starting to write about *Supernatural* at the time, facilitating a web of access for those who were writing about the show and at the same time keeping some level of control over what was written. Want to keep the flow of information going? Don't piss off TPTB by writing about Wincest, or indeed any fan practices that didn't involve words like "higher ratings." Considering the customary content of our interviews so far, and that our reason for writing a book in the first place was to normalize and validate fandom in all its endless variety, we were clearly already headed for trouble.

We were introduced to blogger Rae Hanson, who ran the website Ramblings of a TV Whore. She told us that she'd been a *Supernatural* fan from the beginning—literally before the show even aired, after a friend saw a preview at Comic Con and wouldn't stop raving about it. Rae felt that one of the reasons the show was so popular was because Eric Kripke seemed like such a fan himself. "That adds to why fans are so passionate about the show," she said. "Because the person behind it thinks like them." Rae gave us a little more insight into the personality traits that die-hard fans seem to share, by sharing her own. "I was a big fan of TV anyway, which probably goes back to my parents. I watched soaps with my mother, where you have to always keep watching to see where the story goes. I have kind of an obsessive personality too, it takes over most of my life."

As we've seen time and again, fandom is often as much about relationships and community as it is about a handsome actor or a compelling storyline.

"One of the reasons I got into television fandom," Rae told us, "was that I was away at college, alone, and seeking out someone to talk to. I've met a lot of people through Live Journal, and doing more than just reading, you really become part of the community."

This, of course, is exactly what we'd been finding in our own research—and experiencing ourselves. Rae had also, though, been ashamed of being a dreaded sci-fi fan. "I think oddly enough, it's changed from before I was a blogger. Having connections, having these opportunities to actually visit the *Supernatural* set, I think that has legitimized what I do."

Like us, Rae had tried to reduce the shame of being a fan by telling herself she wasn't *just* a fan. She ran a blog, that's why she watched these shows and felt compelled to write about them, right? It wasn't out of love or passion or (god forbid) because she found the actors hot or just wanted to have FUN. It wasn't because she was lonely and looking for a place she fit in and people she fit in with. It was a job, and that's respected instead of ridiculed. Our culture doesn't encourage fun, after all, especially for women. So we weren't the only ones seeking legitimacy. Was this a driving force behind all the people "in the middle," we wondered?

We asked another blogger, Dan McCallum of DuckyDoesTV, about this. Dan was gay, snarky, irreverent, and an unrepentant fanboy who wasn't afraid to toss around words like "squee." He talked about the difficulty of being both a fan and someone who writes about fandom. "It blows my mind," he said, "that over the last five years, blogs have become a legitimate source of information, advertising, and knowledge. Having access to the creative team and the writers legitimizes what I do, absolutely."

Dan gave us a little more insight into TPTB. He was frankly mystified by how slow they had been to take advantage of social media to publicize their shows. "Some networks get it and some just don't. One network went out there to pull everything from YouTube, and I'm like, don't they get it? These are the things that are making your show so much bigger and more of a cult show, this is what draws more viewers in. And sometimes even the creator of the show is okay with it (Joss Whedon comes to mind), and then the network pulls it? That makes me crazy!"

We also asked whether Dan's connection to TPTB ever affected how he wrote about the show. Was there a price to be paid for legitimacy? We probably should have paid more attention to his answer.

> I would like to say no, but you do think about it. The minute you know they are paying attention to what you write, it's in the back of your head. I'm one of those people who can't change what I want to say, if I want to say shit or the f-word, or worse. It would be weird not to write it because that's me. There have been times I've pulled back and written something in a different way, not so harsh. Some have made this their job, made it a website and not a blog, and then you're hard pressed to find anything opinionated on it. I know people who've been bought by another company, but that's not where I'm going.

Bought by another company, huh? Like a publisher owned by the studio maybe? The cautionary tales we were hearing about the price you inevitably pay for "legitimacy" should have made us wary. As we arrived at Comic Con that year for our second time, however, we didn't want to be wary. We were on the "inside" this time, and that feeling was addictive.

Our access didn't include seats at the *Supernatural* panel, unfortunately, so once again we got up ridiculously early to drive down to the convention center and once again made the mad dash from one line to the next. In our second row seats, we were fangirls to the core. As soon as we left them, we were "professionals." Last year we'd memorized the route and taken off at breakneck speed in fervent hopes of being able to get an autograph. No running this year. No jockeying for position. No mad autograph ticket grab.

We had an appointment and an invitation to the VIP lounge at the top of the Warner Brothers booth. Instead of being swallowed up in the crowd, we could watch them from above.

We were still having a lot of difficulty believing that any of this was really happening to us, even as we were being escorted by a security person past the velvet ropes (okay, they weren't really velvet, but they were ropes) and up the stairs to the VIP lounge. We were shown into a small room with a quiet young woman who had won a studio-run *Supernatural* video contest. Her prize was Jensen. Not to keep, but she was going to meet him and she was understandably nervous. We kept her company and tried to keep her calm until she was eventually escorted out of the room—and Eric Kripke was escorted in, along with writer Sera Gamble, who looked a little shell shocked to have ended up in an unplanned interview. We had mentioned offhand that we wished we could speak to Gamble too, and apparently our wish had been instantly granted. This was another clue that TPTB were not who we'd been thinking they were. Actors, writers, and showrunners are all just as much at the mercy of those shadowy powers as we were. We felt a little guilty that Sera had been waylaid to speak with us.

Eric didn't help by laughingly telling her, "These are the two who sent me the porn!"

Us (blushing furiously): "Uhhh."

Sera (scowling at Eric, who was grinning like a little boy): "You think it's funny. I think it's creepy."

Yes, folks, this is the way we start an interview.

As our research agenda had taken shape over the past year, we were more and more interested in the "reciprocal relationship" between the people who make and produce media and the fans who consume it. We were eager to ask Eric more about how he, as the creator of *Supernatural*, interacted with its fandom. The Season 3 finale had aired recently, so we asked Eric how he felt about the passionate—and divided—fan reaction.

I was generally pleased. Part of the show is to love the process of getting driven nuts. I mean that's part of the viewing experience. If they're happy and content every episode, that means you're not doing your job. It would be a very boring show if at the end of every episode it was like oh, isn't that nice? That wouldn't be very exciting. We got the early pick up and everyone knew we were coming back, but for the record, I was going to put Dean in hell whether or not we had that early pick up. I don't know if it was the least expected choice but it was a nice bold way to end the season. And, I mean, everyone knows he is going to get out.

Maybe not everyone. Eric had joked in an interview that Jensen refused to give him a salary kickback, so they'd fired him and hired Chad Michael Murray, underestimating the way intense emotion can sometimes cloud judgment. Some fans took Eric so seriously that he had to release a statement saying that he was kidding.

"I was thinking in some unspoken way that everyone would know," he confided. "I mean, there are only two leads . . ."

How to communicate with fans—how much information to give and what to keep hidden to maintain some suspense—was a challenge that Eric was explicitly balancing. Keeping fans in suspense was already getting harder in the age of social media.

"It's very hard to do. We have a couple secrets coming up in Season 4 that we have been trying to keep under wraps," Eric said. "So my assistant has been rewriting sides to hide details . . . changing names and making fans try to decipher details. To be honest, sometimes they are right and sometimes they are wrong, but it's kind of a treasure hunt for them to figure out what it all means. There are some major plot points that we try to hide because it takes a little of the fun out of it."

We were gradually understanding that TPTB were far from a single entity—the creative team of *Supernatural* and the studio that produces it had not always been on the same page about how to make or promote the show. Eric was starting to worry a little less about year-to-year survival because the show had gotten an early pick up. That also meant that the studio was letting the creative side do things more their own way.

I used to care a lot more than I do. I feel like in the first couple years, I was really concerned about getting enough viewership to tell the story, just to get going—and you're fighting for your survival every year. I could say there was some turning point this year. We reached syndication so the studio was happy and they started backing off, and with the early pick up, I sort of stopped worrying about the publicity being just right, and promoting our show the right way. It's been really refreshing and fun concentrating on what we should be concentrating on—making the episodes great! I mean, I hope there is a Season 5, but I have just become a lot more like, all I can do is make a good show and I'm not going to worry about spreading the gospel. Whatever is going to happen is going to happen. It is very refreshing.

Eric was talking about something that we weren't worried about at the time—the idea of creative freedom and the reality that creative freedom and pleasing TPTB are often mutually exclusive. Accustomed to the unfettered playground of online fandom, we were used to writing that followed no rules other than those set by the fans themselves. We were spoiled by the norms of free expression and the way a "gift economy" allows writers to say what they want and not care if anyone is going to buy it. There's no money to be made in fanfiction, so there's no audience to please other than your fellow fans who are waiting to read it. In some ways, that makes fanfic writers (mostly women) poor—in other ways, it frees us to be real and write what we want. Eric had already struggled with the mutual exclusivity of artistic freedom and pleasing TPTB. Unfortunately, we didn't understand just how much this applied to our own creative enterprise as well.

Ecstatic to have the creator himself right there, we also asked Eric a few things that we thought fans would want to know. Why did he cast Jared and Jensen? (Other than the fact that they were drop dead gorgeous, that is.)

It was a process of starts and stops. For instance, we were sure Jensen was going to be Sam, positive. And we couldn't find a Dean, and then Jared came in and taped for us, and he was a really good Sam, and looking back in hindsight it was obvious, but at the time it wasn't. We said, okay, we have the better side of riches with Sam, but we don't have a Dean yet, and we looked at it and said, make Jensen Dean, and that made a lot of sense. We called Jensen's manager and they were like, did he get the part? And we said no, but . . . he did get the other role! Looking back, they so embody those characters, but at the time you just don't know. Once you see enough film on them, you see their strengths and you write to those strengths, and the more I got to know them, the more we spent nights drinking, you write those little things into the show. It's a combination of us getting to know them better and us getting to know the characters better whereas now they are so intertwined. If you look at the early episodes of Season 1, there are some clunkers where you see Sam acting in ways he wouldn't really act.

Sera, who had been pretty quiet ever since Eric traumatized her by bringing up porn, chimed in. "You know who you're writing stuff for after a while, and after a while you play to their strengths. You get your writers in a pocket too and bring to the table things you never would have thought of."

Eventually TPTB reappeared and whisked Eric and Sera away to their next meeting. We gathered up our notepads and recorders and walked out onto the balcony area—and right into Danneel Harris, who swept us into hugs and then spun us around! Jensen was with her. Hello, Jensen! More hugs! What? Huh? Danneel remembered us (well really, how could she not after the technical fiasco that was her interview). And Jensen knew us (in the way that you "know" people that has absolutely nothing to do with actually knowing them, true, but better than nothing). Things were said, messages given to pass on, phone numbers exchanged. Now we were sure that none of this was real.

No time to think about it though. We stumbled down the stairs and headed to our meeting with the publisher reps. We were already dazed and confused by our close encounter with Jensen's biceps as we traversed the length of the convention center, and the assortment of Captain Jack Sparrows, superheroes, and Princess Leias popping up in front of us like obstacles in a video game were not helping. So much for our love of fans. That day we just loved publishers. Especially ones whose parent company actually *made* the show we'd fallen in love with.

The publisher reps from DC Comics were lovely. We mean really lovely. Everything about our meeting was lovely. We sat on the outdoor deck overlooking the San Diego harbor, sipped our Starbucks, and shared the outline of our story. They smiled and nodded encouragingly and took notes. A few minutes into the meeting, it became clear that something weird was happening. The publisher reps seemed to be trying to convince *us* to publish the book with them instead of us begging *them* to consider publishing the book for us. Not a done deal, but things looked good. What the hell? It was surreal.

"If you go with us," they said, still smiling, "then you can use licensed photos and put the logo on the book, and we'll advertise for you on websites and in magazines."

We nodded, unable to speak past the rush of excitement and awe.

"Oh, and maybe you can write some articles for the *Official Supernatural Magazine.*"

We knew they were speaking English, but we were having a lot of trouble making sense of the words. Us? Really?

We heard a few comments that hinted that the publisher would like us to write about the show in the way they wanted us to write and perhaps even a few hints that the way we'd been doing it all along wasn't quite going to fly. We wanted to talk about what fans really do and who fans really are, the reasons they love *Supernatural*, and the ways in which they show it. That included fanfiction in its infinite variety. It included all kinds of fanart and not-quite-legal videos and an open acknowledgment that yes, women did objectify men sometimes, and what of it? We didn't want fans to be ashamed any longer, and we wanted to show the world why they shouldn't be. But we were so seduced by the loveliness of the meeting and the promise of an "official seal of approval" that we missed the unspoken message: there was no way the studio would want that book. On that day, we were way too giddy to care. Tell us what to write, and we'll write it! We were all too happy to sell our souls for that heady sense of validation we'd been seeking all along. Our own unrecognized search for legitimacy made us blind to what we were actually agreeing to. All we could see was that the ultimate Powers That Be were on board with what WE were doing. We felt accepted, like part of the *Supernatural* family. We wanted legitimacy so badly that we were willing to do just about anything to get it.

The drive back to our hotel was filled with exclamations of OMG, some of them about the lovely publisher reps, some about the equally lovely chats with Kripke and Gamble. More than a few were about the unexpected thrill of Harris and Ackles even knowing who we were, let alone being excited about our book. We were so busy celebrating our newfound legitimacy that it felt jarring to snap back into fan mode as we threw our giant *Supernatural* Comic Con bags down on the hotel beds and finally exclaimed to each other, "OMG, Jensen Ackles hugged us!"

We spent the next few months excitedly emailing back and forth with the publisher and editors, working on the manuscript every spare second we could grab in between attempts to instill knowledge in our students and happiness in our families. The juggling act was alternately breathtaking and cringeworthy. In fact, we were dropping balls all over the place. There literally were not enough hours in the day for us to fulfill any of our roles with anything like adequacy—the stereotypical challenge for women everywhere was now hitting us with a force the likes of which we'd never known. Life was complex enough when we were balancing career, marriage, and taking care of children; even more complex when we'd both returned to grad school to finish our PhDs. But that juggling act was nothing compared to what we were attempting now.

To make matters worse, our careers seemed, in the view of everyone but ourselves, to have taken a decidedly frivolous turn. Researching eighteenth century literature or narrative therapy was serious business. Researching *Supernatural* fandom not so much. No matter how legitimate we tried to tell ourselves (and anyone else who would listen) our fan studies research was, nobody (including us) was really buying it.

Lynn's daughter worried that her mom wouldn't be there if she needed her. Lynn's son was angry. Her children had been used to having their mother's undivided attention for the past twenty years. Now this sudden "hobby" was taking some of that away. It seemed out of character, unexpected. Selfish. It led to tearful confrontations, shouted accusations. More than once, Lynn came close to throwing the stacks of research articles in the trash can and ripping the Sam and Dean photos off the refrigerator like a two-year-old having a tantrum. Each time, she couldn't do it. Giving up fandom felt like cutting off a limb. The emotional importance of the community was too compelling for her to do without.

While he'd been understanding of her *Supernatural* fannishness at first, as the months had passed, Lynn's partner Doug was less and less so. Especially after that whole debacle with Brian Molko signing her chest. They had other problems too, but they definitely didn't agree about fandom.

"Aren't you just a little worried about yourself?" Doug asked one afternoon as they were driving down the New Jersey Turnpike. "You know, about all this fandom stuff?"

Lynn gritted her teeth. "No," she answered. "What exactly do you think I should be worried about?"

Doug took one hand off the steering wheel to make a sweeping gesture. "Oh, you know, just like how—how *into* it you are. Don't you think you should be, I don't know, outgrowing it by now?"

"Outgrowing it?" Lynn repeated, teeth clenched so hard that the words barely got out.

Doug waved his hand again. "Yeah, I mean, it's so—adolescent. You should spend your time doing more, like, adult things. Things that are important."

Lynn doesn't get angry all that often. When she does, it isn't pretty. "Things that YOU think are important, isn't that what you mean?"

Doug was caught off guard that Lynn, who rarely raises her voice, was actually yelling. He apparently decided that the best course of action was to yell back. "Well, maybe I have a better idea of what's really important than you do recently!"

Things went downhill from there, eventually culminating in Doug pulling the car onto the shoulder so that they could scream at each other without putting the rest of the New Jersey Turnpike at risk of a car accident. Despite all the yelling, there was no real resolution. Doug felt she should give up both the fandom and the research. After a few more weeks of soul searching (and more than a little additional drama), Lynn felt that she should give up Doug.

Talk about outcomes we never saw coming when we started this journey.

Kathy was struggling with family crises of her own. Her daughter was in the difficult process of applying to colleges and needed her mother there, right there, when the stress of the situation got to be too much for her. And Kathy wasn't there. The resentment grew on one side and the abject guilt grew on the other. Every time she went off to another convention "to do research" she felt as if she might as well have been skywriting a message to her daughter that said "I don't care about you." Of course she did care, but it seemed like nothing she could say would outweigh her actions. Her husband was supportive, even encouraging, but she also knew that her frequent absences from home were a strain on him as well. She wondered when he would eventually get fed up with "holding down the fort." And then there was the money. Kathy was still working part time then, one child was recently out of college, and another was about to go. Finances were tight. To compensate, Kathy had taken on teaching an additional course and the task of advising freshmen. The more she advised, the more money she would be given toward research. That money covered her expenses at conventions, but it also meant that much more work. She was exhausted most of the time and still feeling guilty. And while Lynn was giving up Doug, Kathy was beginning to pull back from the one thing that had kept her going in the past. Fandom.

To make things even more complicated, our other juggling act was also becoming increasingly difficult—walking the fine line between fangirl and researcher/insider. We escaped the pressure temporarily for one blissful weekend that fall, when we went to yet another *Supernatural* convention. This one was quite different from the ones we'd been to before. For one thing, it had no celebrities. No photo ops, no autograph sessions, no actor Q&As. Wincon, short for Winchester Writers Convention, was just for fans. Fangirls, to be exact. The same kind of fangirls we were—in academic terms, "participatory fans." The ones who made fanvids, created fanart, posted thoughtful analysis of plot and character, and wrote fanfiction. Fans who didn't just watch *Supernatural* but joined in.

At this point, we were so immersed in the "legitimate" endeavor of writing a book on fandom that we were in danger of losing what had brought us to fandom in the first place—the sense of community, the permission to be real, the pursuit of pleasure and exploration and just plain FUN. We were so busy writing the book that Kathy was no longer writing fanfiction, and Lynn was managing it only occasionally. We sorely needed just to be fangirls again—and Wincon was the perfect place to do just that. Luckily for us, Wincon was also nearby that year—in between our residences on the outskirts of Baltimore. We already knew many of the women who came together at Wincon as their online alter egos but had never met them in real life. Our LJ friend Sarah flew in from California, and we all stayed at Kathy's house. This left us lots of time to squee about Sam and Dean and trade fanfic writing tips and just generally get to know each other. In a way, making friends online lets you get to know someone intimately much sooner than you would face to face—in the safety of the fan community, online, fans share things they wouldn't over dinner. At least not without a lot of blushing and stammering. Through exchanges in comments to each other's fiction, art, and autobiographical posts, we knew each other at a deeper level than many of our real-life friendships. With these women, we didn't hold back. We talked about all those things that we rarely dared to in real life. Stigma, prejudice, misogyny, homophobia. And, of course, sex.

As we drove to the convention hotel, we wondered what it would be like to be face to face with people who had read our most NC-17 rated fanfiction. We'd be lying if we said we weren't nervous—and that we didn't do a fair amount of anticipatory blushing. But the beauty of Wincon was that everyone felt the same way—we were all fanfic readers, most of us writers. Most of us read slash, hurt/comfort, and many of the other shame-inducing genres of fanfiction. Within an hour of arriving at Wincon—for the first time since we'd self-identified as fangirls—we found ourselves shame-free. (Of course, we told no one that we were also academics writing a book on fans—apparently that version of shame was still alive and well.)

At Wincon we allowed our online and real-life selves to merge for the first time. The feeling of wholeness was exhilarating, as fans happily crowded into contests for the best fanvids, attended lively panels on the pros and cons of writing fanfiction imagining the (usually not PG) exploits of actors who are real people, and scribbled down tips for writing better sex scenes. Wincon also offered arts and crafts lessons—this was a gathering of women, so what might be considered "women's work" should surely be included, right? Except at Wincon, the arts and crafts were a bit more subversive than the traditional. For example, a play on fandom's term for an avatar created to ensure anonymity—and frequently start wank—known as a "sockpuppet," was translated into a sockpuppet-making lesson (bring your own socks). This activity culminated in the most irreverent and adult version of "sockpuppet theater" imaginable.

We also made lovely hats. Out of tinfoil.

Recall that "tinhat" is the fandom term for fantasizing two ostensibly straight real people in a decidedly not-straight relationship (*Supernatural*'s version is "J2"—Jared/Jensen). At WinCon, fans took the description literally, grabbing aluminum foil, glue guns, sequins, and sparkles in a make-your-own-tinhat contest. Neither of us won, but we grinned our way through the entire event, cheering on the contestants as they paraded through the hotel conference room, tinhats gleaming. One fan brought her very own Sam and Dean dolls, DIY versions of Andie's by-now-famous Plastic Winchesters. A favorite little girl pastime updated for adults, the dolls were Sam and Dean as variations on Ken (with no Barbie in sight), who quickly ended up in an impressive variety of compromising positions. Dean lost a gun; Sam lost a leg. Fandom, as always, was there to fix them.

Wincon also featured appropriately drunken karaoke and a video (vidding) contest with breathtakingly well done fanvids commenting on serious subjects like homophobia and misogyny on television and much less serious "crack" vids celebrating the epic love story of Sam and Dean in subtext. In a typical mix of fannish interests, it offered a raffle whose proceeds went to charity and a Badfic Idol contest that had people groaning and trying to cover their ears to shut out the read-aloud tales of tentacles, mpreg, and detachable sex organs. There happened to be a World War II veterans convention at the hotel the same weekend, resulting in elderly men with raised eyebrows and a lot of questions as to what all these women of varying ages and nationalities were doing wandering around in their pajamas carrying laptops and why they had no "gentleman companions." One bewildered man asked if we were with an aluminum foil convention.

We had a chance to dress up at WinProm, sing the traditional *Supernatural* songs "Back in Black" and "Carry On My Wayward Son" with fifty other fangirls, and have long conversations about John Winchester's parenting skills with someone you never thought you'd get the chance to meet face to face. WinCon was a place to fangirl other fangirls instead of celebrities. To tell a writer in person that her fanfiction impacted you, changed you, affected you. To hear people tell you the same. At the end of the weekend, physical hugs replaced the virtual hugs that we're all used to giving each other online, accompanied by more than a few real tears. The experience was powerful, both for the lack of shame and for the sense of community. It was as if our online fandom community had been magically brought to life in the real world, without a shred of shame. "I felt like myself for the first time," one fangirl said.

We did too. For the weekend, we forgot about children and partners and even research. It felt damn good.

TEN

. . . . .

Working for the Man

Our honeymoon with the TPTB began in earnest after Comic Con. True to their word, our prospective publishers put us in touch with the editor of *Supernatural Magazine*. Suddenly, instead of writing fanfiction about our favorite show, we were hired to write articles for its "official" magazine. We'd gone from underground, secret, and subversive to sold-at-every-bookstore mainstream. We were legitimate! Our first assignment for *Supernatural Magazine* was covering a convention. Oddly, the magazine had offered no con coverage at all, so we pitched the idea and they agreed. What better way to bring the convention experience to the fans who weren't able to attend? And who better to do it?

Conventions are a rare opportunity to get up close and personal with the actors as well as a chance finally to meet in person the friends you've made online. But conventions are expensive, so the majority of fans never get a chance to go. There's the ticket itself, and who can resist adding in a few photo ops for the chance to sandwich yourself in between the boys? (The only way, alas, actually to experience how tall Jared is or how firm Jensen's shoulders are.) Or an autograph ticket that will allow you to stammer a couple of overly rehearsed compliments and be rewarded with the boys' blinding smiles. Then there's the cost of getting there—which for some fans means flying halfway around the world. Most people also pay to stay at the convention hotel—otherwise they might miss out on Misha Collins grabbing a Starbucks in the lobby. Finally, there's the "stuff": an entire room of stuff, all of it decorated with mouth-watering Winchester boys. If you don't find what you want in the merchandise room, you might not be able to resist bidding in the auction, where fans have been known to bid hundreds or more for an eight-foot Dean-in-a-tux banner. This all adds up to an impressive total. And while the *Supernatural* fandom is composed of fewer teenage girls depending on babysitting money and more professional women taking home paychecks from law firms and libraries and medical practices, many fans don't have the disposable income to shell out a grand or more for a weekend with Jared and Jensen. They do, however, eagerly await every tidbit of information. So we knew that fans were desperately curious to know what goes on at the cons, especially behind the scenes. It was a perfect opportunity for us to share. It was also the perfect opportunity to snag interviews with seven or eight guests, without having to raise a finger. Now that we were "official," the guests would be brought to us. Weren't we special?

We may have been caught up in our own magnificence, but our friends weren't. This was to be another "girls' weekend" with Lana and Kate, and we had good reason to fear that our friendship wouldn't survive the weekend. Lana was responsible for hooking us on *Supernatural* in the first place, but the gulf between us had continued to widen over the past year. There was jealousy (over the time we were spending together more than the fact that we were meeting actors) and disapproval (over the ways we were doing fandom wrong and the fan fiction we wrote) and plenty of misunderstanding all around, because we all continued to follow the rule of "good girls don't disagree, and if they do they sure as hell don't talk about it." On the airport shuttle, we tried to tell ourselves that it would be okay, that we'd be able to "fix" our frayed relationships now that we were all in the same place. We chatted with the other people headed to our hotel, who all turned out to be convention attendees (we'd gotten pretty good at identifying our own kind, even if Kathy still resisted admitting it) from five different states and three different countries.

We arrived on Thursday, the original *Supernatural* broadcast night. The hotel had been prepped to expect an invasion of enthusiastic fangirls, so every television set in the restaurant was tuned to the CW Network, and the bar was once again serving up purple nurples. Lynn wasted no time in ordering one, which the bartender informed us was made with decade-old blackberry brandy. This seemed to be not because it would make the purple nurple better—or purpler—but simply because the hotel had been waiting for something to do with that damn blackberry brandy. Lynn drank it anyway. The hotel restaurant was also in the *Supernatural* spirit, offering special menu items like the Jensen Ackles Filet and the Jared Burger. Although these were the highest-priced entrées on the menu, we had a feeling that more than one fangirl decided this was the closest she'd get to sinking her teeth into Jensen or Jared and took advantage. The bar also offered a tempting Sam-tini or Dean-a-Rita. Sounds silly, but it didn't prevent us from giggling like schoolgirls and making one lewd joke after the other, most of which involved how much of Jared or Jensen we could fit into our mouths at one time or how many of those Sam and Deans (drinks, ahem) we could suck down. Slurp, slurp.

We spent a few hours with Kate, trying to mend fences. It helped that Kate was not really a big *Supernatural* fan herself—she had mostly come along to Chicago to hang out, so our new level of access to the actors didn't inspire any real envy. Kate has always been a different type of fangirl—not only does she jump from fandom to fandom, loving something one day and putting all her collected items for sale on eBay the next, but she has no desire to meet any of the people she is a fan of in person. As we sat in the hotel bar drinking purple nurples, we reminisced about the time we ran into singer Rufus Wainright, then Kate's Number One Crush, at a coffee shop in New Hampshire. We had tickets to his show that night, so Lynn—being Lynn—walked right up to tell him how much we were looking forward to it. When she turned around, expecting Kate to chime in, the sidewalk was empty. Kate—Rufus's Number One Fan—had beat a hasty retreat inside a store, intent on avoiding any contact with the man himself, leaving an incredulous Lynn on her own.

The conversation turned to more memories of shared fannish adventures over the past decade, which reminded us why we became friends in the first place. Nothing could completely remove the awkwardness of us repeatedly disappearing to do interviews instead of hanging out with our friends, but Kate was remarkably understanding. We knew that, if the positions were reversed, we would have been a lot more green-eyed. We still hadn't found an opportunity to talk to Lana, but our conversation with Kate left us hopeful that we'd be able to fix things with her too. As it turned out, we were wrong.

As soon as we left the bar, happily purple-nurpled, we ran into actor Chad Lindberg in the lobby and resumed our double life. Chad stopped to introduce us to his little nephew when a very enthusiastic fangirl, who'd perhaps started sampling the purple nurples at the bar a bit early, walked up and tossed Lynn her camera, announcing that she needed a picture. That wasn't so odd, but her explanation—delivered loudly enough for half the lobby to hear—was. Apparently a friend had just written her some X-rated fanfiction in which Chad was her kept boy. Cue Lynn and Kathy casting a horrified glance at the mother of the little nephew and Lynn taking the picture as fast as she damn well could. Chad, as always, was nothing but gracious, and the fangirl went away happy—and presumably with an illustration for her fanfiction. Chad's nephew, fortunately, was too young to understand the meaning of kept boy, so all was well (except the broken First Rule of Fandom).

Of course, actors don't care about the First Rule, and the inebriated fanfic-illustrating fangirl obviously wasn't feeling constrained by it, so the only ones bothered were us. Up to this point, we'd accepted the norms of fandom as incontrovertible and there for a reason. But the more we interacted with the actors and writers and showrunners and found out that they were pretty okay with fanworks, the more we questioned the ironclad boundaries that fans insisted on keeping around their fannish activities (though not when there were underage nephews standing close by). Was this really just an ugly result of too much fan shame, especially about the racier aspects of fandom? If it really was okay for women to do things that were just for fun—or to lust after hot actors on television—or to write sexy fanfiction— then why couldn't we talk about it?

Perhaps because we had been taught that "objectification" is a dirty word. If a man had walked up to an actress in a hotel lobby and announced that he needed a picture to accompany his porn, we'd be screaming harassment. We had objectified these actors ourselves—lewd jokes, lewder fanfic. We wanted to embrace women turning the tables and celebrating their sexuality, but we were also a bit appalled at what seemed like a crude come-on. Was it that we now knew Chad and therefore could no longer see him as an object? Or was it that the fan's behavior was just rude? We grappled with this for all of ten or fifteen minutes, and then it was time to gather for some serious group objectification as ten fangirls gathered in our hotel room to watch the new *Supernatural* episode. All scruples were tossed aside as soon as Jared took his shirt off. The excitement of a hotel room full of fangirls watching Sam Winchester and Ruby the demon get it on was just about too much to be contained. Oddly, the conversation afterward was more about whether the show had just descended into necrophilia (demons possess dead bodies, so . . .) and less about Jared's biceps. We objectify. And then we watch for the plot.

This was our last purely fangirl moment of the weekend.

The next morning, we got to work. Once again, we endured an impressive array of technical difficulties. Lynn's phone worked only sporadically, leaving her worried about a sick child at home. Our cameras were woefully inadequate for the occasion, and neither of us had had the forethought to acquire something better. (It probably wouldn't have mattered because we're both terrible photographers.) And we had to explain our way into the green room to confused convention volunteers.

"We're doing interviews."

They looked at us, looked at our Gold Pass badges (the clear proof that we were fans), and were having none of it. With the authority of TPTB behind us, though, we insisted in a way that we never would have the year before. Phone calls were made. Feet were impatiently tapped. (We had a job to do, after all!) And finally entrance was granted. Yet from the moment we entered, we felt like imposters. There was still just no way that we should have been allowed in that room. It was the invitation to Jim's house all over again.

Our interview goals were twofold—gather enough information to write an article for the magazine that fans would actually love reading and break the First Rule of Fandom as many times as we could in one weekend. We were still myopically viewing fandom through the prism of fanfiction readers and writers, since that was the fandom niche we happened to live in ourselves. Our goal of wanting to challenge fan shame was still there, but we were determinedly unaware that it was a personal goal too. We *were* those ashamed fans, still struggling toward some kind of legitimacy so that we could stop being ashamed. We asked celebrity after celebrity what they thought of fans. Did they "get" being a fan? Was it something they'd experienced too? This was in part our academic sides asking about the "reciprocal relationship." But it was also our fan side that wanted to know—did these people we were fans of think that *we* were weird? Were they really snickering behind their hands and rolling their eyes every time we turned our backs?

Gabe Tigerman (*Supernatural*'s Andy) was our first interview of the day. He told us that he understood the emotional connection fans have with *Supernatural*. "I think everyone has had an experience of connection with a show at an emotional level, or connecting with the characters emotionally. For me, I was watching *Six Feet Under* at a time when my best friend passed away, and it was like the episodes were speaking to me."

Our experience of *Supernatural*, like that of most fans, was similar to what Gabe was describing. Viewing the show feels intimate—like the characters and themes are speaking just to you (not in a psychotic way, let's be clear about that). Yes, we thought, Gabe definitely gets it. Feeling reassured, we moved along to the riskier First Rule–breaking question: how did he feel about fanworks? After all, Gabe had one in his hand—a fan had just given him a piece of fanart, which he intended to keep.

"I was pretty surprised when I discovered fanfiction." Gabe laughed. "The best man at my wedding happened to Google my name, and the very first thing he ever saw was slash fiction! I'd vaguely heard about this genre, but I never anticipated it being written about me! My buddy emailed me the link and I looked at it on a laptop while at my parents' house, which isn't really the ideal way to discover that."

This had some unanticipated consequences. Reading erotic interludes between himself and actor Chad Lindberg, whom Tigerman had never met, made for an unusual introduction when their paths finally did cross—at a *Supernatural* convention, of course. "I felt like we already knew each other—no, not in the biblical sense! Well okay, maybe exactly like in the biblical sense!"

It didn't stop the two actors from becoming friends or from amusing the fans by playing up their "relationship," scrawling flirty love notes to each other on the 8 by 10 glossies that fans asked them to autograph.

Okay, we thought, first interview down and we'd managed not to knock anything over (other than the poster of Sam and Dean that Creation had thoughtfully provided as a backdrop for our interviews, which kept falling off the wall without any prompting from us). And nobody had changed their minds about this whole magazine interview thing being a good idea and kicked us out! Feeling heartened, we waited for our next interviewee to be led to us, musician Steve Carlson. Although he doesn't actually play anyone on *Supernatural*, that hasn't stopped creative fans from incorporating him into fanfiction, since he's one of Jensen's best friends. What did he think of that (probably quite unexpected) development? Unfortunately for Steve, his mother discovered it before he did.

> She wasn't looking, she's just a proud mom Googling her son, and she stumbled upon it, and it was the first time I had heard anything about it and I was like, this is weird. . . . It's a world that goes on that I don't pay attention to. The only time it kind of bothers me is when it's written from the first person like hey I'm Steve and this is what I did. If you're writing from third person, and that's your thing and you're into that, okay, but I don't like when someone pretends to be me. I think actors are a lot more used to it than musicians.

Obviously Steve had never perused the comms for bands like My Chemical Romance or One Direction. We wisely didn't bring it up. So another vote for "I think it's a little weird but I'm savvy enough not to say that too strongly and I think I'll just leave it to the fans." That was good enough for us—we put it into the "kinda sorta" validation category. With a few interviews under our belts, we felt secure that we had some great information for our article. What we didn't have were photos.

In one of those "ask and ye shall receive moments" that happen all the time in movies and never in real life, Kathy spotted the answer to our problem.

"Look!!"

"At?"

"There!"

Yeah, Kathy tends to be a woman of few words, but this was ridiculous. She grabbed Lynn by the shoulders and turned her in the direction of "there," which was exactly where photographer Lizz Sisson was standing. A Chicago local, Lizz had come by to hang out with her friend, Creation photographer Chris. We had other plans for her. We pulled some strings (us—strings?) and got her a press pass. She was our new official photographer.

With that taken care of, it was time to be fangirls again. We found Kate and Lana and got a chilly reception. Kate seemed okay with the awkward transition, but clearly Lana was still unhappy with us. Dinner with Kate, Lana, and two of Lana's friends, whom she seemed to have brought along to avoid talking to us at all, was almost subzero. We wanted to share some of the amusing things we'd learned in our interviews, but we'd learned our lesson at last year's con when we had offended by talking too much. The fear of sounding like we were bragging, or worse, being coded as BNFs (and hated for it), kept us quiet. It also left us with little to say, since most obvious topics of conversation now seemed out of bounds. The meal was marked by deep silences and purposeful chewing.

Later that night, Creation threw its first karaoke party in the hotel bar. This was supposed to be a chance for fans and actors to "mingle," but at that point Creation's definition of mingling entailed escorting actors into and out of the bar at appropriate intervals. The celebrity guests eventually decided that they were old enough to take care of themselves, broke free from the constraints, played pool while fans knocked out renditions of *Supernatural* traditions like AC/DC's "Back in Black," and occasionally took the mike themselves. It was the beginning of what would eventually become a *Supernatural* con tradition. We had headed to the bar hoping that hanging out and watching other people make fools of themselves while consuming large amounts of alcohol might somehow ease the tensions of the day. If anything, it seemed to make things worse. Lana was not amused, and by this time Kathy and Lynn were distraught. We tried to tell ourselves that we could still repair our relationship with Lana, but that was looking more and more doubtful. In fact, the Chicago convention would be the last time Lana spoke to us.

Six hours later, unable to sleep, Kathy was sitting in the hall outside the green room sobbing into her cell phone, seeking solace and sanity from her husband, who could only lend a sympathetic ear and a virtual shoulder to cry on. A friendship was dying in front of her, and there seemed to be nothing she could do to salvage it.

Four hours after that, we were walking into the green room for our first interview of the day.

Having a photographer set up to shoot the interviews made us feel more "official," but we still had to fight off waves of imposter syndrome even as we reminded ourselves that in fact we were not. This was the first convention for actress Samantha Smith, who played Sam and Dean's mother, Mary.

"It's a unique experience to walk into a room of that many people and not have to win them over." She laughed. "They seem very impressed by how maternal Mary is. Which is flattering to me because that's what she's

Samantha Smith takes her place on the couch. Courtesy of Elizabeth Sisson.

supposed to be. Mary becomes iconic in the boys' life as a symbol of good in all the evil they see."

Samantha's understanding of fandom was colored by her experience of being a fangirl herself. She understood what fans valued about the show and why they gave her character such importance. She also understood why female characters who were introduced as potential love interests were not always welcomed—not out of misogyny, but as fans not wanting anyone to disrupt the primary relationship between Sam and Dean. It was fairly easy for us to relate to her on both counts, affording a different sort of validation.

This was also the first convention for Charles Malik Whitfield, who played FBI agent Victor Henrikson, one of the first recurring African American characters on the show. He told us that he felt comfortable right away. Being at the convention, he said, seemed like hanging out with family. "Taking on a character, it becomes a very intimate and passionate part of you, and it's a lot of fun to interact with fans and get their perspective on things."

Samantha and Malik had both worried a bit about fandom knowing more about their characters than they did. Malik didn't waste time asking just anyone what he should expect—he went right to the experts. Jared and Jensen.

"I asked the guys what to expect—they said you're going to have a lot of fun and you'll meet people who know more about your character than you do. And it's true—they can tell you down to exactly what was *behind* you in a scene!"

Damn straight. Fans are nothing if not observant. But, we wondered, did Malik's surprise about just how much detail fans know translate into some derision? Was this a Trekkies moment, when the audience goes wide-eyed over a fan's obsession with the stitching on his Star Fleet uniform?

Malik admitted that he was surprised by the singular passion of *Supernatural* fans.

> Everything counts. They are not passive! I was very taken aback and grateful about the warm response to the character. I remember I was shooting [the film] *Notorious* in New York City, and someone came up to me and asked, "Are you coming back?" I was like "What?" They meant, of course, *Supernatural*! It's such a blessing. I love the way the fans rock out with the show. A lot of shows get following and numbers, but the interactiveness of this show, that connection is huge, and it's head and shoulders beyond others. A friend of mine called me up after I was on *Supernatural* and was like, "What are you doing on *my* show?" and I was like, "Hey, I thought we were friends! Could you say congratulations, or nice work!?" I think the minute people see the show, it really captivates a lot of people. The story is great, the guys are absolutely dead on. Jensen and Jared are just great. Not only great actors, but great chemistry with each other. That is inspiring.

The choice of words—"my show"—wasn't an anomaly. When you fan something hard, it does become yours. Part of your identity, your support network, your recreational activity, your fantasy fodder. Malik clearly got it—and was happy about it, instead of critical. Chalk up another notch in the validation column. And speaking of chemistry (and trying to work our way around to the fanfic question), we commented on the chemistry between Henrikson and the boys, especially Dean.

"I think the dynamic Jensen and I have, which is fun that we can capture, is we are both 'boy's boys,'" Malik said. "He's a wonderful guy to be around,

and he's accessible. They both are, and that allows for the possibility of connection and lends to the storytelling."

Okay, so that didn't really answer the fanfiction question. We decided to
ask more directly.

> Lynn: "Fans write a lot of fanfiction, and a lot of it pairs characters. People
> have paired the characters of Dean and Henrikson."
>
> Malik (apparently not paying close enough attention): "Mm hmm."
>
> Lynn (giving up on subtle): "As a—as a romantic pair."
>
> Malik: "Uh huh. Wait. WHAT?! Was it the way we cuddled, or what? They say
> what?? I'm confused. What's next? Pair me with Lilith?"
>
> Lynn: "No, it's mostly guy-guy."
>
> Malik (quickly recovering his sense of humor): "Well, if it had to happen,
> they should get married!" He laughed then shook his head. "I'm going to
> have to talk to Dean—I don't know if we can hang out anymore."

One of our goals was to talk to the creative side about the things that fans
constantly debate but you hardly ever hear discussed openly in interviews.
We asked Malik about the strong reaction fans had to an African American
character being killed. It's a topic that Malik is passionate about; he was
working on a documentary about black men in America. He knew about
fandom's reaction to Henrikson's death and felt it contributed something
important to real-world change—if only by making TPTB more aware of
the issue.

"People were very not happy, and I thought, that's good. Any time that
people express themselves, it will change the format in which TV is done.
Take nothing away from the execs, but that doesn't mean they get it right all
the time," he said. "What's great is when you have that interactiveness and
response because it says maybe we're onto something and let's listen to the
response so we can make a show that can stay around. I think it's so cool,
anything is possible with the *Supernatural* fans."

Malik's recognition of fandom as an influential voice in societal discussions of race, gender, and sexuality was about as validating as it gets.

Richard Speight Jr. was up next on our couch (Lynn was starting to think
of it that way, perhaps because psychologists expect that sort of thing in
their offices in any case). This was Richard's first convention, but he was

already fascinated by the unusually close relationship between *Supernatural* and its fans, even if at first he'd been sure they wouldn't give a damn about a guy who just did a few guest shots.

> It was different than what I expected. Having never been to a convention, basically what I know about conventions is what you see on TV—like Trekkies. So when I was first asked to go to this, my response was I've only been on the show twice, no one's going to know who I am! I'm not a celebrity, I'm a working-class actor. My biggest fear was showing up and having nobody recognize me and just feeling like the biggest jerk. I had this image of me sitting under a banner that said like "Meet Richard Speight Jr." and people just walking by. I would be trying to hand out my autograph and people would just be like, no it's okay. I'm fascinated by this culture because it's so new to me. I'm so glad I came to this because I was so nervous the fans would feel ripped off, like I was the crappy opening act. We [actors] don't do this for a living for people not to watch our work. If people watch and like it, it's great to have a venue like this with people who like and want to talk about it.

Richard also got why the show had attracted such a passionate fan base.

"This show isn't about killing demons. It's about relationship—an intricate, emotional framework upon which you can hang anything. I think that's the key and what attracts people to the story."

When we eventually got to the fanfiction question, Richard immediately wanted to know why there's no fanfic for his character, the Trickster, a capricious but powerful god. He sounded a little hurt about the slight.

"Maybe it's too easy—the Trickster would just think of it and make it happen, and that's not fun from the let's look at the alternate universe point of view. The Trickster could make people do it against their will."

Richard had essentially come up with the oft-used fanfic trope of "the curse/witch/demon/sex pollen made me do it." No wonder he fits in well with this fandom. (He would later welcome the writing of a lot of fanfiction about his character when the Trickster was revealed to be the archangel Gabriel.) Our allotted interview time was over, but Richard wanted to keep talking, so we headed over to the hotel restaurant to continue over dinner. Lizz joined us and proved herself much better at herding guests and fending off fans than we were. Richard was stopped repeatedly by fans who wanted a photo or an autograph, and we certainly weren't going to stand

Richard Speight Jr. stops to make a few dreams come true. Courtesy of Elizabeth Sisson.

in the way of fan dreams coming true. Without Lizz's gentle but persistent "We have to move along now," it's unlikely that we would have made it to dinner.

Richard scanned the menu. No Jared Burgers for him. "I can't eat Jared." He smirked, and we were right back to talking about slash. We did our best to explain the fascination, coming up with various cerebral and psychological explanations. Richard's brow remained furrowed in confusion. Finally we threw our hands up.

"Two women together. Sexy?"

Richard nodded.

We just let that hang there for a moment and then the lightbulb went off. "Oh! I get it now."

On Saturday night the Gold Ticket holders headed downstairs for the traditional Creation dessert party. As always, the event lived up to its "speed dating with the stars" reputation, with guests moving between tables so quickly that their handlers advised them not even to sit down. Our table responded by politely rising to our feet every time a guest came over—if they can't sit, well damn it, neither will we! While fans were enjoying a few minutes with the celebrities, they were also scoping out the room where Jared and Jensen would appear the next morning. Which is the best table to be able to see the boys? How early in the morning is early enough to get in line, and how important is sleep anyway? As it turns out, for many sleep wasn't a consideration at all, and "early enough" meant getting on line for breakfast before the dessert party even ended.

Creation had attempted to discourage fans from having sleep-outs (and instituted a different system of preselected tables for the breakfast at upcoming cons), but we weren't surprised that more than a few intrepid people decided to make a night of it. (Fans just love to subvert authority—ask any academic!) By the time we left the dessert party at midnight, twenty or thirty fans were already lining the hallway. Most were in pjs and slippers, propped up on pillows or curled under blankets. At the head of the line was a multigenerational group from Maryland—two sisters, their mother, and one of their daughters, united by their love of *Supernatural*. Another fan was celebrating her sixteenth birthday by sleeping in a hallway, time well spent as far as she was concerned. Nobody in line disagreed with her. The hotel hallway soon became a *Supernatural* slumber party. Throughout the night people came and went in shifts so that each could grab a few hours of sleep. Some had laptops, and small groups gathered round to watch *Supernatural* episodes or read fanfic. Still others talked long into the night, getting to know fellow fans from around the world who were crazy enough to give up sleep for a chance to sit closer to Jared and Jensen. Chad Lindberg, whom we'd interviewed earlier that day, walked down the hallway at 1:00 A.M., wide eyed at the sight of fans camping out. He stopped abruptly when he got to us.

"What are you doing here?"

We immediately felt outed—this time, as fangirls.

"Research," Kathy offered immediately.

"It's our job," Lynn added.

As much as we kept talking about how fans shouldn't be ashamed of being fans, that's exactly what we were suddenly feeling. Would Chad still take us seriously if he knew that we were also there to make sure we got the best seats as close as possible to his co-stars? Would anyone? The vague sense of shame and fear made us instantly defensive.

Chad just nodded, apparently finding our explanation plausible. We breathed a sigh of relief.

Once the sun came up, we joined the rest of the ticket holders in the race for the best table, inhaled a little bit of breakfast, then spun our chairs around to wait impatiently. Half an hour later, the crowd burst into applause as the boys took the stage. You got the feeling that if Jared and Jensen had stumbled in and passed out on the stage for their allotted thirty minutes, the room full of fans would happily have watched them sleep. Instead, they entertained with their customary mix of flirty banter and behind-the-scenes tales. Breakfast with the Boys was over far too soon, but the day had just begun, and the boys' schedules were packed. Photo ops were first, including individual ones with Jared and Jensen, and the provocatively named "J & J Sandwich," which invited fans to squeeze in between the boys. This, as you might imagine, isn't a hardship.

We got permission to have our photo (well, Lynn's photo) taken last, so that we could have some special shots done for the magazine article and the book. When it was our turn in the photo-op room, Lynn was so focused on staying in "professional" mode that she cut off Jensen's attempt at a hug with a foolishly formal introduction and a handshake instead. Kathy resolved to make Lynn suffer horribly for this later. Lynn understood completely.

We explained that we needed the boys to pose for photos for the article and the book. Lynn, always thinking about what she—errrr, fans—would want, suggested that they pose "as if you really like each other." Jensen mock scowled a "nawww, we don't wanna do that." In response Lynn challenged, "Well then what do YOU want to do?" Kathy helpfully suggested that since they're actors, they should just . . . well, act! So they did. Luckily, the result turned out really freaking hot.

Lynn isn't one to be deterred from her agenda, however. She countered with "Okay fine, now you have to do what I want." The boys, interpreting that with no difficulty at all for some reason, slung their arms around each other's broad shoulders with big grins on their handsome faces. Lynn beamed.

After the photo ops, the boys headed to the stage for their Q&As. Fans, many of them still keyed up from their up close and personal photo-op experience, were easily overwhelmed with emotion. One fan walked up to the

Jared and Jensen throw down. Fangirls heat up. Courtesy of Christopher Schmelke.

microphone to ask Jared a question and froze, too overcome to speak. After several unsuccessful tries, she gave up and turned to go back to her seat, tearful. Jared immediately hopped off the stage to give her a hug, while the audience broke out into a chorus of "Awwwww."

Jared got the gold star for tough question of the day when a fan asked what it feels like for Sam to be a necrophiliac (referring to his dalliance with demon Ruby, who was at the time possessing a dead girl), and he fielded the rather unexpected question with sensitivity while Jensen hovered protectively. Fans, also in full protective mode, were just as displeased with the fan's choice of question. Icons online the next day proclaimed: "Dear wanky fan who asked about necrophilia at Creation Con, You have been voted out of the fandom." The specter of the Flying Fangirl still loomed large.

The chemistry between the boys was much in evidence—to the fans' delight. Jensen stole Jared's beanie and threatened to toss it to the eagerly waiting fans. The teasing was accompanied by the kind of heated looks that make fangirls melt, especially when Jared started pleading. Jensen (as usual) relented. When someone asked what their biggest fears were, Jensen looked pointedly at Jared and flexed his bicep, suggesting that what Jared was afraid of was HIM. Jared returned, "Yeah, I'm scared of having little arms one day." Another fan asked if there would ever be a *Gilmore Girls* (Jared's former television show) movie. Jensen immediately squealed like a fangirl and squeaked, "Oh, yes please!" Perhaps the best J2 moment for fans came when someone asked if they would still be friends after the show ended. "No," they said in unison. "Of course not," said Jensen. "I'mma delete him from my phone," said Jared. "Change the locks," said Jensen. "Wait, it's my house!" protested Jared, and the fans, having been reminded of the fandom miracle of the boys living together, broke into a ballroom-size squee of delight. Jared made sure to sign the giant banner hanging behind them directly over the picture of Jensen. On his crotch.

Jensen also got some interesting questions. "What would you be if you weren't an actor?" As Jensen started to go through the choices—fisherman maybe, not good enough to be a pro athlete, sports therapy—a suggestion rang out from the back of the packed ballroom. "Stripper!"

Jensen barely missed a beat. "Or a stripper," he conceded.

The last responsibility of the day for Jared and Jensen was autographs. They were in serious danger of missing the final flight back to Vancouver, and the frantic Creation staff was in the process of freaking out. The boys, however, still managed to be their usual friendly and accommodating selves. No matter what fans asked them to do. One fan had the innovative idea to give the boys pictures of each other to sign. Jared's handler, understandably confused, said "wrong picture," but the fan told Jared to go ahead and "draw all over it." Jared's face lit up like a five-year-old's as he proclaimed that "awesome" and proceeded to go to town, blacking out some of Jensen's notoriously perfect white teeth and giving him silver hair. And a booger. And a thought bubble proclaiming "I'm dumb." Jensen gave Jared a goatee, three ear piercings, silver lipstick, eyeliner, and a beauty mark. He then drew a little stick figure of himself to the side, shooting a tiny rifle at emo!Jared's cheek.

At the end of the day, Lynn collapsed and Kathy went to pick up our photos from Chris—only to find that they had been stolen. By Jared and Jensen. The boys apparently liked the pictures so much that they took our prints with them back to Vancouver.

We flew home feeling accomplished. We'd done our jobs for the magazine and for our own book. Or so we thought. Even though we were "working for the man," we were asking questions that "the man" didn't particularly like. When we sent the article to the magazine, they changed the title to "Hero Worship," thus also changing the entire point of the article and once again casting fans as too invested. Odd for a fan magazine, we thought. But they were paying us, and the change was nuance rather than substance, so we accepted it, not realizing that lines were even then being drawn between allowable and not allowable. Or that we were breaking them.

ELEVEN

. . . . .

The Sweet Spot

For reasons that we'll never really be sure of, Warner Brothers liked us very much that December. So much, in fact, that they offered us a set visit. Could we be on a plane and in Vancouver in a week? Was that a rhetorical question? Screw the end of the semester, forget grading finals, never mind that we were both in the thick of holiday hell. We knew this was going to be our one and only chance and we were taking it.

On the flight to Canada we alternated between composing the all-important questions for Jared and Jensen and just stopping to stare at each other and ask "Is this really happening?" After two years of dreaming about interviewing them, and asking everyone we came in contact with for help (and being put off each and every time), we were realizing our fondest academic—and fannish—wish.

It was snowing when we got to Vancouver. Our first time in Vancouver we never really made it into the city, only dimly aware of mountains and bodies of water nearby because we had seen them from the airplane as we landed. This time we were plopped into one of the posher hotels in the middle of the city, a short walk from the harbor with a view of those now snow-topped mountains. The city outside was lovely and inviting, but we did not budge. Instead, we settled into the hotel and waited for the call from the studio.

It came with alarm bells. Literally.

"You want us to look for what kind of van? Where??" Lynn shouted into her phone, trying to make herself heard over the fire alarms sounding in the background on the *Supernatural* set. "Blah blah blah . . . damn Atmo smoke they use all the time . . . blah blah," Jen, the production assistant who had been assigned the task of shepherding us around the set, yelled back.

"Wait! What kind of van? Where??" Lynn repeated, already catastrophizing about us somehow missing it when it came to get us.

"Wait in the lobby," Jen yelled back, alarms still blaring. "And the van is red. Well, more like cranberry."

"Got it," Lynn answered triumphantly. "A cranberry van! We'll be ready!"

And oh boy, were we.

We gathered notebooks and audio recorders and what little sense of inner calm we could muster and went downstairs to await the cranberry-colored set van. Our driver, RG, gave us a tour of Vancouver on the way to the studios, telling us about the history, the local economy, and the upcoming Olympics. And his love of Payday candy bars. Jen and RG set the tone for a day that turned out to be literally too good to be true. When we arrived on set, things were already running late, which is par for the course on a Friday (Jared jokingly referred to it as "Fraturday," since the night often doesn't end until the next day has technically begun). We assumed that we'd be on set for an hour or two, and the fact that they were running late seemed to be the perfect excuse for getting us in and out of there in record time. Oh well, we thought. At least we're here. This is a dream come true no matter how short the visit.

We still felt like imposters, but this time we were imposters with our own PA! Jen took us around the production office first, where we met Jason Fischer and Anita Truelove, the team who kept the show going and also the front line in dealing with the fans. The office itself was filled with evidence of the fandom's creativity—the walls papered with the fans' postcards and artwork. A fan-made quilt hung in the conference room, and a fan-made *Supernatural* chess set sat on the table. Even the Christmas tree was decorated entirely with fan gifts, crowned by the Lilith-head-on-a-plate that we saw a fan give to the boys at the Chicago convention the month before. It made a perfect tree topper.

After a while, Jen handed us off to Greg, another PA, who gave us a tour of each of the three cavernous sound stages used to film the show. He let us wander around the area where they keep old props, row after row of everything and anything that appeared on film—furniture, clocks, dishes, pictures—while sharing fan stories with us. Most impressive was a fan who pretended to be a PA to get on the set and "worked" for half a day before

anyone realized she wasn't supposed to be there. Greg expressed his grudg-
ing admiration.

"She'll probably go far in life, I'm not gonna lie! I was probably one of
those kids, to be honest, so I can understand." He laughed.

We followed this up by asking more questions about those "wacky" fans.
Did they ever send anything odd?

"Fans know Jared likes candy, so they bring candy a lot. And we get some
great art. Then we get some notes, maybe from people who don't speak English and they just get right to it. Like 'I was walking my dog this morning
and I realized I really love Jared.' We get a lot of rambling ones. I think they
love the show because they feel like they connect with the characters—so
you ramble to your friends, and they think they know these characters so
they ramble to them too," Greg told us, neatly summing up "parasocial
relationships," but with far less pathology.

One thing did puzzle him. "When fans do stumble upon the set and
spend all day waiting to see the boys," Greg said, "they'll be going on and
on all day about what they'll say, and then when the boys actually do come
by, the fans will be absolutely speechless!"

We nodded politely, thinking about our own dumbstruck reactions to celebrity encounters.

"So the boys leave." Greg laughed. "And I'm like, you could have said
'Hi!'—it's like one word, two letters. One syllable."

Greg also introduced us to the third lead on *Supernatural*, the 1967 Chevy
Impala. Or, as fans call her, the Metallicar. This car is far more than just a
car. It is the third star of the show. It represents home to Sam and Dean,
who were raised on the road. It represents a link to their father, who gave it
to Dean when he was old enough to be considered a man. Dean's love for
the car is really his love for his family. When the car is broken, no matter
how broken, Dean will fix it because that's what you do for family. It's also
easier to fix a car than it is to fix a broken life or in some cases your broken
brother. Fans' love for the car represents their own understanding of the
Impala as the emotional core of the brothers' lives. So we approached the
car like something of a shrine, while Greg casually opened its doors and
urged us to climb on in. We hesitated. We were not worthy! He finally posed
us in front of the Impala and took a photo, though we were still having
trouble closing our mouths enough to smile. Seeing how much we obvi-

ously fangirled the Impala, Greg went off to get Johnny, the show's Impala wrangler. He appeared within minutes and ran down the stats for us, beaming like a proud papa.

"The Impala rated no. 8, on most popular television and film cars," Johnny told us, "right after the Dukes of Hazzard car. We have eight in total—two are wrecked, we have one we use for parts, we have one in stage 3 that we can pull apart and take the front end off, and another you can take the back seat out so you can film the front seat from back there. And we have a spare one in case something goes wrong with one of the four main players. We have two stunt cars and two hero cars. Last year they sold the dad's truck [to a fan]—I took them around when they came to buy it and took all the foam out of it where the handguns were, because I was like Oh my God, she's gonna drive it across the border to Dallas!!"

"That's right, we got to see it in Dallas," Kathy offered. She wisely didn't share the story of Lynn's ungainly scramble into the front seat.

We fussed over the Impala a little more, and then Johnny asked, "Have you seen [production designer] Jerry Wanek's work, of all the set dec?"

We shook our heads, still overcome by how nice everyone was being to us.

"Rolling!" boomed through the studio, and we all fell quiet, the two of us still grinning stupidly every time it happened. When they called cut, Johnny went on.

"Oh, you should see it. You have to see it. Hang on, let me go get him."

By now we were cluing into the fact that these were not isolated cases of people being nice to us. Not that we understood what was going on, but we knew that we were not important enough to interrupt Jerry Wanek's day or anyone else's. And yet, again and again, that's exactly what happened. Jerry Wanek came down to meet us, offering more of the kind of detailed inside information that fans are ravenous for and excited to share his contribution to making *Supernatural*. We were transfixed.

"The first season they wanted us to make a deal with Motel 6," Jerry confided, "and I said, you know, these boys are always on the road, and anyone who's traveled the back roads of America, they've stayed at these cheesy little places with a lot of character. Those kind of places are dying out, and we have an opportunity to make that here. If you do Motel 6, it's gonna have to look the same every week. So I talked them out of that."

Another case of studios not "getting it" we thought to ourselves. How does Hollywood stay afloat with so many people making so many bad decisions?

"And then we started pushing these theme motels," Jerry continued, "these different ones, where we like pick out the state bird and say okay, this is gonna be the Bluejay Motel. So we usually take the state, and start with anything interesting about the state. Sometimes we'll have these screens, and they'll have something in them to do with the plot—like in the episode 'Salvation,' there are crosses embedded in the screens in the motel. It just looks like a very interesting geometric, but if you study it, there's a cross in there. And if you look at this one closely, there are skeleton keys there crossed."

We examined the screen he showed us and assured him that fans sometimes really DO look that closely.

"Oh yeah, they do!" Jerry agreed. "They can freeze it and study it. We had one with fish and bobbers 'cause that was in Minnesota and we had it as ice fishing. The mud flap girls was a cool one too—it's getting a little harder, we've done like forty motels."

"So is the pressure on now to top yourself with each new motel set?" Kathy asked.

Jerry nodded.

The first edict for us is like different is just different. So if we're gonna do one like the bowling pin one, another Wisconsin flashback, bowling is big there so we did a screen of bowling pins and balls—but it has to work with everything else in that room. There were black and white pictures of guys bowling on the walls, because being different and getting it wrong is just awful. Even in the room they're shooting in now [for the episode "Sex and Violence"], the palette in there is kinda off—grandmotherly colors, but they have to play with each other and make sense. I think the fans look more closely in this show because there's a lot of symbolism inherent in the show, so fans try to figure out what's coming up.

"Foreshadowing!" we said cleverly.

"Exactly, so we toy with that a little bit. We do that within an episode too, I'll throw a little bone out there, see if they pick up on it before the end of the show. They're pretty good."

That we are. We were probably standing there looking thoroughly entranced, in some kind of fangirl euphoria to be getting all this behind the scenes information about the making of the show. Jerry didn't seem to mind—in fact, he seemed to understand.

"Have you been up to the art department? Because we have like a museum of the screens up there. Come on, we'll go up and you'll meet Lee-Anne [Elaschuk], she does all the postcards. Every motel has their own postcards. And she'll write some funny little stuff like 'meet at Dan's Lounge' and show some sleazy thing there."

We nodded. Did we ever! The office dividers between cubicles in the art department are actually made of the tacky motel room dividers from the show. Brilliant!

"Also this is like fun for the crew. It's like an art opening for me—I watch the crew walk in and their reaction, and I'm like oh no, they didn't get it, I'm gonna have to go a little bit farther. So now it's like every motel, we won't let them see it beforehand," Lee-Anne said.

Jerry showed us a red and black divider for the current episode, with lion heads. "And we had the wallpaper handmade to mirror that. The red and black is a bold statement, and we have the color of the walls, the bedspreads, the floor, lamps—but you have to be aware of how it all ties together."

We told Jerry that one of the things we'd learned from visiting the set was the level of detail that all the crew put into making the show. The wallpaper in the motel set we were on earlier in the day was actually velvet flocked! (Yes, we touched it—we are still children, even on the *Supernatural* set.) We already knew how much fans appreciate detail, but we didn't realize that the crew felt just as strongly.

"I'm really glad about that," Jerry said. "Every episode is eight days, so that's all you get. This year so far, we've built eighty different sets. Have you been in Bobby's fallout shelter? That's on stage 3. We figured it was an old silo on the junkyard that Bobby flipped and cut a hole in it. Because, you know, it had to be iron."

Of course, we nodded. Keeps out ghosts and demons. Jerry was kind enough to share with us two of the set dec books, which reside on our coffee tables. They are, frankly, breathtaking. He added that it was too bad that exec producer and director Kim Manners wasn't there that day, since he had a lot of fan stories. We'll always be sad that we didn't get a chance to meet Kim that day—little did we know we wouldn't get another opportunity. Before we left the art department, we made the rounds to meet the rest of Jerry's miracle workers. Maryanne Liu is the artist behind Dean Winchester's favorite magazine, *Busty Asian Beauties*, a description that she also proudly personifies. We admired the evidence of her work decorating the back wall of her cubicle.

"I designed the tattoo the boys have," she told us. "And I worked on *Dark Angel* too, and that cave painting. And one day this guy came up to me on set and showed me he'd put that tattoo on his arm, this giant tattoo of that cave painting! I was like, oh my God."

We assured her that the protection tattoo she designed for Sam and Dean also looks really nice tattooed on many fans.

"It fascinates me, to do this research," Maryanne said, "because you can't really fake it. As a designer, I have to base it on something real, otherwise there's no guts. We have to deal with copyright issues constantly. If it's more than 100 years old, we're okay, but we clear everything and we're careful about that. So we draw a lot ourselves. Lee-Anne and I do the beer labels—and it makes us feel really good that the fans notice so much."

The art department, by the way, is hardly a place of quiet solemn creativity. The afternoon we were there, everyone was accusing everyone else of stringing up a sock monkey currently hanging by his neck between cubicles with his mouth duct-taped. Poor "Shock Monkey." Nobody would own up to it.

Lee-Anne Elaschuk showed off the postcards that decorated the back of her cubicle, all of which had been used in the show when the boys stay in those seedy motels. "I don't know how it got started," she told us, "but we try to put little things in the rooms that make it look more believable. So I'll make brochures or 'Do Not Disturb' signs. Like Maryanne was saying, a lot of the stuff that we do doesn't get seen."

That's what they think! What passed in the blink of an eye before can now be screen-capped, after all.

Lee-Anne also told us her favorite fan story, which turned out to be about a fan we already knew—Andie of Plastic Winchester Theater fame. Apparently the art department was so taken by her talent that they invited her to the set so that they could admire her plastic boys in person. We were positively gleeful at the warm reciprocal relationship that the show has developed with fans.

Eventually Greg had to go do some work that was more important than escorting some writers around the set, so he took us to Carmelita, one of the props buyers for the show, and said good-bye. We wandered through the props rooms, dodging an inflatable sex doll hanging from the ceiling and almost bumping into a demented looking baby doll sitting on the shelf alongside the giant bins of salt (four different kinds). Typical paraphernalia for demon hunters. And then there was the beer—lots of beer. There's no product placement on the show, so the art department buys 0.5 beer and then designs labels to reflect the "local brews" for each town the boys find themselves in. Part of Carmelita's job is to keep everything neatly labeled and ready to grab. We wished our houses were half as organized!

After some more wandering, we joined Jen the PA and other crew

Everything the Winchesters need is in the prop closet. And then some. Courtesy of Lynn Zubernis.

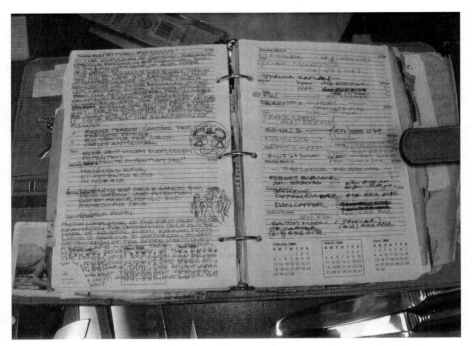

John Winchester's journal is entirely handwritten by a single crew member.
Courtesy of Lynn Zubernis.

members for lunch, taking a moment to giggle at the menu board—someone had drawn a heart and "Da Boyz" in the top right hand corner. Awwww.
Then we returned to the set, where filming had resumed on the episode
"Sex and Violence." Once again, we were taken care of in ways we're completely unused to. PA Molly brought us copies of the sides (the scripted
scenes for that day) and headsets so we could read along and listen, and they
made sure we knew where craft services was in case we got hungry. The
first scene they were shooting was a closed set, because the actress playing
the siren was in her underwear. This was no problem for us, since Jared
and Jensen weren't there anyway. After hearing several takes, we had the
scene memorized, mouthing along with the breathy "baby, bash her head
in, do it for me" and then giggling.

After a dozen or so takes and a few bathroom breaks (for Lynn, of course),
they were rearranging the set for the next scene, this one to take place in

a jail holding cell. With Jared and Jensen. Cue a bad case of nerves for us. It's not every day you get to have the dream of a lifetime come true! Kathy juggled her notes and recorder. Lynn ran to the bathroom again.

"Is this really happening?" we asked each other again and again.

The studio had let the boys know that we were on set and scheduled to interview them and that we were writing a book on the *Supernatural* fandom. In fact, everyone knew—because it was printed right on the sides! However, everyone also warned us that we shouldn't take it personally if Jared and Jensen didn't know who we were. After all, they get interviewed all the time. We nodded. As if they would know us, we thought! So we were not at all surprised when the boys—all dressed up in suits and ties (oh our wildly thumping fangirl hearts!)—walked right by us and went to work. They were filming a scene where Dean and Sam interrogate the siren's latest victim in a jail's holding room. Between takes, the boys chatted amiably with the guest actor, goofing off to put him at ease before he had to tackle an emotional scene. They commiserated with him about the evils of having to wear an ugly orange prison jumpsuit, which he was currently sporting (and which Sam and Dean had to don in the episode "Folsom Prison Blues"). Jensen shook his head, shuddering at what a pain it was.

"You looked good in that jumpsuit," Jared said, leering.

Jensen just shook his head again.

"You look good in nothing too," Jared persisted.

The fanfiction was writing itself in our heads as they spoke.

Jensen was saved from further teasing by the director calling for the next take, but the guest actor was visibly more relaxed, the edge taken off. We sat grinning our fangirl heads off under our jaunty tinhats.

They did a few rehearsals, then some blocking, and then they set the scene for the actual filming. While they did that, the boys wandered out of the holding room set and over to the "circus," the panel of monitors and chairs where the director does his thing. We were seated right behind, and Jared came over to say hello, Jensen right behind him.

"Looking forward to the interview," Jared said, then both boys paused. They took another look at us and said, "Oh, it's you, we know you!" and leaned in for hugs, ruining most of our professional composure. After that, we were left on our own, as we had apparently passed the Ackles-Padalecki safety test.

Our only moment of jarring fangirl/writer discomfort came when we recognized one of the PAs as the woman we met the first time we were on set—our infamous visit with Joanne. We managed to contain our paranoia (is she staring at us?—does she recognize us?), though it did strike us as odd that she at one point attempted to reposition our chairs too far from the filming for us actually to watch what was going on. Since we are unfortunately quite docile and would have dutifully stayed there, we're lucky that another PA came along and moved us, helpfully pointing out that "you can't see from over there!"

Well DUH!

We were still periodically pinching ourselves when Jen apologetically informed us that they were running way behind schedule and both Jared and Jensen had flights to LA that night, so they probably wouldn't have time to sit down with us for an interview. We took this well, proving that we never quite believed it was going to happen anyway. At this point, just being on the set for most of the day, watching filming and chatting with the crew, had been such a utopian experience that it was hard to imagine anything else could be added to the mix, so we just said no problem. And actually meant it.

We had also been told that if we did get to talk to them, it would have to be somewhere on the set or in the studio, off to the side where we could be, we presumed, monitored. Security reasons, blah blah. Once again, we were happy just to be there and perfectly willing to meet with them on the moon, if that's where it would be most convenient. Seems we'd underestimated just how much of a nice guy Jared Padalecki is, however. The second the scene was finally wrapped, Jared headed straight for us, even though he had only a short time before he had to be on a plane and was still in costume. Jensen was right beside him once again, and they took the time to explain to us together that Jensen had to go record some third unit dialogue, but Jared was ready to talk if we didn't mind following him to wherever he had to go. Apparently the "keep the interview on the soundstage" rule had gone by the wayside. We assured them that we absolutely did not mind (and in point of fact would probably have followed Jared off the side of a cliff). Jensen smiled a "see ya later then," and we were off.

It was pouring rain outside, and we trotted after Jared to the makeup trailer like two wet spaniels, jumping over cables and struggling to keep up with him despite the fact that his legs are about six feet longer than ours. We started the interview in the hair and makeup trailer, setting up our voice recorder on the counter while Jeannie scrubbed the makeup off Jared's handsome face. Even with his hair up in a headband and white cold cream slathered all over his face, the guy looked good. Really good.

We led with the rather provocative "so what do you think of the slash" question, which caused Jeannie's eyebrows to fly right up past her hairline.

Jared's response was mostly confusion. "That's what is really most bizarre to me. I was not expecting that. Platonically I know they enjoy that we are great friends, because we *are* great friends and that comes across, and that I can understand." He added: "That's why *Oceans 11* did so well because it just looked like they were having such a fun time. They're goofing around and it's fun to watch and see people really laughing and having a good time. The other part . . . I don't understand, so I have no theory."

Lynn tried the same approach we had used when talking to Richard in Chicago, falling back on the stereotype of guys liking the idea of two good-looking women together.

"Sure," Jared agreed, but he still couldn't quite wrap his head around the way fans had extended that to his relationship with Jensen. "But it's so far from reality that it's just so funny . . . Whatever floats their boat! I guess I'll just take it as flattery."

We assured him that it definitely was. Jared seemed to understand that something about the show pulls people in and inspires passion and participation.

I think this show specifically, being a genre show, and a cult hit and what not, people just link so much to the characters and their plight and it's the whole archetype. You know, why *The Lion King* was so successful, and *The Matrix* and *Lord of the Rings*, they kind of plug into that side of them they don't even know exists. The big thing that has drawn fans to the world of *Supernatural* is that each has turned it into their world. It's no longer about guys on the road or hunting demons, it's connected to some part of them they might not even know exists. That's one of the great things about mythology—the point is to reflect some part of your life. So you start going "Oh, Luke Skywalker kind of doesn't know what he's supposed to be, he's kind of struggling, kind of like me, I'm having my own struggles."

"Yes!" Lynn interrupted excitedly. "You're saying my ideas—that people see their own stuff mirrored in the world of the show and use that world to rework their own stuff in fanfiction, discussion, whatever."

"Right," Jared agreed. "That makes plenty of sense. There's no other logical reason. I don't think any movie or show is that good to be so committed to it unless it's sparked something in you."

The show has certainly sparked something in us, that's for sure!

When Jeannie was done, Jared was up and out of the chair like lightning, telling us to follow him back to his trailer. We got up so quickly and were so dumbfounded that we were going to Jared Padalecki's trailer that we forgot the voice recorder—but no worries, Jared had helpfully picked it up and carried it himself, still talking into it the entire way.

Jared shooed his dogs Sadie and Harley off the sofa to make room for us and offered us drinks. Then, still talking, he started taking off his clothes.

OH.

First the suit jacket came off. Okay, no big deal. Then the dress shirt, leaving him in a thin cotton tight white T-shirt. Sorta big deal. Then he took off his shoes. Then his socks. By this time we were a little distracted. Interview? What interview?

Unaware of the distracting impact of his semidisrobing, Jared swung a chair around and sat down to chat. We took a few sips of the cold sodas he'd thoughtfully provided and tried to regain our composure.

We asked him about his experience of fame, relating Jim Beaver's story of grand-marshaling the *Deadwood* parade and then being completely unrecognized twenty minutes later on the same street. Jared's response, although he certainly didn't realize it, supported what RPF writers say—it's not the real people they're writing about, since all they know is a constructed persona.

"There is a buddy of mine who is also an actor, and he was saying there are so many sides of a person, and especially the sides of an actor. There is the side of Jared that I know, the side that my brother, my girlfriend, my parents know, and the side that the people at work know . . . I think the fans are fans of the Jared that's in the parade, in the Sam costume, the Jared that is playing Sam."

"Fans are very protective of you guys," Lynn said. "And it's a little weird because you're . . . well, very tall . . . and very grounded and competent. But they worry that if someone asked you about fanfiction, that it would upset you. Would it?"

Jared shook his head. "In person, I'm able to tell where it comes from. I'm pretty thick skinned, so I don't take offense too much. It takes a lot to offend me. As long as I know where it's coming from I can laugh it off."

Are there things that do hurt his feelings? Believe it or not, from the start of his acting career, fans have been invested in Jared's hair—for better or worse.

"When I started *Gilmore Girls*, I was eighteen, fresh out of Texas, just graduated high school, pretty naïve—and the fifth episode they cut my hair and the Internet was kind of new and I was like oh, weird, they write about it? Cool! And so I read about the comments and it was like oh Dean has a different hairstyle and a girl was like he looks ugly, he looks like a girl, and I was like that hurts!"

A decade later, fandom is still pretty obsessed with Jared's hair.

But even that, not only is the bad, bad, but the good is bad, even if it says he looks hot, he looks better than he used to. Even that's bad, you get cocky or you get the false confidence or arrogance and you know, just start focusing on vanity, which I don't want to do. My job is to flesh out Sam Winchester however I can, not to take from a billion people, but to play it my way, otherwise all these shows would be CGI [computer-generated imagery], and there's nothing interesting in that . . . I'm not a masochist, it hurts so I stay away. And it's stupid that I'm hurt, but still, but I am hurt.

At that point, we were both fidgeting with our own hair, counting our lucky stars that nobody was scrutinizing it on the Internet. Hair critics aside, though, Jared is an amazingly grounded guy.

"I think I have been very lucky, I've been in the business for nine years and have been very successful, but not too—it's not like I step outside my door and photographers are in the bushes. I am so happy, oh my God, that level of fame, that can't be fun. I love my anonymity, and I love being able to walk around after I work out sweaty and smelly and not someone seeing and writing about it online."

Jared had good things to say about *Supernatural* fans.

I have many times been having dinner and had someone after I got the bill say, "I didn't want to interrupt you while you were eating, but my cousin is a huge fan, can I get your autograph?" So it's not just hey I've seen you on TV, I own you. And I personally love my fans, they're the reason I get to do what I do and make money and have fun and do what I'm passionate about doing for a living and I am certainly grateful, and I haven't had any bad experiences yet. I mean, I've had butt grabs and stuff like that but nothing too too funny.

Butt grabs, huh? We would never in a million years, but hey, we're not blind. It's a damn nice butt.

"One of the funnier things that happened at a con was when that sweet little girl got up to ask a question and started sobbing, and I wanted to say, 'Oh my, it's okay—I'm a fan too,' not of any actor in particular, but if I saw Eddie Vedder, for example, I'd be like uhhhh I—I—I don't even know what I'm going to say . . ."

Jared did an adorably flustered rendition of himself meeting his idol. We grinned. He said:

With musicians, since it's not my calling, I'm sorta like oh that's really cool. Plus, in the last month I've maybe watched 100 minutes of TV that's not sports; however, I listen to music every day. I'm on my iPod every day. Walking my dogs, music in my trailer, so I have the relationship with music that a lot of people have with *Supernatural*. It's on their Tivo, they have it on loop, they're playing the Season 1 DVD and when that one is done, they put the next one in. That's me with music. That appreciation and relationship with music that a lot of people have with TV or characters, or this show, like we're talking about right now.

Oh yes, Jared gets it. Of course, we had to ask what it was like living with Jensen—we would be fandom traitors if we didn't.

"Fans love that you two live together," Kathy said. Jared laughed.

That's so funny. But I guess I figured they would. Yeah, it's great, we're pretty similar guys. We're both, ya know, Texas boys and like the Dallas Cowboys, and drinkin' a beer and watching sports. It's easy. . . . After a long day it's like hey man you want to go like grab a beer, or go to sleep or if Danneel is in town, I won't see them for the week. And if my girlfriend is in town, we're gonna take our own time, but it's a nice situation and he's a good buddy. When times are hard for me, or I've got something I'm going through, it's nice to be like hey man, can I just rattle with you for a little bit, rap about some stuff, and he's like sure, and vice versa. I'm pretty independent and I love my alone time, and I could live alone pretty easily, but it's nice to have a friend.

Us (silently): Awwwww.

"We work out together in the morning with Clif and he's fantastic. He's worth his weight in gold and he's not a small guy."

Understatement!

"Well, the fans love every single thing that you and Jensen do together."

"Of course," Jared agreed, "because in my opinion, every single thing we do is going to be exactly what the fans want us to do. If it got in *USA Today* tomorrow that he and I got in a huge fistfight and I broke his nose and he busted my eye, then they'd be like oh, look how passionate they are and so friendly that they could fight."

Lynn (maybe giggling): "Like ooh, they're having a lover's quarrel!"

"Yeah, and I could go on and say I hate him, I shot him with a gun and wish he died, and they'd be like man, it's so intense what they do on camera that it's bled into real life."

It's true. Fandom is good at spinning things into the way each individual fan wants them to be.

"It has nothing to do with reality. What they think of our situation is exactly what they want it to be and it always will be. You sort of accept that or you don't. It's how I feel about fanfiction . . . They're allowing me to do what I want, so I'll enable them through what they want."

That might be the best definition of the "reciprocal relationship" we've heard yet.

We hadn't asked to take photos, so we didn't take any of the boys, alas, but we did ask to take one of the dogs, and Jared jumped in too. (He also taught us how to get the best pose out of Sadie and Harley by giving us some meat to hold in one hand while we snapped the photo with the other. Worked like a charm!)

Jared gave us his email in case we had any follow-up questions, joking that we'd better memorize it and burn it or at least keep it in a safe place and under a pseudonym, and then he was off to catch a flight to LA, saying good-bye to us with a hug. He walked us back to the set (through the still pouring rain) like the gentleman he is, and we settled in to watch more

Jared with Sadie and Harley (and without shirt). Courtesy of Lynn Zubernis.

filming. It took a good half hour before our heart rates returned to anything close to normal.

"Did that just happen?" we asked each other, still having trouble believing it. How could he be that awesome? Or that insightful? Or that bloody hot?

No sooner did our hearts calm down than someone else appeared to kick them right back up again. Serge Ladouceur, *Supernatural*'s director of photography and the man responsible for the unique look of the show, came up to introduce himself. It took Kathy a moment to react, not because she didn't know who he was but because she couldn't fathom (again) why he would want to talk to us. Serge shared some stories of his little nieces, who are true SPN fangirls, and said that he'd love to talk to us more about our research. And he also helpfully explained the setup for the scene they were about to film and what they have to do to make the stationary Impala on the set look like it was being driven down a dark and rain-swept highway— which involved six or eight crew members bouncing it up and down and walking back and forth with flashlights to simulate movement. Fascinating!

The scene also involved Dean talking to Sam on his cell phone—except that Jensen was actually talking to a PA who was reading Jared's lines, since Jared was on his way to the airport. Also fascinating. (Okay—so everything fascinated us that day.)

Once the scene was wrapped, Jensen disappeared to hair and makeup. Jen warned us that since it was so late we probably wouldn't be able to interview him. We hung around chatting with Jen about her ice skating hobby and where she buys shoes in Vancouver, resigned to our amazing day being over. A short time later, she got a call on her headset. It was Jensen—looking for us!

We had a few moments of panic, thinking OMG, this is it, we're actually about to interview Jensen Ackles, then we were following Jen outside—to Jensen's trailer. HIS TRAILER. Jensen, however, wasn't there. It was pouring rain and we were standing outside his trailer feeling rather stupid and undoubtedly looking somewhat pathetic when the man himself arrived, drink in hand and looking far too perfect in a tight black T-shirt and worn jeans. He laughed and said, "Why didn't you go inside?"

AS IF.

Jen reminded him to offer us drinks, and he protested that of course he was gonna do that, he's a good host. We nodded mutely, overcome at the mere fact of being hosted by Jensen Ackles. He opened his fridge (just like Jared's), but instead of a fridge full of soda, it was a fridge full of bottled water. We laughed and found our voices; Ackles has a way of putting you at ease. His trailer smelled like a Christmas tree, thanks to an evergreen-scented candle that was already burning when we came inside. It smelled wonderful. A little Impala sat on Jensen's entertainment center. Both boys had their mini-scooters inside their trailers, just waiting for them to come outside and play.

"That was a cool scene," Lynn gushed. "Serge showed us how they make the Impala look like it's really moving."

"Oh yeah," Jensen agreed. "There are a lot of elements that go into making it look like it's traveling. Did you notice the guys with the flashlights around the back? And there's also a guy back there with a huge 2 by 4 leveraged on an apple box, and he's just going like this, bouncing the car."

Jensen demonstrated, biceps flexing as he bounced an imaginary Impala up and down. We held onto our composure. Barely.

"And then of course," Jensen went on, "I have to sit there and pretend as though I'm racing down the highway, and so when I'm looking down at the phone and I'm like . . . [he demonstrates quick glances down at the imaginary phone and then jerking his gaze back up to the imaginary windshield]. There's nothing that bugs me more than when I'm watching people drive cars on movies and they're like this [he demonstrates just staring at the phone]."

"They'd be plowing into something!" we interrupted excitedly.

"Absolutely. There would be a massive accident."

No wonder we can never do it the way they do in the movies.

"It was very realistic," Lynn said. "And very quick. I was like, woah, he's done!"

"What's funny is that I didn't even read those lines until about an hour before we shot that scene."

"Wait, what?"

"Which I learned about an hour before we shot *that* scene. I started looking at the lines for that I think during the final takes of the jail scene."

Quick study! We wondered if he was an equally quick study when it came to his fans. Jensen said:

It was kind of surprising when the show really got its feet under it in the middle of the first season and we started getting feedback and recognition of the show. And it was from unlikely characters. The WB was a network focused on a demographic that was obviously much younger. The people coming up and talking to us or writing about the show online, the fan mail, happened to be an older audience and a very intelligent audience. It wasn't "What side of the bed do you sleep on?" and "Do you wear boxers or briefs?" They wanted to know why this character said this and what did they mean by that, and could there be double meanings and how this character relates to that or not. It was kind of refreshing.

Refreshing, right. Though we might have still been stuck on boxers or briefs.

It wasn't just a show about two young guys who try to be sexy or hot, or play that easy card that those kind of shows or networks try to play. It turned out to be a fan base that was surprisingly different. I enjoy the fact that people are interested in the story and characters and why they interact the way they do, which was my initial attraction to the show in the first place. I initially read for Sam and as soon as I was done, I made my case for Dean and he just popped off the page for me. I liked the humor aspect of it and the arrogant air and I just wanted to play that—I liked the chemistry between Dean and his father, Dean and his brother. There was an attachment that I liked that I found in Dean very early on.

Us too. A very *strong* attachment.
From the start, TPTB didn't quite get it.

It wasn't just two guys showing off their muscles as much as they can so we can get a thirteen-year-old girl to buy our posters. In the beginning, publicity was saying these guys are in their mid- to late twenties, we have to put them in *Tiger Beat* and *Teen Vogue*, and Eric was like no, this is not that type of show. It's not Backstreet Boys riding around in a cool car. It's two hardened brothers who come from a really dark past, a really rocky past, and they are going to have a dark future. This isn't a show for the light-hearted. I think that's what drew a lot of people—we were really attracted to the dark, sinister outlook on things.

We eventually got around to the questions that TPTB had no idea we were asking. "Fans like to think of you and Jared sort of as a couple," we said tentatively. Which of course Jensen knew.

It's strange, because being who I am and being who he is, it's just hard to wrap our minds around. For Jared and I, God, it's a good friendship. I think we knew right away it wasn't going to work if we didn't get along. The first season, I forget what episode it was, but we got heated on set and got in each other's face and I mean, we went toe to toe. There were no fists thrown or anything like that, and he ended up taking a walk down the street and cooler heads prevailed, and when we got back to our trailers, I knocked on his door and sat down and I was like listen, man, that can never happen again because if that's the road we choose to go down, we are going to be living a different life. And it wasn't just me, he was actually on the same wavelength, like I'm glad you came by, I need to get this off my chest, we need to come together if we are going to make this show work, because we're gonna be spending way too much time together to not have a friendship. And that's the last fight we've ever had. We've got each other's backs and I support him in the decisions he makes, and will give him advice when he needs it, and he does the same for me. He went through a rocky thing this summer, and I was there for him for that.

"Jared said the same thing about you," we replied, trying not to sound too sentimental.

"It almost turns into art imitating life, or life imitating art," Jensen agreed. "We play brothers on screen, but we're kinda brothers off screen as well. It's a brotherly love that he and I have and it's kind of disappointing to me that people would mistake that for a sexual kind of love."

So for Jensen, it wasn't a matter of being disturbed by the content of fan practices but by a culture that has trouble accepting friendship between men for the lovely thing it is all by itself. Fans don't necessarily think that's the case in reality, though, we pointed out.

"I know they don't," Jensen nodded. "It's a hot fantasy."

Can't argue with that.

I think it stems from—and you can probably help me out with this—that it might stem from their love of the two characters and how much they have invested in these two characters, and there are really no other characters that they want coming into that realm. They don't want anyone to interfere. They want it to be just the two of them, all the time, and I think that's where it stems from . . . So I really think it's just the fact they are left with no other option when thinking of these two characters, and of course these guys are together.

Jensen is a fan of the show himself.

This [show] isn't a mystery. We tell you what we are dealing with and we deal with it, it's layered and layered but we're not necessarily hiding a whole lot and if we do it's questions that get answered. That's one thing I loved about Eric's writing. He poses questions and situations for these characters, but doesn't drag them out through seasons, he wraps them up and then poses new questions. I think with any audience, and for me as an audience and show watcher myself, I like the fact that it's ever evolving and not just one level.

Jensen understood the appeal of Sam and Dean and their bond as brothers from the start.

And I think that was the underlying kind of common denominator that bound everything together. It was the relationship between these two characters, and their love not only for each other but for their family and trying to grasp and hold on and protect as much as they could. We started out kind of positioning the show as a horror show that scares the hell out of you every week, but then there's this underlying storyline going on, this investment into these two characters, that fans really kind of gravitate to and why they kept coming back week after week and watching the show.

We couldn't have summed it up better. And fans can't stand when anything comes between Sam and Dean.

Jensen laughed. "The Catch 22 of that is, just selfishly, I wish that they'd add more characters to get some time off."

We grinned, perhaps evilly. "And it still didn't work, did it?"

No! To be honest, I think the two characters Ruby and Bela were sort of implements of the network and from that standpoint you can't jam some character into a storyline that doesn't make sense. I think that was Eric's biggest concern, that it wasn't organic. Those characters had no merit being there show after show, maybe once or twice or three times, but it seemed contrived, and forcing it down the audience's throat. It's like all of a sudden—it's sort of the elephant in the room.

"To a fandom that will pick up on that," we added.

"And they're not that forgiving either," Jensen said wryly.

We understood more clearly than ever that the network didn't really understand the show. Jensen agreed.

I don't think I'm going out on a limb here saying they might not. I'm not necessarily calling Dawn Ostroff out, but this is not her show. This show was packaged and created and done, sealed and delivered when the WB was the WB and Dawn was not there then, so it was not her show. If you look at the shows she created and delivered, it's *Gossip Girl, 90210*, and so it's a completely different type of show. We are definitely the odd stepchild of the CW and I think that especially this season they have kind of realized it's probably best to let us do what we do. And since they've done that, look at the ratings.

Once again, someone on the "creative side" was giving us an important message, loud and clear. Do what you do. Stick to who you are and what you want to create. Send your own message and don't let others dictate what that message should be. Even with Jensen Ackles himself telling us, we didn't get it. Not yet.

We also asked Jensen about the subject of fame, which we'd become as interested in as we were in fandom. The two, after all, are tied closely together. Fandom had adopted a perception of Ackles as "fragile, shy, and reserved," which wasn't exactly the impression we were getting in his trailer. We asked him about his public persona.

I tend to be a little watchful of what I say or how I act or what I do. It's almost like you put on a coat because you know you're about to go out and be documented. So you kind of put on this professional coat and say a couple funny anecdotes, and respond intelligently and don't cuss, and remember that mom could be watching this and grandma could tune in and see it. I censor myself, not that I'd be throwing curse words around like a sailor, but I'm conscious of it, but I guess that could be seen as being reserved. I also have to understand that they [fans] want to see me and interact with me so I have to bring a lot of my personality and who I am to the table, but I don't bring everything because I want to keep something for me. So if I'm out at a restaurant or whatever I'm me, but as soon as someone says, "Hey can I have your autograph?" it's like a button gets pushed and I flip into a different mode. Not like Jekyll and Hyde, but it's like "Oh yeah, absolutely, how are you doing?" I could be in a fight with Danneel at dinner and if someone comes up it's like "Hey are you that guy from *Supernatural?*" [and I have to be]. "Oh yeah, hey, nice to meet you!" Because it has actually gotten back to me that somebody met me and I was an asshole. A girl came up to me and said, "My friend came up to you and you were an asshole." But luckily I was with a bunch of my buddies and they were like "Are you kidding me?" . . . But it was like a slap in the face.

While Jensen was thoughtfully considering our questions, Kathy noticed Lynn nudging closer and closer to him and thought it might be helpful if she hit Lynn. Not noticeably and not (too) hard, but just enough to remind her what she was doing and that the Flying Fangirl episode would most definitely not be repeated that evening. Jensen, unaware that Kathy had just saved him, proceeded to act out some of the more uncomfortable moments that being "a little bit famous" can create. Or maybe he just thought that it would be prudent to put some distance between himself and Lynn.

"The real weird stuff is when you're at a grocery store or somewhere well lit and public—or an airport, urgh, god forbid an airport, and one person comes up to you in the terminal and they're like . . . [Jensen jumps up off the couch, bounces up and down, and in a high-pitched girly voice squeals] 'Ohmygod ohmygod ohmygod!'"

Lynn and Kathy nearly fell off the couch.

"And then you have like thirty people jostling to see who you are and then you hear this [in a deep manly voice]: 'Who's that?' Meanwhile, you're just going, argh."

Lynn (laughing): "Like ohmygod, kill me now."

"So some people are like hey can I take a picture with you? And I'm like [whispering dramatically] 'yeah, just walk around the corner so it doesn't cause a scene,' so people don't see because then they're staring at me the rest of the whole flight." (Jensen was still helpfully acting this out. Lynn and Kathy were laughing so hard they could barely speak.) Jensen said:

I'm not a household name across the country, but those few that recognize me and make a scene, then I have thirty–fifty other people trying to figure out who I am, and then someone's like "oh, go ask him," and then I have this old redneck guy coming up to me saying [using a hysterically funny accent], "Hey man, who are you? Hey man, my daughter wants me to ask who you are." And I'm like uhh, not really anyone. And then he's like "no, come on man, tell me, who are you?" So then I have to run down the resume, which is completely embarrassing. So when [actors] wear hats or try to stay [incognito], for me I do it not to like hide from fans—I have no problem talking to somebody who likes the show or wants to ask about the show—it's those other people that are uncomfortable, like if someone makes a scene and everyone is looking at you, and I just want to hide.

"And the people looking at you aren't even fans," Kathy noted.

"No, they have no idea, it's like all of a sudden I'm a zoo exhibit. Which is a really kind of odd feeling."

"No one wants to be a zoo exhibit," Lynn said, nodding. "Probably not even the zoo animals."

As with Jared, the interview ended with emails and hugs, and we piled into the ever-patient RG's van for the ride back to the hotel. It was 1:00 A.M. and we had been on the set for over twelve hours.

RG gave us the rest of the impromptu Vancouver tour, along with the guest actor for the episode, Jim Parrack, who was also starring in *True Blood*. Kathy and Jim got into a discussion about *Pilgrim's Progress*. And why not? The rest of the day had been somewhat surreal; there was no reason it shouldn't end with a conversation about a seventeenth-century book outlining the path to salvation. We flew home the next day, still a bit in shock about how wonderfully we'd been treated and the unparalleled (and unrestricted) access we'd been given—to the sets, the crew, the filming, the makeup trailer, and even the boys' personal trailers. If we'd written a description of our perfect fangirl day, the reality would have surpassed it.

TWELVE

. . . . .

The Monster at the End of This Book

We left Vancouver with the interviews that would finish our book. *Supernatural Magazine* liked our convention feature article and let us know it would welcome more. We started presenting our research on fandom at academic conferences and got a positive reception from our colleagues. These people knew us as Dr. Larsen and Dr. Zubernis, an English professor and a psychologist who had some new theories about fandom and how to study it. They didn't know us as fangirls or as fanfic writers or as women who squeed over the latest episode of *Supernatural*. They didn't know who we were on LJ or Tumblr. We quickly gained acceptance in the still-new field of fan studies. Kathy was appointed the Fan Culture area chair for the Popular Culture Association, and several publishers expressed interest in our academic books on fandom. As researchers, we felt equally accepted by *Supernatural*'s "creative side." We stayed in touch with most of the actors we'd interviewed and some of the crew. We emailed back and forth with Sera Gamble and Eric Kripke, who called us "the official reporters of the fandom" and thanked us "for all you do for the show."

This should have been the happy ending for our book, but alas, that's not quite the way the story turned out. As in any story based largely on hubris, we were heading for a fall. We had been warned, but you never really see it coming.

Six weeks later, we were back in Vancouver for a very different kind of set visit. This one had been arranged months in advance and involved many forms, waivers, disclaimers, and identity verification. Two friends had bid on and won a set visit for four, the proceeds to go to charity. The two other people who were originally going to accompany them had to pull out, which left two slots open. In keeping with what we later realized was a serious inability to understand that the world of television studios works quite differently than the real world, we figured that we should take advantage of being on set again to do some more work. We emailed the editor of *Supernatural Magazine*, who had been so enthusiastic about our convention article, and pitched what we thought was a fabulous and mutually beneficial idea—interviewing some of the people we'd met in December: the buyer from the props department, director of photography Serge Ladouceur, and the production staff. The editor jumped at the idea, and we dutifully informed TPTB of our good news.

We arrived in Vancouver thinking that everything was fine, at least as far as TPTB were concerned. In reality things were far from fine. Beloved director Kim Manners had just passed away, and the loss was still raw. We were also sharing the set visit with *Entertainment Weekly* reporter Alynda Wheat, who was writing what everyone hoped would be a cover story on *Supernatural*, finally gaining it the wider audience it so richly deserved. A studio rep had come along too, presumably to make sure that Wheat got the story she needed and the network wanted.

Grief, tension, and a group of fans touring the set do not mix well.

We went to work as soon as we arrived, while Julia and Alison were taken on their tour of the set. On our way to start our interviews, we ran into Clif the bodyguard and stopped to talk for a few minutes. We apologized for not sending him the photo we had taken of him in sparkly headgear last time we were on set and promised to email it to him when we got home. Lynn gave him her business card so that he would recognize the email when he got it. As we were leaving, we asked if the boys knew we were there. Clif replied rather ominously, "Oh, they know."

Something in his tone bothered us, but we tried to shrug it off.

Jen took us around the production office again so that we could take more photos of fan gifts and front office paraphernalia that we missed last time. Once again, we gave out a business card to several other people we were introduced to. Normal everyday human interaction, as far as we were concerned. Dangerous subterfuge as far as TPTB was concerned. We were soon "invited" into a conference room where we were told in no uncertain terms to stop talking to people we were apparently not supposed to be talking to. Never mind that six weeks earlier the people we weren't supposed to be talking to were coming to meet us. We were confused, embarrassed, humiliated, and completely caught off guard. We apologized (somewhat reluctantly, since we were having a hard time believing that we had done anything *wrong*), pulled ourselves together, and went back out there to do our job, trying to hang onto our professionalism while feeling more like the imposters that we had always feared we were.

Things went downhill from there. Our interview with Chris Cooper, who's been the prop master on the show almost since its inception, and two of his staff, Robyn Stooshnov and Carmelita Fowler, was punctuated by tears when we offered our condolences over the death of Kim Manners. The technical difficulties that had come to characterize so many of our interviews recurred when our tape recorder once again malfunctioned. Our next interview, with Jason Fischer of the production office, ran more smoothly, but again the mood was subdued. Even Jason's amusing stories of fans sending underwear to the boys barely made us crack a smile. When we were done, Jen shepherded us back to the set, where we assumed Julia and Alison had been living a fangirl's dream watching filming, just as we had on our last set visit. Wrong!

They had been watching filming, but not the way we thought. They were set up in a small cluster of set chairs about ten yards from where filming was actually happening, behind a giant floor-to-ceiling black drape which effectively prevented them from seeing anything going on—except on the single monitor provided. Without headsets. So they had a visual, albeit on a small screen, but they couldn't hear, except for snatches of Jensen's "Dean voice," which occasionally carried across the ten yards and over the black barrier—just enough to be an intermittent tease. Complete openness had shifted to information blackout.

At first, we assumed that Julia and Alison must have been treated to an introduction and some time with Jared and Jensen while we were working. But no, they informed us with dismal faces, they had been behind the curtain all along. Again and again, crew members came by and said hi and asked innocently, "Have you met the boys yet?" Again and again, Julia and Alison shook their heads, increasingly hopeless and frustrated. This was a fangirl nightmare. The boys they had come to see (and had paid a small fortune to see in person) were right there, only ten yards away, almost close enough to touch. And completely out of reach.

Finally they decided to ask—politely—if they could say hello to Jared and Jensen. The PA dutifully went off to find out and came back ten minutes later smiling, so we were sure the answer must be yes. Hopelessly optimistic, that's what we were. Instead of Jared and Jensen, she handed Julia and Alison each a copy of *Supernatural Magazine* signed by the boys. She was still smiling. Julia and Alison were not. We all stared at the magazines as if they were pieces of dried dung. Surely nobody could actually think that an autograph is what is expected from a set visit, when fans could get that at any fan convention for free as part of their package. And at a convention they could get it in person, not shuttled back and forth by an intermediary PA.

Over the course of our research, it had become obvious that TPTB really do not understand fans. Obvious, though still inexplicable. Weren't we, after all, the customers? Didn't they want our love and loyalty and dollars, euros, and yen? They were remarkably good at pick-up lines but had little idea of what it takes to sustain a long-term relationship. By now we were used to seeing this, though still dismayed over the treatment that Julia and Alison received. But there was Alynda Wheat, also behind the big black screen, also sans headphones (though she had of course gotten her interviews earlier). Were they really going for a trifecta of idiocy that day—annoying cast and crew, fans, and press in one hot mess of miscalculation and obliviousness?

Alison and Julia were inconsolable—and mad as hell—on the drive back to the hotel. Who could blame them? As we pulled up to the hotel, we saw another set van pull in ahead of us. Out jumped Misha Collins, the newest addition to the *Supernatural* cast. He was so new that nobody had interviewed him yet, so we had arranged one through the network (before we were chastised for overstepping boundaries). We introduced ourselves and arranged to meet in the bar in an hour. Attempting to salvage something of the day for Julia and Alison, we invited them to sit next to us while we conducted the interview.

Once Misha joined us, Lynn launched right into what fans wanted to know. "So how do you think Castiel feels about Dean? Because you play it in a very subtle conflicted way. Does he like Dean, does he hate Dean, does he want to take Dean apart?"

Misha interrupted to deadpan, "Does he want to take Dean to bed?"

Julia and Alison froze. Did he just say that? Their day was picking up!

Misha Collins. Where does SPN find all these gorgeous guys? Courtesy of Karen Cooke.

"You're very okay with the homoerotic subtext," Lynn observed. Misha just grinned and then promptly turned the tables, asking *us* about slash.

"From a psychological vantage point what needs is this fulfilling?"

Lynn immediately offered one explanation. "Fanfiction can be a kind of self-narrative therapy. People sort of write to put their own stuff out there in a displaced form, using characters to tell their own story. It works like a form of group therapy because then you have the support of the community. You post it online, then the support of the community comes out and it rallies around you, and now you've got normalizing and validation."

"Huh," Misha said. "Interesting."

Misha hadn't been to any conventions yet, though he had recently signed on for several of them. We offered a quick course in Conventions 101.

"As soon as you walk out onto the stage there will be clapping and cheering."

"Sounds like a fantasy," Misha observed. "I have a friend who was on the last *Star Trek* series and he was telling me about his conventions a few years ago, and I was thinking, wow, I hope my career never comes to that.

It sounds so pathetic. Then I got the first call and I was like, WHAT????
FANTASTIC, sign me up."

An hour into our half-hour interview, Misha got an irate call from the
network rep, admonishing him for being late for the telephone interviews
he had scheduled.

Bad *us*. Again. But we had one more faux pas to make before the end of
the evening.

Serge Ladouceur, the director of photography, who'd asked *us* about doing an interview the last time we were in Vancouver, had offered to meet us
at the hotel after they were done shooting. He called around 10:00 P.M. to
ask if we were still up for the interview. Of course we were. Serge sat with
us in the hotel bar for two hours discussing the crucial role that cinematography plays in SPN. Although the show is fantastic in more ways than one,
he explained that they want *Supernatural* to look like it could happen in real
life, which means specific lighting and working with a colorist (appropriately nicknamed "Sparkle") to adjust the contrasts and colors. Having actors
who look like Jared and Jensen makes Serge's job a little easier.

"They're so good technically that I can have them perform little adjust-
ments in their acting so they would catch for instance that little ray of light
that I want them to catch as they step into a dark corner. That helps me keep
the show on the dark side. And they are indeed very photogenic. I can use
almost any type of light on them and they'll still look good. I can light them
as I would a beautiful woman."

Damn right, we said, grinning. Our chat with Serge was so fascinating
that two hours had flown by before we realized it. Serge seemed to enjoy it
as much as we did. He even emailed us the next day with another interview
that he'd done for an online blog that never ran. "You were actually interested," he said. "So feel free to use this too."

Serge's generosity provided the grace note to an otherwise frustrating
trip. Yet we flew back from Vancouver still smarting from our inadvertent
rule-breaking and consequent on-set hand-slap. We got another when the
studio found out that we'd met with Serge until midnight—never mind
that it was his idea and that we'd all enjoyed the chats. Our hands, by this
time, were sore from all the unexpected slapping. Even worse, our fangirl
sides were sorely disappointed. We'd spent a day on the *Supernatural* set
and hadn't caught even a glimpse of Jared or Jensen.

Back in the United States, we shook off the soreness, salvaged what we could from our once again mangled interview recordings, and wrote three more articles for *Supernatural Magazine*, thrilled to see their titles on the covers. We kept working on the book, periodically emailing updates to the prospective publisher. They kept responding with encouraging one-liners, pronouncing the book "fun."

If we hadn't been caught up in the euphoria of unexpected success, we might have paid more attention to the other messages contained in those brief emails or the not-so-subtle hints dropped in our meeting with the publisher reps. For one thing, the publisher had little interest in our academic theorizing; they wanted a book that would sell to fans. Lots and lots of fans. They didn't want "dry" research, even if it did go a long way toward actually explaining fandom and what makes it tick. Even if we knew damn right well that fans themselves wanted to understand fandom. TPTB just wanted a fun story, not an intellectual one.

And then there was the sex part. One email included the odd comment that "of course you'll have to tone some parts down—like the sex," but we shrugged that one off. After all, there was no actual sex in the book. Nobody sneaks into one of the boys' trailers and seduces him or sleeps with a guest actor to get access to the green room. As far as we were concerned, our book was downright tame. Surely they couldn't mean that we weren't allowed to reference sex at all—how can you write a book about *Supernatural* fandom without talking about how hot the actors are or what sort of fanfiction fans like to read and write about them?

We ignored that reference as an aberration. Or a bad joke.

It wasn't. TPTB wanted a fun book, period. With nothing controversial included. Never mind that our reason for writing the book in the first place was to "set the record straight" and argue against the shame that women feel when they indulge in "frivolous" pursuits like fandom. It had been deeply, vitally important to us to show fandom as the healthy, positive thing that it could be. We wanted our book to do something that had never been done before—to celebrate subversive ideas that women were entitled to do things just for fun, that women longed for a community of other women where they could be real, that women were every bit as interested in lusting after hot guys on TV as men were in ogling an endless array of hot girls on film.

That was exactly what TPTB didn't want us to write. They had dangled a publication contract in our faces and we'd grabbed for it, ignoring the plethora of attached strings. If what we wanted to write was too controversial, sure, we'd leave those parts out. If that's what we had to do to get published, well, we'd just have to suck it up and go along. After all, we were in a good place. We were on the inside. Accepted, legitimate. As we finished up the book, we went to another *Supernatural* convention in nearby New Jersey.

New Jersey felt comfortable. We drove there, since it was only an hour from Lynn's house. Now that we regularly corresponded with many of the actors by email or texts, we could set up our own interviews. We knew the Creation owners and staffers, and they knew and trusted us. In fact, at this convention they eventually just gave us a key to the green room so that we could interview to our heart's content. We met up with Richard Speight in the hotel bar that evening and settled in to chat. *Supernatural* guest actor Todd Stashwick came over to join us. We were all so engrossed in conversation that at first we didn't realize that we were attracting attention. Eventually Kathy noticed the circling fangirls (and yes, she was most definitely putting herself into another category). First they pulled up chairs at nearby tables, and then those chairs were inched closer and closer to ours. As we were watching this slow ballet of encroachment unfold, a harried Creation Convention volunteer walked into the bar with a very tired and somewhat dazed Misha Collins in tow. It was his first convention, and he had just arrived from LA, jet lagged and famished. When the volunteer, who knew us by now, saw us sitting with Richard and Todd, she brought Misha over to us and sat him down, giving us instructions to "protect him" while she went to get him some dinner. Clearly the volunteer was on the same page as Kathy. We were not fangirls in the eyes of Creation. Misha seemed happy to see familiar faces and settled himself on the couch between us to join the conversation.

The moment the volunteer left, the perimeter around Todd, Richard, and now Misha was breached, finally and completely. Fans pulled up chairs and joined the conversation while looking at us with all the interest you would accord a speed bump. We were in the way, slowing them down. Clearly they did not see us as fangirls either. Never mind that we were squeeing on the inside to be curled up on a couch with Misha Collins.

New Jersey gave us back a little bit of the happiness that our last trip to

Vancouver had so effectively dampened. We started to feel good about ourselves and the project again. We all but had a contract, and we had all of the interviews that we now needed to move forward. We were in a good place.

For us, being in a good place has always been a dangerous proposition. Our pessimism comes to us by experience as well as by nature. Nevertheless, we were still in our happy places when Lynn got an email a few weeks later from the publisher.

Not only had they suddenly done a 180 and decided not to publish our book, but we were essentially barred from having any contact with anyone having anything to do with the show! It was the dreaded cease and desist email that every fan fears. Cease and desist from *what* wasn't exactly clear. From writing the articles you hired us to write? From doing the interviews you helped set up for us? Or was it really from telling the "truth" about fandom?

Lynn's first reaction was disbelief. Was she reading it wrong? This couldn't be what it sounded like, could it? The second was horror. Cease and desist? That meant lawyers. Lynn picked up the phone and called Kathy. By the time she started relaying the contents of the email, Lynn was in an all-out panic.

We were at a loss to understand what we had done wrong. All our interviews had been arranged by the studio, with the exception of the one with Serge, who had happily volunteered. The timing of the interviews, which had been arranged to take place on what was probably the worst of all possible days, just a week after the death of Kim Manners, when everyone on set was still grieving and the pain was raw, was not our doing. The less than flattering article that came out in *Entertainment Weekly* shortly after that set visit was also not our doing. Considering the mood on set that day, it should have come as a surprise to no one that the article published during a surge in the show's ratings would actually be about the show's demise, with both Eric Kripke and his two lead actors calling into question whether or not they would continue after the end of the fifth season of the show. Fandom, predictably, felt gutted by the article. Presumably TPTB were less than happy as well. Clearly they weren't happy with us.

Our rational selves knew that we were being blamed for a series of internal problems that had nothing to do with us or our book. Of course, it didn't feel like it to us at the time. We just felt wrong. Terribly, terribly wrong, shamed and infantilized. We were naughty children and were being sent to our rooms. Permanently.

Once the initial shock wore off, Lynn was still worried. Her partner, who was much more understanding of her fan interests than Doug had been and who also happened to be an attorney, reassured her that she had nothing to worry about, but Lynn wasn't easily reassured. Kathy, in contrast, was just mad. And defiant.

And then she was happy.

In the end, she realized, TPTB had done us a favor. We were poised to write a book that we did not want to write, sanitized first and then polished into a shiny story of fandom that ignored most of the things that make it tick. We'd been saying all along that fandom is about passion. On some primordial level, whatever we are fans of gets the blood up and the hormones pumping. It doesn't matter if it's a television show or a hockey game—love is love. Fans will readily tell you this, but TPTB, for reasons that still remain vague to us, have been slow to admit it. Never mind that they are in the business of selling passion and sex and desire. Never mind that they cast impossibly pretty people in their television shows and films. Never mind that they often mount (yeah, pun intended there) over-the-top ad campaigns that emphasize sexual subtext over plot. They don't seem to have a problem with any of this, but they do seem to have a problem with fans acknowledging it, indulging in it, and celebrating it. We were back to boundaries.

And we still didn't know why they were there or what they were for.

Neither did Misha Collins. He was talking about actors, but the same applies to anyone who enters the arena of fandom and fame—or who, God forbid, tries to straddle the line between the two.

"There's this strange phenomenon that happens, and it is definitely some sort of normative force," he said. "I don't know where it comes from, but there's a certain set of basic rules that as an actor coming into celebrity you almost inherently understand. You know that you're supposed to interact with your fans in a certain manner, sort of distant, reserved, strong boundaries—but then if you take one step back and analyze it, to what end? What is it that you're really protecting?"

Nobody seemed to know, but breaking those boundaries is dangerous. As it turned out, the book we wanted to write could not be written. We had planned a "hybrid" book that had our academic voices side by side on the page with the fans' voices. One that would break boundaries and push limits. That isn't what the studio publisher reps wanted—while they had never been clear about what it was they *did* want, it clearly didn't include the things we wanted to say. They didn't want to hear about fans finding community or women looking for validation or that one of the many reasons we love *Supernatural* is because Jared and Jensen and Misha are effing hot. They didn't want us asking questions about fanfiction or about how badly TPTB misunderstood the show.

Once our studio deal was off the table, we got picked up by an agent and started trying other publishers. We were repeatedly told that there was no clear market for our hybrid story. Academics would not take it seriously and fans would think it too academic. "Who would buy it?" was the question we heard over and over.

Finally realizing that our attempts to be both fan and academic hadn't worked out all that well for us and that we usually had to choose one over the other, we also realized that the same held true for the book. It could not be both simultaneously any more than we could. That left us with two stories to tell. One is the story of fan communities and the alternating current of celebration and shame that electrifies the experience for many fans, the scholarly outcome of our years of research. That book was published in 2012 as *Fandom at the Crossroads*. The other is this book, our own circuitous arrival at this moment of clarity.

By the time we finished our research, we had managed to break every rule. We'd blundered through doing things our way, discovering the joys of fandom and the realities of power that blocked us from getting where we wanted to go. We'd courted TPTB and offered to sell our souls to do it their way. We'd had our dreams come true and then watched as they fell apart. We'd strained and sometimes lost relationships we valued in our pursuit of fandom. As we discovered ourselves, we had to renegotiate who we were with our children and partners and friends—and with each other. Surprisingly, as we split our identities into researcher and fangirl, we had to look at who each woman was and eventually find the person who was underneath both.

Misha Collins had navigated a similar journey.

I don't like to play by the rules. I had a moment when I first got on *Supernatural*, when I was like "Oh my god, people are paying attention to me and I have fans, maybe I should cultivate an image and like try to seem really cool." I had this sort of moment of being commercially self-conscious and it took me maybe a month to realize no, this is just not fucking who I am and I don't wanna behave that way and I'm not gonna do that. And then I started being like, "Here, here's a picture of me in drag, fuck it," which is so much more liberating and relaxing.

He's right. This feels so much better. So thank you to TPTB for ditching us. We found our Fangasm anyway.

GLOSSARY

. . . . .

AU: acronym for "Alternate Universe" or fanfiction that places characters from the original show/book/film into non-canon scenarios. For example, Dean and Sam are doctor and patient (or werewolf and vampire) instead of demon-hunting brothers.

BNF: acronym for Big Name Fans or fans that have attained a certain prominence within the fandom. BNFs are not always looked on kindly by other fans.

CANON: the world according to the creator/writers of the original show/book/film. Canon "errors" (anything that fans don't particularly like) are fixed by rewriting them in fanfiction.

CRACK FIC: a story so bizarre or implausible that it is said the writer must have been on crack when she wrote it. This is not a bad thing.

DESTIEL: slash pairing of the *Supernatural* characters of Dean Winchester and the angel Castiel. The pairing gives rise to, among other things, **wing fic.**

EMO: from "emotional," a person who experiences extreme emotions or feels things deeply. Often applied to certain genres of music, to fanfiction which is intensely emotional and thus intensely satisfying ("emoporn"), and to Sam Winchester.

FANFICTION: stories written by fans featuring the characters from the fanned book/film/series. These stories often reinterpret the characters (understatement), fill in gaps in the story line, or focus on less prominent characters.

FANFICTION.NET: one of the first online fanfiction sites, hosting fiction from hundreds of fandoms.

FANON: interpretations of the original text/actors by fans that become part of the fandom history and eventually become as widely accepted as the actual facts.

FANZINES: a pre-Internet method of distributing fanfiction. Fanzines (or "zines") were often mailed or passed around at fan conventions, often literally under the table.

FIRST RULE OF FANDOM: to tell no one about fandom. This is a comment on the widely held belief that fan activities should not be shared with anyone outside fandom, especially the people on the other side, such as actors and writers. The rule is enforced much like the first rule of the movie *Fight Club* on which it is patterned.

FLAME WAR: a heated online argument between two individuals that results in those involved posting personal attacks on each other. Sometimes started purposely by users (known as trolls) who want to cause trouble. Common fandom advice: Don't feed the trolls!

FRIENDS LIST: the other members who "friend" you on Live Journal. Your friends list or f-list will see (and perhaps comment on) your posts, and you will see theirs.

GEN: fanfiction that does not involve characters in a romantic relationship. *Supernatural* has lots of gen fanfic. No really, it does!

GENDERSWAP: fanfiction in which male characters are suddenly (usually magically) turned into women, or vice versa, with resultant body part confusion.

HET: fanfiction in which the romantic pairings are heterosexual. *Supernatural* does not lend itself to het, since most of the recurring female characters are swiftly killed off.

HURT/COMFORT: fanfiction in which one character is injured or otherwise rendered vulnerable, giving another character the opportunity to care for him. Very popular in all fandoms.

ICONS: avatars that fans use to accompany online posts, often reflecting whatever is going on in fandom at that time, whether wanky or humorous.

J2 OR JSQUARED: fanfiction romantically pairing actors Jensen Ackles and Jared Padalecki. Mathematically incorrect.

LIVE JOURNAL (LJ): social networking site used by fan communities to post fanworks and discuss fans' favorite series/book/film. Thought of (perhaps erroneously) as a "safe place," more anonymous and less visible than Facebook or Twitter.

LURKER: someone who reads or watches what goes on in online fandom but doesn't actively participate.

MANIP: short for "photo manipulation." Photos are usually altered to place two characters or actors into erotic positions. When done well? Hot. Not so well? Hilarious.

MEME: a concept or pattern that spreads from person to person via Internet sites such as blogs, journals, social networking sites, and YouTube. There are hate memes, love memes, and everything in between.

META: metacommentary or intellectual discussion centering on larger ideas and issues raised by the fanned series/book/film. Also known as "thinky thoughts."

MPREG: fanfiction in which a male character finds himself pregnant. What?

NEWBIE: someone new to fandom, who does not yet understand the culture and norms.

NSFW: acronym for "Not Safe for Work," a warning appended to fanworks, especially images, that may not be appropriate to view in the workplace. Fannish translation: Gimme!

OTP: abbreviation for "One True Pairing" or the couple that a fan believes to be the only one possible. Pairing one member of the couple with a different character/person is considered unthinkable. The spark for some of the most passionate fan infighting.

PARASOCIAL INTERACTIONS: one-way relationship posited to exist between fans and the famous. Not exactly the pinnacle of mental health, according to early research.

PICSPAM: a blog or journal entry consisting of a series of pictures, often centered around a central theme (such as motels of *Supernatural* or shirtless Sam Winchester) and featuring the poster's comments.

PWP: acronym for "Plot? What plot?" or "Porn without Plot," often short pieces of fanfiction whose sole point is to get two characters into bed (or on the floor, the couch, the hood of a car, against a wall, and so forth).

RPF: acronym for "Real Person Fic," fanfiction written about actual actors, musicians, athletes, politicians, and others. Many disapprove of RPF, claiming that it is unethical or an invasion of privacy to write about real people as opposed to fictional characters. Of course, the "real people" in the fic bear little or no resemblance to real life anyway.

RPG: acronym for "Role Playing Games," played online; fans assume the roles of their favorite characters and act out collectively written scenarios.

RPS: acronym for "Real Person Slash," a subset of RPF that pairs two (usually straight and male) actors, musicians, athletes, or others romantically.

SHIPPING: pairing two characters together in a romantic relationship. Results in "ship wars" when fans disagree about which characters should be paired and which shouldn't.

SHOWRUNNER: the person who is responsible for the day-to-day operation of a television show. *Supernatural*'s creator Eric Kripke was showrunner for the first five seasons, followed by writers Sera Gamble and Jeremy Carver.

SLASH: fanfiction in which two same-sex characters are romantically paired. Slash most often refers to male/male pairings, with "femslash" used to refer to female/female pairings. Slash is the most popular type of fanfic in *Supernatural* and in many other fandoms.

SLASHWINK: the acknowledgment in canon of the *possibility* of a slashy relationship between two characters. Increasingly common on television, if the network thinks it might attract more fans.

SOCKPUPPET: a false online identity, usually created for the purposes of stirring up trouble or acting as a foil for the person's main online persona.

SQUEE: the sound that a roomful of happy fangirls makes, sometimes only audible to dogs.

SUPERNATURAL WIKI: started in 2006, the "Superwiki" is an extensive online information resource and compendium of fan knowledge about both the show and the fandom. The creative team is as likely to use the Superwiki as a resource as the fans are.

TINHATS: fans who see evidence of a "secret" romance in every gesture between two celebrities, and whose tin(foil) hat will permit no other signals (such as "they're just friends") to permeate their brains. But hey, there was that time when the boys were . . . okay, never mind.

TPTB: acronym for "The Powers That Be" or those who are in charge—usually studio executives, who, like referees and umpires, are universally thought to have no real knowledge of their own business. Draw your own conclusions as to the accuracy of this view.

TUMBLR: a microblogging site where users can post text, photos, and videos. Highly visual, Tumblr is valued in fandom for its ability to "bring the pretty."

VIDDING: making fanvideos, which are usually mash-ups of clips from a film or television series set to a popular song. They range from feel-good and fun to erotic to dark and disturbing. Metacommentary vids critique the show, the fandom, and the culture.

WANK: trouble in fandom, usually centering on the objectionable actions or comments of another fan. Wank often starts when it is felt that someone has gone "too far" or when one fan's OTP or shipping preference doesn't match another's.

WINCEST: a mash-up of "Winchester" and "incest," the controversial pairing of Sam and Dean Winchester in a romantic relationship. The first Wincest fic was written the night the pilot aired, long before writer Sera Gamble referred to *Supernatural* as the "epic love story of Sam and Dean."

WING FIC: a genre of fanfiction in which one of the characters unexpectedly sprouts wings.

INDEX

. . . . .

Ackles, Danneel. *See* Danneel Harris

Ackles, Jensen, xii, 5–6, 19, 27, 49, 58, 72–74, 101–102, 133–134, 137, 178, 199–202, 212; on appeal of *Supernatural*; on fame, 225–227; on fanfiction, 33; on the "flying fangirl," 30; on friendship with Jared, 222–223; interview with, 220–227; on *Ten Inch Hero*, 85–86

Asylum Convention, 19, 33; the "flying fangirl," 27–31, 169; interview with organizer, 168–170

Beaver, Jim, 114–115, 118, 151, 163; on being a fan, 29, 65–66; Eyecon T-shirt, 144, 154; on fame, 155–158; on fan conventions, 153; on fanfiction, 124; on the "flying fangirl," 28; interviews with, 120–126, 151–158; on slash, 124–126; on Wincest, 154, 168

Big Bang Theory, 2

Busse, Kristina, 20

Carlson, Steve, 117, 119–120, 161; on being a fan, 67; on fanfiction, 191; interview with, 190–191

Castiel, 33, 102, 124, 146, 231

Celebrity Worship Syndrome, 10

Chicago. *See* Creation Conventions

Cohen, Matt, 97–98

Collins, Misha, 170, 185, 235; interview with, 231–233, 237–239

Comic Con, ix–xi, 3, 69–74, 171–179

Creation Conventions, 61, 185–186; Chicago, 95–100, 104–110, 186–202; Dallas, 148–159; Los Angeles, 129–140; New Jersey, 235

Dallas. *See* Creation Conventions

David Mackay, 81–82, 84–86; on being a fan, 66

Eyecon, 159–165; interview with organizers, 167–168

fan conventions. *See* Asylum, Comic Con, Creation Conventions, Eyecon, Something Wicked, Wincon

fandom: addiction as a model of, 11–12, 20–21, 59–60; as community, 14–25, 17, 19–20, 37, 182–184; investment, 5, 10–14; and sexuality, 4, 39–49, 131; therapeutic value of, 10, 12, 20–25, 47–49, 63, 89–90, 105–107, 182–183. *See also* fans fanfiction, 14–16, 33–35, 43–48; slash, 44–45, 83, 100–104, 110, 162–163; zines, 14, 84, 161. *See also* Wincest

fans: attitudes toward, 3–5; definitions of, 3; pathologizing of, 2–4, 10–13, 22; power of, 3–4; shame felt by, 1, 31–33, 39–41, 47–49, 56–57, 62, 83–84, 90–94, 109–110, 183, 189. *See also* fandom

Ferris, Samantha, 98, 107; on being a fan, 66–67; on the "flying fangirl," 28; interview with, 113

A Few Good Men. See Fort Worth

Fifty Shades of Grey, xii, 3, 17, 33, 44, 47, 84

Fort Worth, 37–39, 49–58, 83

Gamble, Sera, 7–8, 72, 74, 143, 175–178; on the appeal of *Supernatural*, 7–8; on fanfiction, 112–113

Hanson, Rae, 173

Harris, Danneel, 56–57, 64–67; on fans, 139–140, 178; interview with, 131–140

Horton, Donald, 13

Impala. *See* Metallicar

Jackson, Michael, xii, 4, 121, 157

Jenkins, Henry, 61; attitude toward *Supernatural*, 9

Kripke, Eric, 61, 72, 74, 111, 114, 129, 166, 228, 236; on being a fan, 142, 173; on fanfiction, 143–144; inter-

views with, 141–144, 175–177; on slash, 143

Ladouceur, Serge, 219–220, 229; interview with, 223

Lehne, Fred, 129, 131; on fans, 149; interview with, 148–151

Lindberg, Chad, 129, 187–188, 190, 198–199; interviews with, 131, 159–160, 165. *See also My Big Break*

Los Angeles. *See* Creation Conventions

Mackay, David, 81–82; interviews with, 84–86, 131; on being a fan, 66

Malin, Adam, 76, 95–100, 167; interviews with, 95–97, 131, 133; on success of *Supernatural*, 100

Manners, Kim, 68, 80, 168, 208, 229–230, 236; in fanfiction, 143

Manns, Jason, 35, 119; on the "flying fangirl," 29–30; interview with, 161–162

McCallum, Dan, 173–174

McCutcheon, Lynn: absorption-addiction model of fandom, 10

Metallicar, 7, 75, 205–206, 219

Morris, Betsy, 67–69, 76, 79, 81, 85–86, 171

My Big Break, 159–160, 165. *See also* Tony Zierra

Orlando. *See* Eyecon

Padelecki, Jared, xii, 5–6, 101–102, 164, 199–202, 212; at *A Few Good*

Men performance, 53–55; on fame, 215–216; on fans, 216–217; on fanfiction, 214; on friendship with Jensen, 217–218; interview with, 213–218; on popularity of *Supernatural*, 214

parasocial relationships, 22

People's Choice Award, 9

Peterson, Karla, 171–172; attitude toward *Supernatural*, 9–10, 23

Plastic Winchester Theater, 55–57, 71, 209

Potter, Harry, xii, 1, 7, 12, 35

Rudski, Jeff, 12

San Diego. *See* Comic Con

Schmelke, Chris, 105–108, 170–171

Shyamalan, M. Night, 64–65, 160

Singer, Bobby, 28, 122–123, 152

Smith, Samantha: interview with, 192–193

Something Wicked Convention, 81–83

Speight, Richard, Jr.: interview with, 195–197, 235

Star Trek, 2, 7, 61, 68, 84, 96, 149, 155, 170, 232

Supernatural, x–xi, 5, 17, 77, 94; appeal of, 7–10, 214, 221–224; set dec, 206–210

Teen Wolf, 101

Ten Inch Hero, 62, 64, 68, 71, 79, 81, 85–86, 171

Tigerman, Gabriel: on fanfiction, 190; interview with, 190

Twilight, xii, 3, 7, 40, 86

Vancouver, Canada: fan pilgrimages, 86–88; Something Wicked Convention, 83; *Supernatural* set visits, 90–92, 203–227, 228–231

Vernon, Sharon, 79, 82, 86; on the "flying fangirl," 27–28

Wanek, Jerry: interview with, 206–208

Whitfield, Charles Malik: on fanfiction, 195; interview with, 193–195

Wincest, 33, 35, 48, 77, 102, 124–125, 146

Winchester, Dean, xi, 5–8, 14, 17, 34, 88, 111–113, 122–123, 205

Winchester, Sam, xi, 5–8, 17, 34, 88, 146–147, 188

Wincon, 182–184. *See also* Fan Conventions

Wohl, Richard, 13

Yalom, Irving, 20–21, 41

Zierra, Tony, 159–160, 172